MAR   2021

THE NEXT SMART STEP

KELLY WATSON AND JODI ECKER DETJEN

THE NEXT SMART STEP

How to Overcome Gender Stereotypes and Build a Stronger Organization

Kelly Watson and Jodi Ecker Detjen

imagine!

At the time of publication, all URLs printed in this book were accurate and active. Charlesbridge and the authors are not responsible for the content or accessibility of any website.

An Imagine Book
Published by Charlesbridge
9 Galen Street
Watertown, MA 02472
(617) 926-0329
www.imaginebooks.net

Library of Congress Cataloging-in-Publication Data
Names: Watson, Kelly (Consultant), author. | Detjen, Jodi Ecker, author.
    Title: The next smart step : how to overcome gender stereotypes and build a
    stronger organization / by Kelly Watson and Jodi Ecker Detjen.
Description: [Watertown, Massachusetts] : Charlesbridge Publishing, [2021] | Includes
    bibliographical references. | Summary: "A guide to understanding the challenge
    of gender imbalance in organizations, implementing solutions, and equipping
    readers with the tools we all need to ensure change that is positive and enduring"
    —Provided by publisher.
Identifiers: LCCN 2020021432 (print) | LCCN 2020021433 (ebook)
    ISBN 978-1-62354-538-3 (hardcover)
    ISBN 978-1-63289-227-0 (ebook)
Subjects: LCSH: Sex role in the work environment. | Sex discrimination in
employment—Prevention. | Sex discrimination against women—Prevention.
| Diversity in the workplace. | Corporate culture.
Classification: LCC HD6060.6 .W347 2021 (print) | LCC HD6060.6 (ebook) |
DDC 658.30081—dc23
LC record available at https://lccn.loc.gov/2020021432
LC ebook record available at https://lccn.loc.gov/2020021433

Printed in the United States of America
(hc) 10 9 8 7 6 5 4 3 2 1

Cover design by Ronaldo Alves
Interior design by Mira Kennedy

CONTENTS

INTRODUCTION   1

PART 1: THE CHALLENGE: BARRIERS AND BIAS   17

  1 It's All Made Up 19

  2 Unconscious Bias   29

  3 Flawed Assumptions and Bad Habits 43

  4 Organizational Bias 57

PART 2: THE SOLUTION: REFRAME AND RENEW   73

  5 The Power of the Reframe. 75

  6 What Women Need to Do 79

  7 What Men Need to Do 96

  8 What Organizations Need to Do 110

PART 3: MAKING GENDER EQUITY HAPPEN:
           TOOLS AND TECHNIQUES   127

  9 Promoting Leadership 129

 10 Building Gender Equity from Vision to Reality . . . 135

 11 Making and Measuring Progress 152

CONCLUSION   186

POSTSCRIPT   191

ACKNOWLEDGMENTS   195

APPENDICES   197

BIBLIOGRAPHY   221

ENDNOTES   229

INDEX   243

ABOUT THE AUTHORS   249

INTRODUCTION

TERRY WAS A BRIGHT, CURIOUS CHILD who loved hearing stories about astronauts and outer space while growing up. Other kids built buildings or cars with Legos, and Terry built spaceships, watched every space movie, and dreamed about visiting another planet or the moon.

Terry got a telescope at five years old and used it to make a map of the stars. When friends wanted to learn about planets or constellations or stellar distances, Terry was there. Favorite field trip? The planetarium. Favorite subjects in high school? Advanced placement science and math—and Terry aced it all, learning how to code sophomore year and winning a rover-building contest.

Terry's future unfolded from these interests and strengths: top of the class in college, internship with an aerospace company, and eventually a seat on the Mars exploration team. Smart, confident, hard-working, and dedicated, Terry is now living the dream, paving the way for a new era in space exploration.

Terry, in all likelihood, is a man.

Somewhere else there is another Terry—a woman—who also aced her science and math classes. She is equally smart, confident, hard-working, and dedicated. But her college counselors told her she wouldn't have good work-life balance with an aerospace career and she should think about the social sciences instead (advice many women receive). Her friends told her she was weird because she liked math. ("That's not normal for girls!")

But Terry persisted and landed her dream job in aerospace. Or so she thought. There was no seat on the Mars team. From the beginning, some

1

of her work colleagues eyed her suspiciously, assuming she got the job because of affirmative action. They openly challenged her technical abilities, talked over her in meetings, and dismissed her ideas. She was paid less than her male colleagues because she hadn't asked for raises as often as they had, and the organization went along with her reticence. When Terry had a baby, other women told her good mothers raise their own children, and she should prioritize her family. Her boss steered her to an operational role with less travel and critical responsibility. And when she invented a breakthrough technology, management told her she was just lucky, and if she did it again, *then* they would give her a bonus.[1]

THE DESIRE FOR EQUITY

You get the picture. We like to believe that everyone has the opportunity to realize their career dreams. And the first Terry—the male Terry—got that opportunity. What's more, he might even have expected to have the career he envisioned and probably didn't question that he would be paid what the work is worth. And why not? It is normal for a man like him to have a meaningful career.

The second Terry wants what the first Terry has—a great career. She is willing to work just as hard for it. But even today the odds are stacked against her being as successful as her namesake. Especially if she is a woman of color. Women get blocked so often, they leave organizations and even careers. Or they box themselves in to lower-level jobs or limited contributions. The few who make it through often find there aren't women in sufficient numbers to make change; rather it is they who ultimately get changed by the organization.

The Next Smart Step is driven by a desire to turn a wish—that all people have the opportunity to realize their career dreams—into reality. That women like Terry should have the same expectations and achievements as Terry the man. That gender equity—fair treatment for women and men, according to their respective needs—moves from aspiration to actuality. That seems reasonable, right? Maybe you picked up this book because you are a woman who wants a career without barriers. Or maybe you're a man who wants to know how to help change organizations to support women. Maybe you're a leader who has already tried to make change and you want to do more. Or perhaps you've made some honest mistakes and want to learn how not to do *that* again. That's great, and we are glad you want to learn.

But gender equity isn't only about fairness: it's also about effectiveness for individuals *and* organizations. Because an organization that does not have equity and that primarily hires and promotes white men at the expense of not just women but people of color and other groups that traditionally lack opportunity—such an organization is narrowed to one perspective, one type of background, one model of success. And while two men may be somewhat different, they are not nearly as different as a man and a woman would be. So gender equity helps everyone. And *The Next Smart Step* will show how organizations reap the benefits when employees have many different types of backgrounds, skills, and perspectives—cognitive diversity—and put that to work for better, more innovative results.

Organizations need women's voices to be part of the conversation. Women make up 50 percent of the population and now nearly 50 percent of the workforce, yet less than 20 percent of top decision-makers.[2] When women aren't involved in the conversation, policies get made that don't benefit them.[3] Products get developed that don't fit them.[4] Drugs get developed that don't work for them.[5] And workplaces get designed that don't suit them.[6] There is now significant research that suggests women make a disproportionately positive impact on the economy through their workforce participation.[7,8] Further, women's leadership contributions have been shown to have a significant positive influence on company earnings.[9] So everyone needs to get better at including women and leveraging the advantage they bring.

MEDIAN WEEKLY EARNINGS BY DEMOGRAPHIC GROUP, 2019[*]		
	Men	Women
Asian	$1,380	$1,138
White	$1,025	$843
Black	$768	$683
Hispanic	$757	$661

Gender equity is also about leadership. Leading diverse teams and fostering inclusion are key twenty-first-century leadership skills. Our world is increasingly connected, which means organizations have access to a wider range of talent, background experience, cultural context, and unique points of view than ever before. Tapping into that potential and leveraging it effectively is critical for leadership success. It can also provide organizations with a unique point of differentiation (translation: competitive advantage) because so few organizations are truly maximizing the potential that diversity has to offer. For individuals, being among the first to excel at leading diversity will mean better opportunities for personal

---

[*] Bureau of Labor Statistics, "Usual Weekly Earnings of Wage and Salary Workers Third Quarter 2019," U.S. Department of Labor (October 16, 2019).

leadership impact. So it is also the aim of *The Next Smart Step* to teach these skills and maximize this advantage. We want to help you do that so you can influence others and drive change in your organization.

We believe that what women and men do as individuals to address their biases about themselves and others is foundational to organizational change. Organizations are merely groups of individuals, and the unconscious bias of individuals is compounded when people form groups. Based on our combined decades of research and working with organizations large and small across the US, the methods outlined in this book provide leadership tools to help male and female leaders improve their understanding of diversity and inclusion and their ability to apply this understanding in the workplace to build more inclusive teams. *The Next Smart Step* also outlines a consulting process for organizations to help you learn how to assess your own organization or team and address any gaps. There are concrete solutions to common organizational problems you can apply immediately. These three areas of focus—individuals, leaders, and organizations—are our three pillars of gender change. If all Terrys are to succeed equally, everyone needs to change, even Terry.

VISIONING: GOING BEYOND THE WISH

We all may wish things were different for Terry, but while asserting that is great, it is not enough. Many leaders make the mistake of thinking that simply by being aware of a wish, it will happen. "We are going to improve diversity," or, "Diversity is a big priority for our organization." The problem is that leaders often miss the next step—envisioning what the wish means for people and organizations. Or they think about the good stuff that could happen for individuals, but not necessarily how it will look and feel when the job gets done. And they forget to consider how it might impact everyone else. While leaders may get support for the broad desire for "diversity," they don't usually get buy-in for the changes that diversity actually brings. What we need is for leaders to envision a truly diverse organization, and think about how that differs from today, so they can get the engagement they need to enact lasting organizational change.

The wish for gender equity requires a different way of thinking and a different way of working. Radically different. It's not just about inviting more women into organizations; it's about truly engaging them to make organizations better. It's not about recruiting diverse people and then molding them to "fit in" with the homogeneous culture already there. And it's not about keeping women at the bottom of the organization or in "pink-collar roles" with no influence on leadership or decision-making. Instead, it's about a workplace that actually engages *all* the Terrys. What does that look like?

Before you get scared, when we say radical we mean looking at gender equity from a different viewpoint altogether. A difference that is achievable. We have worked with dozens of organizations to help them remove barriers for women. We've worked with hundreds of men and thousands of women. We began our journey by studying women's careers and uncovering the ugly impact of organizational barriers and unconscious bias on the dreams and aspirations of many career-focused women. And although we started with the premise that work-life balance was the main problem hindering women, we discovered that this assumption was flawed. In fact, we learned that women themselves often make decisions based upon many flawed assumptions. Through our workshops and women's leadership-development programming, we have helped individuals uncover their assumptions to challenge and change them. Our work has empowered many women to "lean in" to their careers in whole new ways as they navigate male-dominated workplaces.

The Next Smart Step builds on our foundation of training and consulting work and the research behind it, with the goal of helping women and men improve their leadership skills and organizational approaches. We recognize the reality that the important efforts women have made to remove their own biases and barriers are not enough—because organizational biases and barriers remain. Men need to include the women on their teams. Leaders must change their approach to managing women and use measurable leadership competencies to manage inclusive workplaces. (Later in this book you'll find a gender scorecard, developed to help organizations objectively and systematically remove bias from their processes.) Most importantly, this book will give you an approach that has led to improvements in the numbers of women retained and promoted in the real-world organizations we've worked with.

> ### CHANGE MEANS CHANGE
>
> "You think change comes without change? You think you can open the door and then keep the rooms on the other side exactly the same? Come in, come in, sure—but don't touch, don't sit on the furniture. Watch where you're stepping. That's not change, man—that's a dinner party. All the guests come and then all the guests go home."
>
> from *The Guest Book*, by Sarah Blake[*]

---

[*] Sarah Blake, *The Guest Book* (New York: Flatiron Books, 2019), 436.

Organizations need more than a desire to improve gender equity; they need a vision of what that looks like. Leaders need to ask themselves: What would gender equity look like for our organization? What would increased diversity look like? (Think race, age, and ability level too.) What faces would we see when we walk in the door? How would people be dressed? What would people eat? How would they move around? How would decisions be made? Who would make them?

These questions are important because sometimes people get stuck. "We hired a woman executive once, but she didn't want to join us for our weekly cigar-smoking sessions where we strategized about the business. She was fully welcome to join us; we were being inclusive," said one COO. (Yes, this is a true story.) "We have been meeting weekly like this for fifteen years and all of a sudden she comes along and wants to change the venue. Why should we? She wasn't willing to fit in."

Take a moment to think about your own organization. Using your senses as a starting point, what do you see? Hear? Smell? A more diverse workplace might mean different noise, different colors, and different smells. It might mean a workplace that resembles a bustling city rather than a stifling office. You might hear different languages, smell different foods, and see different ways of bringing people together.

It could also mean that work happens differently, in different places, and at different times of day. It might mean there are breast-pumping rooms, prayer/meditation areas, and massage stations, not just cigar rooms. Today's pool tables, video games, scooters, and beer kegs might be supplemented by volleyball courts and spa water. And there might be daytime breaks for parents to pick up school-age kids or coach soccer. Or there could be people using walkers or wheelchairs to get around.

What will executives be doing? It's likely they won't frequent the same country club with their wives anymore. And certainly not strip clubs like in the past. Social situations at work, such as cultural celebrations and birthdays, may be more robust. And there could be subtler changes, such as more collaboration, less competition, and more creativity.

Most certainly there will be more conflict: the good, healthy kind that comes when people with different perspectives speak up and banter ideas around. It might get raucous! There will also likely be a wealth of skills, experiences, and different ways of thinking that will result in radical ideas, innovation, and the production of something extraordinary. It may be uncomfortable too, especially for those who come from more traditional or homogeneous organizations. Or for people who don't like to debate.

But discomfort often precedes growth and development, and the prize will be worth it. It could also change the decision-making time frame. Slow things down. Including a wider variety of perspectives and debating their impact will probably take longer. This might feel less agile. But maybe fewer mistakes will be made.

Think again about your own organization. How will having more women at the top change things? Will it change the social fabric—what executives do together when you aren't working? Will it change the decision-making structure—who decides, how they decide, and who has to buy in? And will it change what formal and informal networks look like? Hierarchy might give way to flatter organizational structures that include more relevant perspectives or a new organizational structure altogether. Processes like hiring and promotion will likely change, as would definitions of success. Will these be small changes for your organization? Or does this seem like a different planet?

Visioning in this way—asking and answering critical questions—helps us move beyond only wishing for change. It helps us see that true gender equity requires a change in leadership skills. It demands more facilitation, conflict resolution (or not letting positive conflict go too far), maintaining the diversity of teams, and finding ways of fighting bias and groupthink. And it forces us to consider: How will existing employees upgrade their skills to this level?

In Appendix A you will find a mind-map tool to guide a visioning exercise and help you think about what your organization could look like with gender equity and/or diversity at all levels. Part of that exercise is recognizing that not everybody will embrace this vision. Anticipating resistance is critical so it doesn't come as a surprise. Let's face it: unconsciously, many people like organizational culture just the way it is, especially if they have been successful there. Homogeneity, especially if you are in the majority group, can feel very comfortable.

In the old command-and-control structure of most organizations, difference was considered threatening, so people unconsciously worked to identify and exclude it from their teams and organizations. Difference often meant dissent, and dissent was highly discouraged. But the workplace has evolved to more egalitarian organizational structures. Now it is more commonly recognized that dissenting opinion is good—it keeps teams away from groupthink and the echo chamber. Difference yields innovation and creative outcomes. And as hard as it seems, this ability—to manage and cultivate difference successfully—is what the future holds for leadership.

THE NEXT SMART STEP

Over the past forty to fifty years, American corporations led predominantly by white men have embraced marked, significant change. They've moved from a top-down, authoritarian leadership approach to more dispersed and empowered leadership. This globally accepted model is taught as standard at universities throughout the world. This innovative shift in leadership is partly why Western companies continue to lead the world in performance. It's a framework that enables strong talent and ideas to rise and be heard. The foundational history of openness and acceptance of difference in places like the United States are actually advantages: they produce more ingenuity. Homogeneous and hierarchical societies, on the other hand, make it harder for individuals within organizations to manage difference because people are generally so unused to it.

Making organizational leadership more diverse is the next step in this egalitarian trend. It is about embracing a distinct global business advantage, the culture of diversity, and putting it to work for your organization. Many business schools offer core courses about working in diverse teams. Some universities have installed "managing diversity" as a core developmental skill across all disciplines.[10] The challenge for businesses is that while diversity is touted as critical to success (69 percent of senior leaders say it's important[11]), leaders don't know how to leverage it. Most of them weren't trained in bias awareness or fostering inclusion, and they are still much more comfortable with homogeneous teams. So, it's time to catch them up—fast!

Fostering diverse teams doesn't come easily or intuitively to most people. We all learn to key in on people who are similar to us, to look for commonality, and to alter our behavior—copying gestures, language, and ideas—to fit into the broader group. It's comfortable to be the same as everyone else. Remember how awkward it felt in middle school to be different or how nice it felt in high school to finally find your clique? We bet most of that transition meant finding your people, and maybe to some extent, modifying your own behavior or appearance in some way to manufacture sameness. Some people took bigger risks and joined more diverse groups while others did not. Some were accepting of difference, and some—think about the bullies—were not. Already the seeds of inclusive leadership skills were sprouting in a few, though most of us were nudged toward sameness and conformity, not diversity.

In fact, despite research that shows diverse teams outperform non-diverse teams, people keep hiring sameness.[12] Why? Some say it's because similar people seem easier to manage, quicker to integrate, and harbor less team conflict. That may be true, but we think it is something bigger. We believe a stronger force is at play, rooted in a more emotional personal place for those who lead: it's more fun to hang out at work with people you like. And why are those people easier, quicker, and less dissonant to manage? Because the intrinsic emotional motivation—the fun—keeps leaders incentivized to make it work.

Think about the last time you enthusiastically advocated for a colleague who you don't particularly like as a person but who brings a unique or helpful skill set to the organization. Hard, right? Have you ever defended the mistakes of someone you like at work? Or advocated for them to get a second chance? Were they really deserving? Would you be able to devote similar passion for a perceived outsider? We all struggle with this. It is an invisible tide that seeps into hiring, promotion, and firing decisions.

And then there is the classic tech startup story—a fast-growing company is started by two college buddies who hire friends and family to build their empire. In these stories, the founders don't seek the best possible candidates when hiring, they seek the best candidates they like. It especially helps if they already know them. And we get it—people spend a lot of time together at work, so it is human nature to want that time to be fun. But it squashes diversity and merit right out of the candidate pool when you unconsciously solve for a different variable entirely!

Here's the real kicker: it's harder to like people who are different from you. Think about your preferences in music and how influenced they are by the music business. The first time you hear a song, you might not like it, but once you hear it hundreds of times, you find yourself humming along when it comes on the radio. There's a reality that all music producers understand: you don't know what you like; you like what you know and what is familiar to you. So the music business works hard to expose you to their clients' music as often as possible until you like it.

People do the same thing: seek out similarities and commonality—things you know—to determine if you like someone. Of course, shared values play a big role in our relationships, but again, not as much as having a similar background. If Sally is a person who values honesty, and her colleague Jonus is honest, then they share an important value. They can appreciate and respect each other. If what they are being honest about is also something they agree on, they will probably get along and even like each other. For example, if Jonus expresses his concerns to a client about the viability of a project he and Sally are working on, and she shares those concerns as well as the desire to be open and honest with the client, then they will get along.

But what if their honesty centers on a different point of view or perspective? What if Jonus is a staunch socialist with a background in labor organization, and he expresses his honest concerns to the client that the part-time workers on the project are the company's attempt to exploit people by avoiding paying them benefits? Whereas Sally's background in consulting makes her think that having part-time workers on the project offers a compelling opportunity to bring people incremental paid work they otherwise wouldn't have? Not only do they disagree, but their shared values about honesty are suddenly less important than their different perspectives. Well, then it is a heck of a lot harder to like each other. And it takes two very big people to leave that client meeting and go grab a beer together. To create and lead diverse teams requires new skills: it takes training and disciplined practice to become proficient at managing people who aren't like you, especially if the difference makes them unlikeable to you.

It's a cop out to say, "Some guys just shouldn't manage women." Think about it. If a man isn't very good at presenting, he would be coached. He certainly wouldn't be promoted or allowed to avoid presenting. But organizations let people off the hook when it's about gender. They don't get feedback; they are given a pass to run all-male teams.

Working with difference is a skill that can be cultivated by anyone. Women too. In fact, not all women are proficient at including other women at work. Some actually work against other women out of fear or intimidation. Everyone starts in a different place on their own personal journey. The key is to identify where the gaps are in skill sets and provide support and training as well as sufficient practice and feedback to develop those skills. Chapter 9 of this book shows how anyone can learn this. We will even give you the opportunity to assess your own skills or those of your team members as well.

SOME RADICAL THOUGHTS

In our research and workshops, we have developed three key insights that are the foundation of our vision of turning the wish for gender equity into reality. The feedback we have received from our clients is that these insights are perspective-changing. At first blush, they may seem innocuous. Read on. We promise they will dramatically change your viewpoints. And it's from this perspective shift that change can start.

Key Insight #1: the meritocracy doesn't exist.

What? Really? Merit is fundamental to most people's core thinking about the workforce. "We only hire the best and brightest regardless of gender, race, creed, color, background, sexual orientation, etc." and "We are an equal opportunity employer." But numbers don't lie. Would it surprise you if I told you that a disproportionate number of CEOs are tall, white, heterosexual men named John? [13] How does that make you feel if you are short? Latino? Named Luis? Gay? Female? Does it make you feel like you are less good at your job? Less deserving of a high position? Less qualified for leadership? So what does this data imply? In a fully functioning meritocracy, the only logical explanation is that people who don't fit these characteristics are less good. Let that sink in.

Many men and women justify this disproportion with unconvincing excuses. John *is* the most popular boy's name. Women entered the workforce en masse in the latter half of the last century and haven't had time to rise (it takes time!). Many women take time off to have babies, which naturally slows career progress. But the fact is, even once all these factors are considered, the data say the same thing: the representation is disproportionate. In Western countries, being tall has been associated with an increase in salary between 9 and 15 percent.[14] Are you 15 percent better at your job than your shorter peers? Are you 15 percent worse than your taller ones? What if, when deciding salary increases, management took your whole team and lined them up against the wall and ranked the increase in terms of height. Would that roughly represent your value? Would that be fair?

In a true meritocracy, given that women are as good as men, they would be represented fairly at all levels. But they are not. Believing that the meritocracy works means believing that women are actually less good than men at leadership. We know (and the data shows[15]) that isn't true, but there is a large segment of the workforce, including many women, who unconsciously believes that it *is* true. If people believe that, then how can they effectively lead inclusive, gender-balanced teams? The first step is to acknowledge the facts about the meritocracy's flawed reasoning and their own internal biases against women.

Later in this book we will explore the pervasiveness of bias. Remember this height example because it illustrates something important: privilege is invisible to those who have it. If you are tall, you probably aren't aware that your height gives you an unfair advantage at work. You may even have an emotional reaction to this news and want to reject it. What does it say about your abilities? That you are a fraud? You have this reaction because this data contradicts your meritocratic ideals. Shorter people, on the other hand, probably already sensed this reality as they were overlooked, dismissed, or even marginalized for their height at some point. We've all heard of the "Napoleon Complex," a phrase used to attribute negative personality characteristics to short men. Are those stereotypes legitimate? Of course not! But do people with height privilege unconsciously perpetuate them as a means of protecting the meritocracy and their own legitimacy? Sometimes. These are all important things to think about as you consider your own privilege and how it impacts your unique perspective about the meritocracy.

We all wish there was a true, working meritocracy, especially those who don't benefit from privilege. But wishing and having are two different things. When everyone assumes that a meritocracy works, they become closed to thinking that it needs to be fixed. If they question it, then it puts their own abilities in doubt. And it is tempting to think that because there has been some progress for women that the struggle is over and the meritocracy works for women. It doesn't.

Key Insight #2: WOMEN ARE NOT MORE BIOLOGICALLY PREDIS-POSED TO CERTAIN ROLES LIKE PARENTING AND NURTURING OTHERS.

Many people still assume that women are so biologically different from men that they naturally should prioritize home and family. Girls play with dolls, boys beat each other with sticks. It's nature. Okay, we know: said out loud, this seems like blasphemy. Feminists everywhere are burning this book. But we said it because deep down it's true. The unspoken pressure to conform to long-held gender roles and to limit career aspirations for parenting (or give up family to have a career) is extremely strong. Women everywhere are counseled as early as middle school to pick careers that offer work-life balance over income potential. And roles that are nurturing like Human Resources (HR) and Nursing. Because of strongly held stereotypes about gender roles, women, especially white women with college degrees, may start out with a meaningful career that dominates their attention until they get married and have children. Then they face pressure to pull back and invest in their husband's career or focus on raising children until the kids leave the nest. Or they struggle to fit in work while feeling guilty for not being perfect at home. Or they give up having children, thinking that is the only way to achieve true career success. Women may want to put their careers first or at least treat them equally to family, but everyone else acts like that's too selfish and cold. And many women unconsciously think that having babies means we are the ones who should raise them.

It's sad, because all this is based on made-up, culturally ingrained gender roles. Worse, many people unconsciously behave as if every woman is working only to pass time until they become a mother. This assumption is made even about women who have no intention of having kids, or who don't subscribe to traditional gender roles. Workplace behaviors are modeled around it. You find that hard to believe? Notice when you ask people what they do to help move women into leadership roles, their first answer is usually about helping women balance motherhood with work. On-site daycare. Flextime. Maternity parking. Those offerings are based on some pretty big assumptions, right? Interestingly, even women who start out with the intent to buck stereotypes often end up falling into them when workplace and social pressures nudge them hard in that direction.

Our research shows that almost everyone makes assumptions about gender roles, including women, and those assumptions are limiting. Men are expected to go to work, have a career, provide for their family, and take out the trash. Women are supposed to take care of the family and make a nice home (and women living at lower socioeconomic levels are expected to keep working plus do all this). Society says that bucking these rules emasculates men and makes women less likable. These assumptions are especially dangerous because they tend to be unspoken and invisible. In fact, we tell our sons and daughters they can be anything they want, but then we question whether our sons can earn enough as a nurse, and we caution our daughters that surgeons don't enjoy good work-life balance. All because of unspoken gender rules underneath. In Chapters 6, 7, and 8, we encourage you to question foundational assumptions and reframe them to open up new possibilities for yourself and others. We will show you how to recognize when unspoken gender rules are influencing your decisions and what to do about it.

KEY INSIGHT #3: *GENDER EQUITY AND INCLUSION ARE A BUSINESS PROBLEM, NOT AN HR PROBLEM.*

Yes, we know. This insight is also controversial and may make those of you in Human Resources want to raise your pitchforks in protest. But let's face it, treating gender equity like it is some kind of benevolent social good initiative or accommodation instead of just plain smart business has contributed to holding women back. There is a lot of research on the positive impact of women's work on business, but let's boil it down to a simple fact—when leaders exclude half of the talent pool from their search, they end up with less talent. Their workforce is less talented, so their output is less good. Period.

So why do so many gender initiatives start in HR and focus on fixing or training women to fit in better? We get that nothing really matters to a business (and yes, nonprofit organizations) unless it makes money. Social good, award-winning products, environmental stewardship—these are all nice things to have after the company is profitable; rarely are they considered integral to corporate strategy. As soon as profitability is threatened, HR initiatives such as bringing more women into the organization are seen as "nice to haves" and are shed. In fact, they often need to be justified financially—and incrementally—to be implemented in the first place. Think about the diversity conversations you have heard in your organization. Do they start with having to prove why adding women will help the company financially? Have men ever had to prove as a whole gender that they benefit companies?

Most diversity initiatives start in HR and, as such, come from outside the business. They lack compelling bottom-line impact and are seen mostly as overhead—discretionary costs that can be dropped in tough financial times. These initiatives usually ask the business to compromise something in favor of a nobler goal. The entire foundational premise is that diversity is abnormal or unnatural for business, and it's something that requires investment to get done. And the return usually isn't measured, only the costs are. What is needed is a shift in thinking—one that starts in the business itself.

The Next Smart Step is grounded in our operational business experience, an understanding of the business drivers that impact the bottom line. We get it: any business-improvement initiative must be driven by positive return on investment or it isn't going to be a priority for the long term. We understand that change happens when the math gets done, and we encourage organizations to do the math: counting, reporting, and calculating return is all a part of our solution.

This operational approach is unusual in a world where most companies are merely checking the boxes for women, offering a benefits-based approach with on-site daycare or sending high-performers to expensive conferences without understanding what really holds them back or how solutions can achieve any type of strategic goal for the organization. Or teaching people how to be politically correct, saying the right words while stifling the real conversations. Companies like that spend a lot of money trying to look good without any sort of real progress for women or any measurable financial return. Instead, our approach represents the next generation of gender progress.

This book is not about throwing out the baby with the bath water, however. Let's first acknowledge the good stuff. There has been progress towards gender equity in the last hundred years, particularly in the United States. Women are now 55.4 percent of university students,[16] including 49 percent of business majors.[17] And 36.8 percent of those who earn an MBA are now women.[18] More women than ever before are starting businesses, spending longer in careers before having children, and rising through leadership ranks. Women are making headway around the world: in Saudi Arabia, women are getting driver's licenses for the first time, and in America women are leading Fortune 500 companies. This is great!

But while these statistics are encouraging, they also lead many to assume there is no work left to do. To assume that generational attrition will do the rest, that women will naturally rise through organizations when given enough time or when older men retire is flawed. Because that's not happening. The World Economic Forum estimates that it will be 170 years before gender equity is achieved.[19] That's long past when generational attrition should have worked (it should have already!). Workforce participation for women has stalled since the turn of the twenty-first century,[20] and there are fewer women engineers in Silicon Valley now than there were in the mid-1990s.[21] There may be a lot that is going well for women's advancement, but powerful counterforces are stalling progress. It's time to fix the system.

FIXING THE SYSTEM

The Next Smart Step offers a unique, three-part approach to solving the gender equity problem, a roadmap for how to change individuals, leaders, and organizations as a whole.

In Part 1, we examine some of the assumptions underlying how most of us think about gender. We show how many of these assumptions are flawed and, in fact, completely made up! We then explain unconscious bias, both the external stuff we get from others and the internal stuff we buy into ourselves. And we'll show you how much of this has been unconsciously embedded into our organizations. Once current behaviors are better understood, and once we can see why we behave this way, the path to fixing it becomes more clear.

In Part 2, we offer a model for change. Based in cognitive behavioral therapy, our approach seeks to challenge biased thinking and reframe flawed assumptions to create new decision options for people and organizations. There is specific work to be done by women, men, leaders, and organizations, which we identify. We also show you how to manage resistance when it inevitably arises.

In Part 3, we provide practical tools for designing more diverse organizations. We offer a comprehensive way to identify and measure inclusive leadership competencies in leaders so we can up our talent game. We also share our consulting process for assessing barriers to gender equity throughout the organization so that policies and processes can be changed for the better.

Please note that throughout this book we talk about the specific problem of gender inequity. Our expertise is with gender. But that in no way minimizes the inequity that exists for other underrepresented groups. And we know that intersectionality—the interconnected nature of membership in more than one underrepresented group—compounds the effects of bias and inequity. Our recommended approach, while focused on women's examples, can also work well for these other groups. And the benefits of gender diversity can be magnified by including all types of diversity in a company.

We also apologize in advance if we refer to any group or gender using an outdated term or reference. We recognize that gender is a social construct, and it's not always binary. Our intention is to showcase examples and vantage points from our experience, and we are always learning new perspectives. We hope you are too.

No one person or organization has ever gotten gender equity completely right. There are many good deeds, partial role models, and works-in-progress. That's okay. We all need space to learn. So we share examples and anecdotes of things that work and things that don't. Maybe some of it describes people familiar to you or pockets of your organization. Getting it right on your team is a nice place to start. Because eventually, those pockets will join and change larger pockets until the majority of the organization has changed. It will never be perfect—people are human after all. But our goal is to make diversity and gender equity the norm, not the exception.

You've taken the first step. You're reading this book. Thank you. Now join us for the journey. You will be glad you did.

PART 1

THE CHALLENGE: BARRIERS AND BIAS

1

It's All Made Up

IMAGINE FOR A MOMENT THAT seventy-five years ago, World War II ended differently, and the fascist powers did not surrender until nuclear bombardment had irradiated many parts of Europe and Asia, and a global food crisis emerged because of the lack of suitable land for planting. Imagine that women in the United States, who had been running factories and many companies while men were at war, decided that food production was so important that they sent the returning men, blessed as they are with innate physical strength, out to farms to grow food to feed the world.

What if, using their innate empathy and connection skills, women managed business and government so the men could be free to focus on the important physical work of farming. Let's say that as women consolidated power and wealth, they passed legislation to stipulate that only one family member could work in business so that the other could farm. And since it was obvious who was better physically equipped for farming, the men stayed home on the farm. Of course, the entire culture would elevate farming as glorious and beautiful, and so important for society, so revered, and so honorable. But of course farming would be unpaid, because after all, shouldn't men simply do their duty, knowing they are doing what nature intended?

The world today might look completely different, like this: Folk songs connect the long history of farming to the present. Young boys are given toy farms to play with. Special holidays are set aside to honor farm service, days on which the women fumblingly hold the tiller so men can have breakfast in bed. Teenage boys are steered towards farming school. The most physically fit men become objectified, with Mr. America contests and an industry of magazines focused on the male body. There would be no point in hearing what farmers had to say, as their intelligence is irrelevant and, before long, probably considered absent. And if anyone tries to innovate farming to make it less labor-intensive, then an organic movement might arise to show how family farming by hand is the only socially correct way for farming to happen.

Can you imagine how frustrated a man who wasn't interested in, or particularly physically suited for farming, might feel in this scenario? Or how limited his life options might be? Even if he was particularly gifted in another field, he would be socially ostracized at work and constantly made to feel as if there were something wrong with him for wanting to pursue a passion other than farming. His male identity would be constantly under attack for daring to want something else. If he were able to work outside the farm, there would always be the expectation that his career was his second priority, after number one—the farm. Any time he took off from work would be assumed to be about the farm and that would make him appear less committed to the job. If he hired anyone to help on the farm while he worked, he'd be letting the household down by not truly farming or leaving it in less capable hands, especially if something went wrong. Because only by personally farming was a man really farming. The more wealthy and successful his wife became, the more it would be encouraged that he give up his work and make his farm the most beautiful and plentiful so his wife's status would be elevated.

You get where we are going with this. We indulge in this exercise in alternative history to show how a perfectly plausible social construct can be rationalized by flawed gender-science assumptions. It makes it easy to see how today's gender-based social constructs about women and their social roles is equally false. Because these kind of assumptions about biological traits or innate differences due to gender are, in reality, *all made up*.

Imagine the farm scenario being believed by most men and women and reinforced as an accepted set of gender rules. Well, much of what women have been historically allowed to do for a career has been culturally defined and socialized into us. Then it has been back-end justified based purely on a binary, presumably nature-based, definition.

How Did We Get Here?

Let's take a step back before we move forward. How did we get here? How did we end up with a workplace dominated by white men where women struggle for fair representation? And in the United States, women have had the right to vote for a hundred years, right? Why is this still a problem? Why do barriers still exist?

In our consultation work, people often immediately jump to a nature argument: men are naturally better workers, better leaders, and better built for work outside of the home. In fact, many people who hear the word *leader* still imagine a white man.[22] After all, people assume, "cavemen" hunted for the food and "cavewomen" cooked it. But research suggests that prior to agriculture there was actually much more gender equality.[23] Early human women didn't stay home and clean the cave; they were out gathering food-stuffs. Yes, there was some gender specialization, but if we want to go back to early days, that story suggests better gender equality than we have today.

Even after human societies became agrarian, gender power differences and role differentiation were not clearly defined. Yes, there were societies which relied on men's brute strength to plow, but there were other soci-eties that relied on hoeing, which was done by both men and women.

But as society moved toward increased specialization and trade, where the struggle for food lessened and a wider variety of commer-cial roles emerged, the worth of women's work roles diminished. In the 1100s, "English common law, a combination of Anglo-Saxon and Norman traditions, led to the creation of coverture, which is the belief that married men and women are one financial entity. As such, married women [could not] own property, run taverns or stores or sue in court. Those financial rights could be enjoyed, however, by widows and spin-sters. Over time, coverture was corrupted into the view that women are property of their husbands."[24]

Women lost significant rights as individuals. Whether to protect tradi-tion, wealth, and power, or in fear of political instability, governments legislated and institutionalized gender roles.[25] It became illegal for women to work outside of the home, own property, or have a bank account. And even though democracy spread in the West, women had no legal right to vote, and policies were entrenched in the political system.

The system started to tell a story that physical strength was worth more, so men were more valuable. Yet even jobs that didn't require strength came to be seen as male jobs, as long as they were able to generate wealth. Women were relegated to unpaid or less-valued work. They had neither the political power to make change nor the physical power to resist. How can such a condition be said to be natural? Historians concur, noting that, "there is nothing 'natural' about this system."[26]

But women and men *are* different and have different innate strengths, right? Doesn't biology tell us that? "My son behaves so much differently than my daughter," or "He's all boy." Well, it turns out not so much. The differences between men and women make it seem easy to place everyone into one of two categories, male and female. But the science behind these differences tells us that gender difference is not really that clear-cut. It's much more nuanced. There is actually more variation among members of the same gender than there is between the conventional binary genders. And many people don't subscribe to either gender.

These differences appear big when we think in terms of stereotypical ideals—men or women as representations of the ultimate example of their gender. Such a construct creates a set of characteristics intentionally set in opposition to each other. But researchers note that the science doesn't support the large gender assumptions.[27] Much more of the differentiation is due to socialization rather than physical difference.[28] Jodi has two sons, one with brown hair and one with blond hair. Each has a very different personality from the other and their approaches to life are often described as polar opposite. Yet we don't stereotype those differences with a binary categorization and say that all brown-haired people behave a certain way. That would be ridiculous. If we did, an entirely different socialization and resulting role allocation could occur!

These so-called ideal gender definitions exist at the extreme opposi- tional ends of a scale, and very few of us fit either mold perfectly. The majority of us exist somewhere in the middle. And of course the ideals themselves change over time. Different generations see these definitions very differently. Not that long ago, women were thought incapable of running marathons; now there are more women marathoners than men. If the reason was based on nature or biology, how could it change so drastically? Of course, it couldn't change; it wasn't true to begin with. *It's all made up.* Before women had the right to vote, it was generally believed that women were too emotional to make such decisions. Now it is broadly considered a basic human right. Appendix B provides more eye-opening examples of how attitudes about what women can and cannot do has changed over the past century.

A CHANGING WORKFORCE—BIT BY BIT

A closer look at the history of gender and the workplace illustrates the arbitrariness of these supposed ideals. The place of women in the work- force has steadily changed, as well as the perception of specific industries as masculine or feminine. World War II is an interesting starting point because of significant changes in the workforce made necessary by so many men being away at war. Of course, women worked prior to that.

Women have always worked, especially at lower socioeconomic levels, and during the Victorian Age women worked extensively in textiles, service, retail, workhouses, and on the farm. And enslaved women worked extraordinarily hard physical jobs. But World War II marked a more formal definition of "women's work."

As the timeline on page 24 illustrates, over the last ninety years or so, there have been several shifts in attitude and practice around the role of women in the workplace. Sometimes the shifts are progressive; often they are not. The trend towards women gradually growing their numbers in the workplace and in positions of leadership is improving, albeit very slowly. But each time women move forward, the goalposts that mark success change. It's no longer good enough to simply care for their children; for example, now mothers are expected to entertain them and enrich their education with carefully curated after-school activities and developmental interventions.

WE CAN DO IT

A famous World War II advertisement aimed at getting women to work said, "'What Job is mine on the Victory Line?' If you've sewed on buttons, or made buttonholes on a machine, you can learn to do spot welding on airplane parts. If you've used an electric mixer in your kitchen, you can learn to run a drill press. If you've followed recipes exactly in making cakes, you can learn to load shell."*

And note that acceptable careers for women shift, too—from teachers, nurses, and secretaries to women engineers. (And why do we need to name a gender in front?) You see, to label a job feminine or masculine is also *all made up*. Have you ever noticed how once an industry becomes too "female," men stop entering it and wages go down?[29] The veterinary industry was once dominated by men but is now mostly populated by women (except in industry leadership roles), and this feminization is expected to decrease veterinarian salaries over time.[30]

These shifts can also be the result of automation. When the complexity of a job is reduced, it is often deemed more feminine.[31] For example, in 1910, slicing and wrapping margarine was considered men's work. "Despite the shortage of boys, and the problems with discipline, it took some time before . . . management decided to hire girls on a large scale. The innovation that triggered this change was the introduction, in 1915, of a machine that looked like a large egg slicer, which cut slabs of

---

* Karen Westerberg, "What Job is Mine on the Victory Line?" *Cobblestone* (2007).

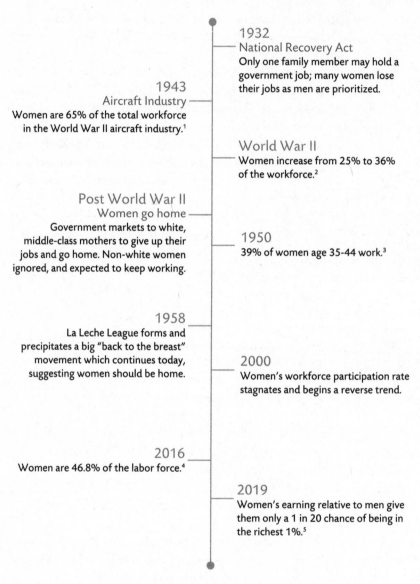

1932
National Recovery Act
Only one family member may hold a government job; many women lose their jobs as men are prioritized.

1943
Aircraft Industry
Women are 65% of the total workforce in the World War II aircraft industry.[1]

World War II
Women increase from 25% to 36% of the workforce.[2]

Post World War II
Women go home
Government markets to white, middle-class mothers to give up their jobs and go home. Non-white women ignored, and expected to keep working.

1950
39% of women age 35-44 work.[3]

1958
La Leche League forms and precipitates a big "back to the breast" movement which continues today, suggesting women should be home.

2000
Women's workforce participation rate stagnates and begins a reverse trend.

2016
Women are 46.8% of the labor force.[4]

2019
Women's earning relative to men give them only a 1 in 20 chance of being in the richest 1%.[5]

Women in the Workplace: Shifts in Attitude*†

---

* Paula England, Paul Allison, and Yuxiao Wu, "Does Bad Pay Cause Occupations to Feminize, Does Feminization Reduce Pay, and How Can We Tell with Longitudinal Data?," *Social Science Research* 36, no. 3 (2007): 1237-1256.

† All timeline citation information begins on page 240.

margarine into pieces of more or less the same size."[32] The job became a woman's job and the pay dropped.

The opposite also happens. Once an industry becomes more visible or lucrative, it becomes more masculine. In the 1950s, most computer programmers were women. But in the 1990s, as the personal computer took off, men entered the computing business en masse and squeezed women out. One woman we worked with commented, "Silicon Valley didn't used to be like the old boys' club. When the Internet was first invented, 40 percent of tech was women." But she noticed that as the industry got more mature and became more lucrative, the men sharpened their elbows and moved women out. It became so competitive that women decided because of family and life obligations and their dislike of the "bro" culture, that they didn't want to compete.[33] The result? Computer programming is now considered men's work. It's all completely *made up*.

This phenomenon is not recent. Consider the history of the three different industries below.

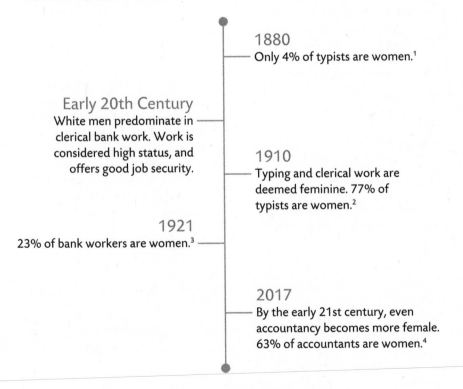

1880
Only 4% of typists are women.[1]

Early 20th Century
White men predominate in clerical bank work. Work is considered high status, and offers good job security.

1910
Typing and clerical work are deemed feminine. 77% of typists are women.[2]

1921
23% of bank workers are women.[3]

2017
By the early 21st century, even accountancy becomes more female. 63% of accountants are women.[4]

The Feminization of Jobs: Clerical Work

Mid 20th Century
Women are called "computers"[1] and computing is considered "women's work."[2]

1984
Women are 37% of programmers.[3]

Mid 80s - mid 90s
Commercials and movies highlight computers as "boy's toys." Math puzzles created to determine who would make a good programmer focused on boys in math.[4]

2014
In less than 30 years, women decline to less than 20% of computer science majors.[5]

2016
But there are some bright spots: Carnegie Mellon has 48% women in its incoming School of Computer Science class[6]—one of the only universities to do so nationally. They created a separate track that doesn't require prior experience and changed their culture, reducing a known barrier to entry.[7]

2019
At the University of Michigan School of Engineering, women are 50% of the engineering faculty, role modeling to young women that it's possible.[8]

The Masculinization of Jobs: Computer Programming

"It really amazed me that these *men* were programmers, because I thought it was women's work!" —*Elsie Shutt, hired by Raytheon in 1953*[34]

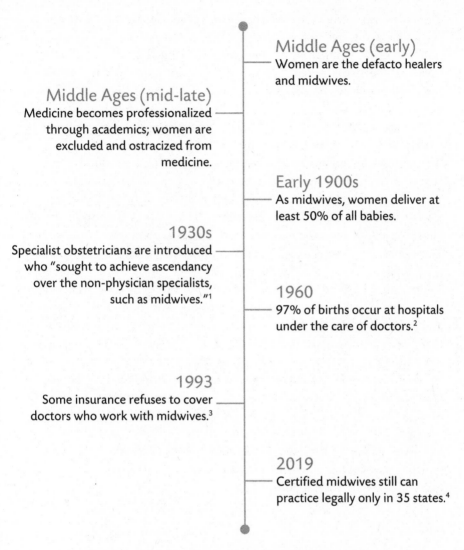

Middle Ages (early)
Women are the defacto healers and midwives.

Middle Ages (mid-late)
Medicine becomes professionalized through academics; women are excluded and ostracized from medicine.

Early 1900s
As midwives, women deliver at least 50% of all babies.

1930s
Specialist obstetricians are introduced who "sought to achieve ascendancy over the non-physician specialists, such as midwives."[1]

1960
97% of births occur at hospitals under the care of doctors.[2]

1993
Some insurance refuses to cover doctors who work with midwives.[3]

2019
Certified midwives still can practice legally only in 35 states.[4]

The Masculinization of Jobs: The Business of Birthing Babies

Each of these examples shows how a job, once considered the domain of only men or women, transitioned to the domain of the other gender. The essence of the story is that these assignments are all made up based on bifurcation of roles and on a single criterion: gender. It's this history that we need to recognize honestly so we can change the future. The good news is: *because we as a society have made it so, we can unmake it, too.*

Why should you care? Because we all want to have an impact that aligns with who we are, to pursue our passions and métier. It's that simple.

These arbitrary gender barriers stop that from happening. Why should gender have any role in determining which career we end up in?

Two young women we've worked with wanted to be surgeons. The father of the first woman told her, "You can't have a family and be a surgeon!" So she changed her goal and is now a nutritionist. The second woman interned at a surgery, saw the lifestyle role modeled by the mostly male surgeons, and concluded, "I can't have a family and be a surgeon!" She's now a surgical nurse practitioner. Simply because of gender norms, there are two fewer, potentially brilliant surgeons in the world. Isn't it way past time to change these restrictive, made-up gender definitions?

Here's something we hear a lot: "But what about birthing and breast-feeding babies—men can't do that, right?" This line is used to justify all kinds of things. Yes, many women birth babies at some point in their life. Those who do are pregnant for nine months. They have the baby, which takes a day or two. Some breastfeed, sometimes for six to twelve months. Some women birth more than one child. Taken all together, on average, this would mean a one-to-three-year interruption in a woman's career, assuming that is all they did. One to three years. In a career of thirty to forty years, that is a very small percentage of the total. Of course, not all women do this and not all mothers take time off for pregnancy or to breastfeed. And it's now increasingly common for men to take parental leave.[35] So we are talking about designing an entire system around something that happens for *some* people for a very small amount of time. It's absurd, really.

Appendix C includes a short history of women's rights. And yes, there have been changes for the better. But progress has been slow and barriers remain—and will remain as long as this made-up narrative and the biases that come with it are not addressed.

2
Unconscious Bias

WHY ARE THESE MADE-UP SITUATIONS still accepted? A key driver is unconscious bias, a tendency deeply embedded in human thinking. This is such an important and pervasive barrier that we dedicate this chapter to documenting biases that exist. We know it's a negative place, but don't let learning about unconscious bias crush you into believing it can't be fixed. It can. We just need to define the problem before we explain how to turn bias on its head.

Ohio State University defines unconscious or implicit bias this way:

> Also known as implicit social cognition, implicit bias refers to the attitudes or stereotypes that affect our understanding, actions, and decisions in an unconscious manner. These biases, which encompass both favorable and unfavorable assessments, are activated involuntarily and without an individual's awareness or intentional control. Residing deep in the subconscious, these biases are different from known biases that individuals may choose to conceal for the purposes of social and/or political correctness. Rather, implicit biases are not accessible through introspection. [36]

Let's break down this definition:

1. The brain often makes quick decisions that are often invisible to us.

2. The narrative on which these decisions are made was built over a lifetime of our own personal experiences.

That is, there is no cognition or intent behind the decision-making process; it's simply an automated response based on a person's individual socialization. It's not our fault. But we can do something about it. We need to know and accept that this is happening to all of us.

Understanding unconscious bias is important because, unmitigated, it can work against any group that holds a minority position in a given situation (including white men) or that doesn't fit the dominant group's stereotype. So, in leadership positions, it works against women because the majority group has traditionally been white men. Boys, especially Asian boys, are stereotypically said to be better at math and science, a bias that works against girls, Hispanics, and African Americans.[37] Bias shows up in job roles too, protecting the incumbent group. For example, it can be difficult for men to become nurses or daycare workers, and it can be challenging for African Americans and women to gain tech roles.

Bias doesn't negatively impact only hiring, it also shows up in promotions and whether or not people ultimately stay in a particular job or career field. It impacts whether a person feels psychologically safe or included in their work or school environment. It also affects whether or not someone's perspective is integrated into decision-making. In this way, unconscious bias reinforces stereotypes because out-groups remain out-groups and are thus unable to influence or erode stereotypes.

BIAS 101 – A REFERENCE GUIDE

Putting a name to each different type of bias helps us recognize it when it occurs.

LEADERSHIP BIAS

In our work, we've seen significant bias in the workplace around leadership. This is a deeply rooted bias because, for most of us, history shapes how we feel. And historically, people conflate leadership with masculinity.[38] Furthermore, the traits that male leaders from the past have displayed are assumed to be the characteristics of good leaders. People feel that good leaders are strong, assertive, decisive, calm, and tough. And when men behave this way, people naturally feel good—it confirms our expectations. When women exhibit these characteristics, people feel awkward, as if it is unusual or out of character for women. So we struggle to explain it. We either decide she is not a normal woman, or we change the words used to describe those characteristics; instead of "strong" she is "brash," instead of "assertive" she is "aggressive," and instead of "tough" she is "bitchy."[39]

Compare these definitions of top leadership skills:

- *Entrepreneur Magazine*: Focus, confidence, transparency, integrity, inspiration, passion, innovation, patience, stoicism, wonkiness, authenticity, open-mindedness, decisiveness, personableness, empowerment, positivity, generosity, persistence, insightfulness, communication, accountability, and restlessness[40]

- *Harvard Business Review*: Strong ethics and moral standards, provides goals with loose guidelines/direction, clearly communicates expectations, flexible, is committed to ongoing training, communicates openly and often, is open to new ideas, creates a feeling of failing or succeeding together, nurtures growth of others, and provides a safe environment for trial and error[41]

Does your definition of leadership also include these skills? Notice that many of these traits are gender-neutral and some are even stereotypically female traits. Yet organizations often credit men with being better leaders than women, with male examples of leadership exemplified as the natural model. Clearly the leadership skill itself is not as important in the definition of a good leader as one would expect. At the end of the day, people mostly think of leadership as male merely because leaders in the past were men.

Here are some examples of leadership bias we've heard in our workshops:

- A female ad-agency executive told us that "women did not fit into the senior management circle" because they tend to overcommunicate, take too long to say things, and use too many words. She said she was successful because she was succinct but could understand why she was the only woman in leadership because other women don't seem to innately possess this skill.

- A senior leader in an entertainment company was given similar feedback when she was turned down for a promotion that should have been a sure thing. During the debrief, she was given a list of reasons why, even though she had met all the criteria formally spelled out for her for the role, it was given to a male colleague who hadn't met all of the requirements. Her tendency to "overcommunicate" was cited, although without specific example. She was also told that she needed to "push back on senior executives more" but was confused because the winning candidate was commonly described by peers as a "butt-kissing yes-man."

- Men in an organization with almost all men from the mid-level up said that the number-one way to get promoted—what the company valued most—was working hard. But the women felt they were doing the majority of the actual work, and very few women were promoted. They said that "being friends with executives, golfing, and going to lunch" seemed to be valued more highly than working hard because that is who they saw being promoted.

These are just a few examples of what we have encountered professionally. Now ask yourself: Who springs to mind when you think of great leadership? Is it a man? You wouldn't be alone.

SYSTEM 1 AND SYSTEM 2 THINKING

Nobel laureate Daniel Kahneman pioneered a new way of understanding how the brain makes decisions and the pitfalls of trusting them. He highlights the trade-offs between what he calls System 1 thinking, where the brain operates automatically and unconsciously, and System 2 thinking, which is more deliberate, conscious, and logical. He points out the cognitive bias inherent in System 1 thinking and what happens when we over rely on it.[42] It's easy to find examples in our work and in popular culture of how System 1 thinking negatively impacts women.

- *"One hundred percent of the resumes we get are from white men. Therefore, there are no women candidates available for this job."* Using System 1 thinking, people are influenced by irrelevant numbers, such as the size of the candidate pool for a single job posting. Called **anchoring bias**, this refrain ignores the actual number of women candidates in the market. It also ignores how unconscious bias can affect a company's marketing process for candidates: how job descriptions are worded, where job ads are posted, how many women's faces show up in the company's marketing materials, what is reflected in the press about the company, even what products the company sells—all of which have been found to influence the size of a single job's application pool.[43]

- *"We are hiring plenty of women at lower levels in the organization, so naturally this problem will solve itself in time. We have only men at the top because there were only men at the bottom when they were hired."* With System 1 thinking, the answer that comes most easily to mind seems right, an example of **availability bias**. The belief that this problem will solve itself over time is a common trap that leads people to dismiss the need for gender equity intervention. But it isn't true. The management consulting company McKinsey & Company predicts it will be more than a hundred years before gender parity is achieved in organizations.[44] Cornell University researchers predict gender equity in computer science won't be achieved until 2100 or beyond![45] That's not your grandkids, that's your grandkids' grandkids. Further, women have graduated with bachelor's degrees in larger numbers than men since 1981.[46] If the quote above were correct, then shouldn't there be *more* women than men in leadership? Yet less than 13 percent of corporate leaders are women.[47]

- *"I feel bad for men these days with all of the sexual harassment allegations. How do they know that some innocuous thing they do won't end up getting them in trouble?"* It's common to substitute easier questions for the harder question at hand, another feature of System 1 thinking known as **substitution bias.** This bias allows a quick response to a question or comment by using a ready and obvious answer to a different question. In the above example, when harassed and assaulted women come forward to address their perpetrators after years of victimization, the response to the problem often relates to a completely different question: whether or not men will be frivolously and falsely accused going forward. The leap to a substitute issue further demeans the women who are victims and blocks the development of solutions to the complex problem of sexual harassment.

- *"Susan Fowler took her harassment complaints to Uber's HR department, only to have her concerns dismissed because her harasser was a star-performer."*[12] **Optimism/loss-aversion bias** is when System 1 thinking overestimates the good and underestimates the bad. This example at Uber shows that the good—someone is a star-performer—so far outweighs the bad—harassed women—that the behavior was allowed to continue unchecked. [48]

- *"If we have quotas for women, we will end up recruiting and promoting people who are less effective."* Using System 1 thinking, brains are fooled by context, and people fall into what is called **framing bias.** People think quotas, for example, will interrupt the meritocracy by rewarding group status over merit. But as we often point out, this assumes a working meritocracy, and we know the system isn't a working meritocracy to begin with. Historically women were blocked, both legally and socially, from working. White men benefited because they were unencumbered by legal barriers, which is how they came to dominate. Statistically, at least some of those candidates weren't as well qualified as some people in the blocked groups. Moreover, those in leadership built cultural and systemic barriers to outsiders. Research shows these cultural and systemic barriers will not entirely disappear until a minority group reaches at least 25 percent of the total group.[49] Until then, a minority group is dominated and shifted by the majority. This is why tokenism hasn't worked. A single underrepresented group member can't sufficiently sway or impact the group dynamic.

- *"The guys on our floor have been giving Sally 'the business' for years, whistling when she arrives at work and offering to take her to lunch. She has always been really good-natured about it. But recently, Tim gave her a playful smack on the butt when she walked by. Everyone thinks she should report Tim to HR but Sally just blushed and hid at her desk."* As Kahneman's research has found, for some reason we often consider prior decisions relevant in current decision-making, a tendency called **sunk-cost bias**. In economics, it's throwing away good money hoping to turn around the bad, like the surge of hopeful marketing spending almost every company makes right before filing for bankruptcy. People's brains remember how much money, time, and effort has been invested and consider that in the next decision, even though it has no relevance. Often when a woman experiences sexual harassment, she fails to report it because she considers all the times she has tolerated low-level unwanted sexual innuendo in the past. There is often a belief that, because she tolerated it before, it would be inconsistent or unreasonable to discourage it now. As much as hindsight has revealed to her that she likely should have spoken up sooner, she may refuse to let go of the previous flawed decision-making. And so perpetrators of sexual harassment continue get away with their behavior in the workplace and victims continue to feel guilty and shameful.

- *"Let's promote Bob instead of Ellen. Just last week he was telling me about this excellent deal he closed. And while Ellen's numbers look as good as his on paper, she has been out on maternity leave for the past six weeks, and I can't remember her closing such an impressive deal before that."* Kahneman's research with colleague Barbara Fredrickson showed that the human brain also doesn't tend to remember perceptions of duration, a phenomenon called **duration-neglect bias**. Memories of prior events are based on remembering peak and end experiences. People like an event if it ended well or had a moment of great enjoyment and have an unfavorable memory if something tragic happened or if an experience ended on a low note. Annual review meetings can be particularly challenging for women, especially those who don't self-promote or speak proudly about their accomplishments, and for those who may have taken some time off during the year; they may find it harder to get a positive appraisal for the same quality work. [50, 51]

ORGANIZATIONAL BIAS

Kahneman's ground-breaking work has been reinforced by other thought leaders, including Howard Ross, who studied the impact of bias and applied his research to the corporate context. He describes three ways in which unconscious bias manifests itself when we make decisions about ourselves and others:[52]

- *"He's just like I was at that age. He'll make a big impact on our organization [just like I have]."* When people favor employees or candidates who remind them of themselves, they fall victim to **affinity bias.** Think about how often someone gets hired because of this bias. In fact, it has often been seen as a good thing. However, this bias is often based on physical traits and similar background experiences, not on merit or capability. And it corresponds to the dangers of unconsciously building homogeneity on our teams.

- *"Maybe I'm just not cut out for a career in finance."* **Unconscious self-perception bias** or Claude Steele's highly researched **stereotype threat**[53] is when people buy in to negative stereotypes about themselves and as a result perform less well. When women struggle in a male-dominated environment, it may have more to do with expecting to struggle than any actual skill deficiency.

- *"I always knew she was too emotional."* When someone performs in a way that agrees with a stereotype, people believe it; but if they act against a stereotype, it's rejected as coincidental. **Confirmation bias** is why women are commonly seen as having "feminine" leadership traits such as empathy, compassion, and the ability to nurture, and are less often described as strong, decisive, or strategic. It is also why when a woman does display strength, for example, it is dismissed as pushiness or some other negative characteristic. It is very difficult for our unchecked minds to accept counter-stereotypical information.

Joan Williams and Rachel Dempsey have documented four types of implicit bias that negatively impact women in the workplace.[54] In their research about women in the legal profession, as well as other high-stakes workplaces, they noticed some common trends that hold women, especially women of color, back from achieving their true potential.

- *"Your performance was pretty good, and you are almost there. Let's review this again at next year's promotional cycle."* Groups stereotyped as less competent often have to prove themselves over and over, because of what is called **prove-it-again bias**. Williams and Dempsey found that women's accomplishments are often seen as one-offs or lucky, particularly if they violate a stereotype, such as a requirement for highly technical skills or strong decision-making. Men's accomplishments are seen in aggregate. Further, a woman's accomplishments are often considered less significant compared to the same work done by a man. As Iris Bohnet notes, "When performance is observable, successful women are rated as less likable than men."[55] This is where intangibles are often drafted into the evaluation process: language like *fit* and *executive presence*. On the other hand, "When performance is ambiguous, successful women are rated as less competent than men."[56] For women to prove performance, there always seems to be one more opportunity needed or an extra step in the process that isn't required of most men.

- *"I think she is too much of a bitch to be the leader we need."* Williams and Dempsey write that a narrower range of workplace behavior is often expected from women, which they call **tightrope bias**. Women are expected to balance the stereotypical masculine traits of a leader with likability and femininity, an often contradictory challenge. If she comes across as too assertive, she can be labeled as bitchy. Unlike men's, women's performance reviews often contain assessments of subjective qualities and personality traits, rather than a focus on results or measurable skills.[57] If a woman spends too much time adjusting her behavior to walk this tightrope, she can be seen as inauthentic. And note, this tightrope is enforced by both men and women leaders, not only men.

- *"Whenever I walk by her desk, she is always away at some appointment with her kids."* Mothers, Williams and Dempsey found, are stereotyped as less competent or committed, whereas fathers are seen as breadwinners who shouldn't take time off. This bias is called the **parental wall**. Whenever a mother is away from the office, it is often assumed she is home with her kids, and she gets penalized. She is not seen as someone who can be good at work and good at being a parent.

- *"I wonder how she got that role. I heard she slept with the boss."* **Tug-of-war bias** says that underrepresented groups tend to fight and are suspicious of each other's success. They tend to be harder on each other with a real implication for career progress. This bias can be the root of much woman-versus-woman conflict and can lead to women accusing each other of tokenism or "sleeping their way up." There is also the assumption that if one woman earned a leadership role, there is no space for another. So it forces women to compete rather than work together.

Finally, there is a phenomenon that occurs when bias happens throughout multiple stages of a process: **cascading bias**. For example, when a company uses traditional hiring practices, such as hiring candidates from similar companies in the same industry or graduates from a select number of "brand name" schools, it is at risk for compounding the selection biases of all of those companies or schools. It is well documented that Ivy League schools skew to wealthy, white students regardless of ability or talent.[58] But when companies assume that candidates from these schools are better qualified than candidates from urban colleges, for example, they perpetuate a biased candidate pool.

Trusting competitors' hiring practices can result in the same cascade. When a company recruits candidates who hold comparable positions at other companies, it compounds whatever biases those companies hold. Also, when companies use hiring committees to vet candidates or discuss an employee's readiness for promotion, the unconscious biases of each of the committee members are triggered, as well as the tendency for groups to be subject to politics and groupthink. Unconscious biases are not mitigated by simply adding more voices to the conversation—they are actually further exaggerated.

UNCONSCIOUS BIAS—THE HIDDEN IMPACTS

Unconscious bias is, of course, *unconscious*. Without careful self-scrutiny, its principle dangers are hidden to us. In addition to the external impacts of bias, such as reinforcing stereotypes and keeping women underrepresented in powerful roles, there are also internal impacts.

Social psychologist Claude Steele, who has spent a lifetime studying stereotypes, has documented the very real physical damage that can occur when people work under the effects of stereotypes. He contends that being aware of negative stereotypes for a group you belong to, even subliminally, causes performance-limiting anxiety, including both physical and mental effects. The constant subliminal awareness that your positive actions will be dismissed and your negative actions reinforced by the stereotype, or that you feel you need to represent all women when you lead, raises the heart rate, takes blood away from cognitive function, and lowers performance. It is actually enough stress on the body to reduce a person's lifespan.[59]

And it can be completely unconscious. The performance impact is stunning.[60] A famous Harvard study had two groups of similarly-skilled Asian women take a math test. One group was reminded through demographic pre-test questions that they are Asian (and thus a member of a positive math performance stereotype group), and the other group was reminded of their gender (and thus a member of a negative math performance stereotype group—Barbie thinks "math is hard"[61]). The group with the gender stereotype threat performed significantly less well on the test.[62] Similar tests show the same documented effect—stereotype threat—negatively impacts performance.

The impact is not short term, either. Long-term physical effects of stereotype threat, such as increased anxiety, heart rate, and blood pressure, are cumulative and life-shortening.[63] Also, the poor performance that can result reinforces or confirms the group

THE TRICKS BIAS PLAYS

Knowing there is bias doesn't make it go away—Howard Ross offers a training session where he walks participants through a series of examples of the tricks bias plays on the brain, everything from showing lines that appear to converge (but don't) and images laced with stereotypical props intended to nudge thinking. The audience buys in. They agree there is bias and they actively want to eliminate it from their decision-making. Then he breaks them into groups and each is given a resume to evaluate. They evaluate as individuals first, then as a group, rating the resume on a scale of one to one hundred. He records the results on the board and gets a range of between forty and about ninety. Then he reveals that the resumes are all identical except for the name and photo. Even after an entire workshop predicated on knowing that people have unconscious bias, nobody can help how brains work, even if they are willing and try!*

---

* Howard Ross, "'Everyday Bias: Identifying and Navigating Unconscious Judgments' | Talks at Google," https://www.youtube.com/watch?v=v01SxXui9XQ.

stereotype on an individual level, further increasing performance anxiety, reinforcing the performance impact, and so on in a vicious cycle. It's as if women at work are carrying a backpack of emotional baggage all day, every day, for their working lives. Think of the physical and mental toll this takes. These internal impacts alone should compel anyone who wants to optimize human capital to address the problems of unconscious bias.

The math-test study above illustrates the impact of priming on a person's level of stereotype threat. If a person is primed—or reminded in advance—that she is capable, she performs better than if primed negatively. Again: this process is completely unconscious.

Microaggressions can reinforce impact. Small reminders of stereotypes, delivered as insults or slights on a regular basis, microaggressions can be couched humorously or dismissively. "Don't drive with Inga—she's Asian" or "You don't sound like us. What country are you from?" or "You should smile more." Although the receiving party can feel like these are intentional, many perpetrators are quite ignorant of the negative impact. They tend to deliver microaggressions as a way to maintain their own in-group status without overt malice toward the recipient. But the effect is the same: remind someone of a negative stereotype and their performance will suffer. It's a form of priming.

Unconscious bias is dangerous because its impacts are felt whether or not malice is intended. Understanding what it is and how it occurs is critical to recognizing the impact on human behavior and decision-making.

In our consulting engagements, we have found that most corporate recruitment efforts target graduates from a short list of name-brand schools, woo only candidates who hold the same role at another firm in the same industry, or tap into a network of people who have similar backgrounds. When we question organizational leaders about these tactics, we hear a common response: "It's easier and avoids risk." Well yes, it does make recruitment and training easier. Going outside the box takes more time and makes comparative judgment harder. Also, when you hire stereotypical leaders—tall, male, white, Ivy League—nobody faults you if they fail. "Who knew the Harvard guy wouldn't work out?" But when you hire a nontraditional candidate (yes, there is even a name for this) and they don't work out, your decision-making is questioned. You get blamed for *not* succumbing to bias.

There is as much variability in the workplace performance of graduates of the top schools as there is from other educational experiences. So our underlying assumption that these selection processes yield the best candidates is inherently flawed. And these selection errors are compounded when the processes of other organizations are weighed more highly than our own discernment.

There is a hidden cost to unconscious bias and the way it cascades—a smaller supply of qualified labor means a higher price for that labor. As the leadership pipeline constricts, this effect compounds, and the price of labor at the top keeps rising. One reason executive salaries have become exponentially higher than entry-level salaries is reduced supply.[64] Bias plays a big role by artificially narrowing the candidate pool. This is a self-perpetuating problem.

If this bias information is new to you, don't despair. We didn't know most of it when we started doing this work. And growing up in a biased world, we didn't see it, even when it was directly affecting us. Just because women are victims of bias doesn't mean they don't unwittingly impose bias on others. The tendency is deep and hidden. It's invisible.

The problem with bias invisibility is twofold. On the one hand, not knowing it is there causes people to falsely attribute 100 percent of success or failure to merit.[65] While nobody admits to believing that women are less capable or qualified for leadership, that is nonetheless the subtle implication of a merit-based system where women aren't as successful. It also provides a perceived rational explanation for gender inequity, one that in many cases puts the responsibility for the lack of representation and progress on the women themselves. While women do share in the responsibility to drive their careers, work hard, promote themselves, and remain focused on goals such as senior leadership, it is also imperative that men and women understand and mitigate the impact of unconscious and unintended biases along the development pipeline.

Secondly, denial of the problem eliminates the possibility of understanding, empathizing, and ultimately, solving it. Studies show that organizations that believe they are meritocracies are often much more biased than those that understand that bias happens.[66] So the leaders who recruit, evaluate, and promote based on merit are deficient in critical skills and further perpetuate bias. Qualified candidates and employees are overlooked, held back, or slowed. They can become frustrated and leave, costing money in turnover, or they stay but are underutilized. Low bias awareness in an organization usually signals stronger likelihood of many underlying systemic problems.

"I always hire the best person for the job, regardless of gender, race, or any other factor." We hear this claim a lot. Managers tell us there is no bias in their processes. They believe strongly that they only hire the best people for the job, that they employ rational decision-making, and cultivate a meritocracy. If women are not represented, they say it is a problem of numbers—there are not enough women in the pipeline, and the situation will change once there are. Or women choose to exclude themselves from the pipeline because of the type of work. This is commonly cited in legal, consulting, or Big Four CPA firms because of the need for "billable hours." People think that women choose not to enter these fields because they don't want to do the work, particularly when they become mothers. For tech jobs, such as coding or engineering, people commonly think women exclude themselves because they aren't interested in science.

But as Kahneman's research shows, the majority of our decision-making is based on flawed System 1 thinking. In our consulting projects, we often document this feedback and then explore the data. Most often we find the real story. For example, a software firm may say their population of new hires represents the demographics of the software market, but we do the research and show the client the number of graduates and compare it to their on-campus recruiting pools. Generally, the clients are shocked when they see how their perception compares to reality because they truly believe their system and process is above bias.

Part of the problem is that believing in bias often carries stigma. Who wants to admit to negative behavior, even if it is unconscious? Nobody likes thinking that they are biased. Or that their processes are flawed. And the big question it raises is, "I thought I got here solely because of my talent and hard work—didn't I?" There is even a fear, and not an unfounded one, that if the environment were truly biased in their favor, changing it could make them less able to compete. This fear can restrict the impetus to change when those in charge of ridding the system of bias feel they are themselves vulnerable to being displaced.

Awareness of unconscious bias and moving from System 1 to System 2 thinking provide the best foundational opportunity for mitigating its effects. Once you know bias is there and begin to see examples around you, you can work out how to slow down and make better decisions.

Finally, it's important to note that women often have internal unconscious biases. That may seem strange—how can women be unconsciously biased against themselves—but our own research over many years has shown that women often buy in to some of the common external biases against women, unquestioningly, in a way that dictates their own behaviors and responses.

These behaviors don't always help careers progress. In fact, the extent to which women buy into the stereotypes is often directly correlated to performance. For example, a woman who feels a lot of conflict between her role as a parent and her career tends to be less successful at work and more encumbered with guilt than a woman who sees the roles as compatible and complementary.

The larger the role conflict, we found, the larger the performance gap. Some women see career and family as a binary choice. Even women who are not parents can experience conflict between their roles as friends or extended family members and their career goals—with a negative impact on performance.

Women haven't only been victimized by unconscious and conscious bias; they have also perpetuated it. Women throughout the ages have helped enforce some of society's rules by policing other women and raising children in their image. For some, this is a conscious act, done perhaps to protect traditional roles or models of femininity. For others, it is an unconscious implementation of what they've seen and been taught by external social cues. The solution to diminishing bias is not only a challenge for men and organizational leadership—it is also critical to acknowledge the work women need to do to change our own behavior.

And don't worry—we'll get to solutions later on. In the meantime, have a look at Appendix E for a self-assessment tool to help show where you are on this journey of discovery. Recognizing unconscious bias and learning to think differently is a twenty-first-century leadership skill. But before we get there, let's consider some of the bad habits and flawed assumptions that bias and complacency can lead to, for both men and women.

3
Flawed Assumptions and Bad Habits

OUR LAST CHAPTER'S CONCLUSION is worth repeating: recognizing unconscious bias and learning to think differently is a twenty-first-century leadership skill. And a key part of the learning process is the recognition of flawed assumptions and the bad habits they give rise to. Because as you would expect, unconscious bias shapes attitude, which in turn shapes behavior—something we have seen over and over again with workshop participants across the country. Men and women, in different ways and from different perspectives, fall prey to presuppositions, which condition how they behave in the workplace. Finding out what we assume, it turns out, can tell us a lot about why we act a certain way.

Let's begin by examining the underlying hidden assumptions that are so prevalent and unquestioningly accepted in our culture that we don't even notice how they govern how many women behave in workplaces that, let's face it, are designed primarily by and for men.

THE IDEAL WOMAN: DO IT ALL, LOOK GOOD, BE NICE[67]

For many women in the workplace, the goal is to balance their perceived role as a woman with that of a worker, which are often seen as incompatible. The ideal woman has been conditioned by some common rules of femininity. Those rules? Simple: Do it all, look good, and be nice. Follow these, and you will be praised. Reject them at your peril.

Chasing this ideal, in our view, causes women to buy in to the rules unconsciously. These rules are not even questioned. Think about how women widely hated Yahoo's former CEO Marissa Mayer when she went back to work so soon after having a baby. Or how Hillary Clinton was heavily criticized for wearing pantsuits and sounding "patronizing" during her presidential campaign. And most people don't like to think about women getting rich from their work and driving around in a Ferrari—many of us would much rather see them work selflessly for passion or philanthropy. Women hear this message loud and strong. Nobody wants to be criticized for not being woman enough.

The problem with these feminine rules, though, is that they are in direct conflict with what it takes to be successful in the workplace. Doing it all instead of delegating causes burnout and limits leadership development. Looking good, especially striving for perfection, often is a misallocation of critical resources, like time and creative energy. Being nice can mean under-resourcing critical projects and setting them up for failure. So, understanding the root cause of these false assumptions is the first step to breaking the habits they lead to.

Have you ever felt like the highest compliment you could pay a woman is to tell her how "you don't know how she does it all?" Try it—she will glow! She works all day, she gets home and cooks a nutritious meal for her family, and then shows up to the PTA meeting with a homemade pie. Her kids take customized bento boxes for lunch. Her partner gets a well-coordinated tribute to their favorite rock band for their birthday. At work she organizes the office potluck, runs the local employee resource group, and still manages to be the first to submit her expense reports. She is detailed, organized, and amazing—a magician. Other women see her achievements and crave the "does it all" label too, so they secretly compete to raise it to the next level.

The do-it-all rule has, deep down, some primary

GETTING INOCULATED

Some women have been what we call inoculated against these rules. Perhaps their mother worked or they had some kind of epiphany. We hope these "woke" women can help inoculate the majority of women who don't see these harmful rules and help them become more aware.

assumptions or core beliefs that unconsciously fuel it. "I am primarily responsible for my home and family, and my career is secondary. I show commitment by the amount of time I dedicate. Anything I do for myself is selfish." These assumptions women hold have significant consequences and are worth looking at in some detail.

Many people believe that women are primarily responsible for home and family, and career comes second, which tends to be at the root of why most women assume their career must be deprioritized when they have children. It's why most women still make dinner (70 percent of women vs 46 percent of men), spending fifty minutes a day preparing food compared to twenty minutes for men.[68] (Interestingly, while the percentage of men who cook has increased over the past five years, the amount of time women spend cooking has also increased!)[69] This is also why women are criticized as bad mothers for working too much or not spending enough time parenting. "Those children behave so badly. I hear their mother is at work all the time."

As we have seen, men are assumed to be primarily responsible for earning a living and providing for the family and feel less worthy (and masculine) for losing a job or earning less than their wives. Society has built many structures around these assumptions. Even the fact that daycare and flexible hours are seen as important workplace benefits for women (not men) reinforces these assumptions. You don't have to agree with these assumptions. Just know that our research uncovered them as a pervasive foundation, or reason, why women feel such work-life conflict. We want you to notice how often it drives some of the choices you see women make.

For many women, the career-life balance struggle is about time management. We get lots of requests in our work to help women balance time. But these requests are based on the assumption that the amount of time a woman gives to each task indicates her commitment to it. To be a good mother, "to raise her child," she has to personally change each diaper. A good employee is one who works long hours—in the office where people can see her. This assumption is also used as justification for women doing everything themselves, handling every task personally rather than delegating. It's as if they have to prove their commitment by doing it all themselves.

Have you ever noticed that when a woman takes time for herself, she's often labeled as selfish? Or how at a dinner party, the women go into the kitchen to help clean up while the men have another drink? Women have been schooled to sacrifice their self-interests for others. This assumption causes women to submerge their ideas and needs in discussions or resource requests. "Well, the company is struggling financially this year so I guess my bonus can wait." They volunteer to stay late to take on the extra burden of work, they tidy things up, and they organize everything. Think about how often women step up when a call goes out for volunteers, or how guilty they feel if they don't. We have heard women actually apologize for *not* volunteering. Most women fear asking for a raise; they are squeamish about looking too greedy. In fact, pretty much the worst possible insult (or microaggression) you can perpetuate on a woman is to imply she is selfish. Or done backwards, it's huge to compliment women for their selflessness, which is a very common reinforcement of this assumption.

The ideal woman also has to look good. Here too, a couple of false assumptions underlie the rule: "I need to be perfect. I am not good enough."

On first blush, the look-good rule seems to be all about personal appearance. And women don't spend more time getting ready in the morning for nothing. Showing up with air-dried hair and no makeup definitely garners labels for women that don't apply to men who do the same. But it is deeper than that. It means spending more time on little details, preparation, and checking boxes than on producing content. Because women feel they can't just do something; they have to do it 110 percent. There is no room for good, only great. Mistakes can't happen, and if they do, they need to be buried and dealt with privately.

Youth sports coaches often note how the main difference between boys and girls in organized sports is how much more dramatically the girls fear mistakes—so much so that the girls are less willing to try new moves or practice challenging skills. This is particularly true if a mistake is highly visible or gets called out by others. The girls retreat, hide on the field, and avoid trying again. They internalize failure as unworthiness and sometimes even leave the sport. Boys, on the other hand, seem to let go of their mistakes more readily and even use getting called out to dig in and try harder the next time. But with sports, as with any kind of learning, making hands-on mistakes is integral to the process. Nobody learns when they leave. Think about how often you have seen women struggle with an all-or-nothing attitude. There is often no room for middle ground.

We have found there is an endless loop in many women's brains that constantly tells them how important it is to be perfect. It is reinforced daily by little things in the external environment. Girls in school are rewarded for sitting still, keeping quiet, and following rules. We tell them how good they look and compliment their clothing. No wonder some women can't seem to send an email without making sure it is perfectly written!

This tendency has big implications for a woman's willingness to take risks. A woman who takes a leap and falls short of expectations runs the risk of shattering the illusion of perfection. It can be easier to master smaller roles, and can feel satisfying for her to languish there being excellent, rather than to venture into the unknown.

Falling short of perfection, which is inevitable, means that many women feel they are not good enough. Reinforced by highly Photoshopped magazine photos of society's idea of the perfect woman, normal women are reminded daily that they fall short: not pretty enough, not smart enough, not worthy enough, you name it. At work, even well-meaning feedback can be received as reinforcement of a woman's internal perceptions of incompetence. Ever have a woman break down and cry after receiving negative feedback? Did you wonder why the emotional response seemed out of step with the level of the criticism?

Research shows that the less confident a woman is, the more time she will spend in the morning to look good.[70] We have no doubt this is the case with looking good at work as well. Women consistently report far less confidence than men on a wide range of topics where their actual performance is similar.[71] The less confident she is, the more she may avoid risk for fear of making a mistake. And in this way, she actually slows her own development, making mistakes less often and burdening each error with the potential for catastrophe.

As well as doing it all and looking good, women are expected to be nice. Women have been taught that being liked is required. This comment always gets a laugh from our audiences—especially from women who have read Lois P. Frankel's controversial book *Nice Girls Don't Get the Corner Office*.[72] But let's face it—the traditional rules of femininity dictate that women should be pleasant and get along with everyone. Nobody wants to be seen as "the bitch" when they are assertive or have their voice considered shrill. The result of this fear can be conflict avoidance, resistance to negotiation, and an unwillingness to draw boundaries. And while companies invest in training women to get better at negotiation, they miss that some foundational assumptions are working against them in the background, dictating feminine rules. It's why they are better at negotiating for others than they are for themselves.

Underlying this fear of being seen as a bitch are two other core assumptions: "I'm not entitled to rewards" and "If I follow the rules, I'll be taken care of."

Women often believe they should find intrinsic joy in pursuing their passion rather than money or power. This belief is reinforced by many career and life coaches who implore women to do something meaningful, not just a job. Once we spoke to a group of young college women, many of whom wanted to go into finance and make money. But people in their life were encouraging them not to, saying things like, "It's too competitive or too much about the money." One of our interviewees said, "Wall Street is soulless," and therefore not a place for women. The message is loud and clear: money for women is a bad thing. Of course, everyone gets this message to some degree, but for women, it is trumpeted from the hilltops. Perhaps it is meant as a consolation for leaving underpaid jobs to balance family obligations, but it can be damaging. It can end up justifying women earning less or entering (and staying in) a field that is less financially lucrative. Maybe this is why there are so many women in nonprofit roles (where, even there, they are often paid less than men for the same work).

And it's more than just money. Women are not supposed to want to drive the fancy sports car or golf on Saturdays. They are supposed to work hard and then come home and work harder, glowing in the aura of having contributed to society. Because enjoying visible rewards would be what? That's right—selfish. Do you see what we mean?

Women also often feel they have to be recognized by others and rewarded versus asking for rewards themselves.[73] Microsoft CEO Satya Nadella reinforced this belief when he advised women not to ask for raises, but to keep their heads down and wait to be noticed. People who don't ask for raises, in his mind, have a "superpower of good karma," and the pay will naturally follow their good behavior.[74] But this is not what happens. Women make less than men from their first job out of college, and this compounds over a lifetime.[75] One study found that white women make 79 cents for every dollar a white, non-Hispanic man makes in the United States.[76] Latina women make 53 cents,[77] and African American women only 61 cents.[78] That's in part from waiting for karma! We've had senior leaders tell us not to teach women to negotiate because their HR department doesn't want to have a bunch of unhappy women suddenly asking for raises. This disproportionately hurts women who already ask less often anyway because they expect they will be fairly compensated in a system that isn't fair.

Decades of research suggests that this assumption stops women from pushing for more money.[79] But it's about more than money. Women are pressured to sit back and wait longer to be promoted or gain resources when they are understaffed. The squeaky wheel does indeed get the grease, but women are not supposed to squeak.

THE IDEAL MAN: EARN IT ALL, LOOK STRONG, BE THE MAN

We are all influenced by cultural gender assumptions that impact how we live and work. And we all tend to internalize these assumptions, resulting in flawed decision-making and damaging behaviors. For men, these assumptions can be summarized by a simple set of rules: the ideal man must "earn it all, look strong, and be *the* man."

Earning it all means assuming that as a man, you have to be a successful provider. That is, many men believe that their primary responsibility is to earn a living, and their home life is secondary. They are expected to work, work, work, and if they don't bring home the bacon, they are not real men. This is the granddaddy assumption of them all. It permeates cultures and generations. And yet, as we discussed in the history chapter, it is also made up. Single women are the largest growth group in real estate purchases.[80] More than 64 percent of women are now the primary, sole, or co-breadwinners of their family,[81] and yet we can't seem to shake the cultural belief that men must provide.

Society continually pressures men to live up to this assumption. The pressure points come from all sorts of sources: self, work, spouse, in-laws or partner. In a qualitative study we conducted, where we interviewed men about their career and life (see page 97), we heard a lot from them about these pressures:

- "It's my wife's right to stay at home. I can't really question that."

- "Employers assume it will always be the man who goes to work. If we both have a meeting and something at home comes up, it is harder for the man to leave."

- "I get pressure to work more from my wife."

- "I feel pressure to work and provide for my partner."

- "When I lost my job during the financial crisis, I was devastated. It put pressure on my marriage, and I felt like I lost my mojo. I struggled with relationships and was afraid of bumping into people and having to explain. I told people I was consulting rather than admit I was unemployed."

These pressures are so strong that, "even when wives' jobs yield higher incomes, men are still likely to perceive themselves as the primary provider."[82]

Let's consider an example. Charlie and Maria are both career-oriented with great jobs. They work in finance, making good money at the same firm—that's how they met. Both are smart, capable, and ambitious. Then they get married. They remain the career-oriented power couple until their baby, Pete, is born.

Maria takes eight weeks maternity leave; Charlie takes two weeks vacation—at their company more than that is frowned upon. Charlie gets a boost in pay—of course he needs one because he now has a family to provide for.[83] But when Maria comes back to work, everyone assumes she would want to work less, and even though she doesn't change her approach at all, her bonus gets docked for her time out of the office. Their friends start to pressure Charlie to focus more on work, and they indicate that Maria should handle the family in support of Charlie's rising career.

Charlie stops helping with daycare pickup and drop-off because he's got to be at work early and stay late. He figures that it's natural that Maria take the lead on these things. Soon she starts to get bossy and protective of her dominance in the household and relegates Charlie to simple tasks that "he can't possibly screw up." What's more, she withdraws more and more from work, claiming the family tasks take up time, which means he needs to spend more and more time at work to compensate. She doesn't seem to understand that without his income, the family would be broke. He resents that he never sees his family, his kids see him as a less competent parent, and to Maria he is never doing enough or around enough. And at work, he feels owned by the company, fearful about taking risks, rocking the boat, or even taking too much time off. He can't help but wonder what happened.

Does this story sound stereotypical? You'd be surprised how often similar scenarios are presented in our workshops. Maria behaves according to her own assumptions about femininity, as we have already discussed. But what about Charlie? He should be happy, right? He has a great job and a wife at home looking after the family. It's all a man should hope for, right?

But Charlie is working all the time. He's not allowed to do otherwise. He can't have a passion career; it has to pay the bills. He has no work-life balance, either. Worse, he likely doesn't feel he is entitled to it. Men increasingly struggle with work-life balance[84] in part because they haven't tackled the main assumption about being the provider—that men are responsible for providing for the family.

Both men and women struggle with work-life balance because of the same gender-limiting assumptions. What's stopping them? It's the unconscious bias that they all buy in to. Men have been socialized to act and behave in a certain way.[85] A story we've heard in our work, hundreds of times, unfolds. It's a story that starts as a dream and turns into a reality that ends up constraining choices. The societal bifurcation of gender roles strikes again.

Many people assume it's different for younger generations, because the world is changing. But change is really slow, especially when people start having children. In 1994, fewer than 30 percent of high-school seniors thought that "the husband should make all the important decisions in the family." By 2014, nearly 40 percent subscribed to that premise.[86] Other research concurs: among millennials surveyed, only 26 percent of women think that their career should take precedence of over their partner's compared with 50 percent of men.[87] And while two-thirds of dads surveyed by Boston College thought that child care should be evenly split, only a third actually practiced that.[88] One of our interviewees, who is unmarried, said he wants a wife who will stay at home and take care of kids. But if she wants to work, "she will do so because it is meaningful, not because she needs to provide for us. I will support her choices." The provider assumption is alive and well and will likely continue exerting influence on future generations if left unchallenged.

Another part of earning it all is the assumption that men have to look successful and important. They have to show others that they are successful, often with fast cars, expensive watches, showy homes, or the status of their kids' school. A man can pay undue attention to his body, his leisure pursuits (note the growth in weekend competitive cycling), the age or beauty of his wife, or even the fact that she doesn't have to work because of his ability to provide. Sometimes this pressure is so strong, it sends men into an endless treadmill of working harder, earning the next promotion, buying the next expensive thing, and then having to work harder to pay for it. As one of our interviewees said, "I am a family guy. I haven't taken risks so my wife can stay at home. I am certain that has slowed my career progress." Another said, "My wife said my car was beneath me, so I bought a new car." And this set him up to need that next promotion, and so on.

Boastful behaviors in the workplace are another manifestation of the need to earn it all. Taking credit for others' ideas, displaying false confidence, and aggressive self-promotion all stem from a need to look important. Many men describe the feeling as having to constantly sell themselves or risk falling behind their peers. "Fake it until you make it," is another common attitude.

In our interviews, some men shared they felt they couldn't be authentic at work because they had to adopt a persona that wasn't their own to be successful. They thought that working late would show their commitment, even if they didn't really get incremental results. And all of this was hidden because they were supposed to be the provider and show off the spoils of their efforts. Men are just as restricted by the provider rules of manhood as women are about the primary parent rule of femininity.

Now let's consider men's assumption that they need to look strong. Seen all over the media[89] and within companies, a type of toxic masculinity permeates workplaces. Using physical size or a loud voice to influence others is one manifestation of this assumption. Another is competing even when collaboration might be a better approach. Displaying a win-at-all-costs mindset is seen as an indication of strength. Men are usually socialized against weakness and can even be judged negatively for showing warmth or emotion. They can't get away with having too many soft skills if there isn't an off-setting strength indicator in their toolkit, such as being decisive or powerful.[90]

It isn't that strength, competition, or being unemotional at work are bad; it's that for men these characteristics tend to be the only option, even when it doesn't work for the situation or impacts others negatively. The problem is that being strong is a constraining rule rather than a guideline to help men choose what's required in any given moment or situation. As one of our interviewees put it, "I can't truly be myself at work." Another said, "I hide that I am a softie."

A corollary of the looking-strong assumption is that men need to protect others. "My role is to provide, preside, and protect," said one interviewee. While this drive is honorable on its surface, particularly if it means standing up for someone who is being harassed, it is generally a bad idea when the recipient doesn't need it. In a misplaced attempt to avoid hurting feelings, some well-intentioned men give women easier assignments to help them be successful or fail to provide the hard feedback needed for growth and development.

Mansplaining is a sign of how men see women as weaker and in need of an additional explanation to understand tougher concepts. We have observed male managers make unnecessary assumptive accommodations for women in the workplace, such as avoiding having them travel, excluding them from after-hours client events, and nudging them toward pink-collar work, such as training or organizing, so they will be surrounded by other women and thus more socially comfortable. In many cases, unneeded protection can actually be harmful to the recipient's career path.

Now let's consider the third rule, be the man, which carries with it a range of false assumptions. Fortunately, this set of assumptions, which can be exhausting for men, is slowly becoming more and more challenged thanks to the work of sociologist Michael Kimmel[91] and many others. The reasons for these assumptions are different for different men. Some see women as an outright threat, so demonstrating masculinity can offset the rise of femininity in the workplace. Others unconsciously believe that while women have been making great improvements, women are still simply less capable at work or as leaders. In this case, being "the man" can re-emphasize that there is a difference. And the third, probably most dangerous, assumption we have uncovered is the need for some guys to prove worthiness at work through sexual prowess. Getting her to believe he's a stud can make him feel that all is well with the world.

A male leader once asked us, "Why would we want to encourage gender equity in our company? Our leadership team is all male, and we are not going anywhere soon. We would have to remove a man to add a woman." This reflects a deep-rooted fear that if women gain power, men will be displaced. This fear explains many workplace behaviors, from intentionally sabotaging women's advancement to ignoring or reinforcing existing structural barriers for women.

It can also be subtler, such as excluding women from the social fabric of the organization or reminding women through microaggressions that they don't really belong. Telling sexist jokes, talking about women's bodies, or even calling out how a woman looks can reinforce this feeling. As we learned in the previous chapter, priming can make a difference to performance. Sometimes men can unconsciously prime women to perform less well by reminding them of their gender or making them feel like their presence is unusual or unwelcome.

When men, in reaction to the #metoo movement, ask, "What if I'm wrongly accused?" they are expressing their fear that a movement of women who have finally found the power to talk about rampant harassment and assault will somehow morph into massive, runaway, unlimited targeting of innocent men. Such a fear reflects how deeply rooted this displacement assumption is. "When I am at work with women, I can't help but think about HR. I am afraid to get in trouble," one interviewee told us. Men who buy into this assumption feel deep down that their own grip on power is so tenuous and insecure, that it is unable to withstand the power of anyone else.

Then there are men who aren't concerned that women are a threat because they don't think women are actually as good at the job. This assumption underlies a lot of corporate leadership development efforts for women. There is the belief that women's leadership skills are less intrinsic than men's and therefore need to be shored up through special training and development.[92]

Women in technical jobs often describe having to prove their technical skills over and over again despite their educational background or demonstrated performance. It is the same for women in finance. Of course, as we know from history, women have had to overcome many made-up biases about what they can and cannot do. That bias is alive and well. But for those still caught up in the gender-makes-skills paradigm, it is very tough to shake the belief that the women they work with are less good, and it's because of their gender.

Sometimes this assumption results in men mentoring women in a very patronizing way. It's not done with the belief or intent to make them as successful as they are, but rather to make them grateful for the help and indebted to their benefactor. Sometimes it can even feel creepy. One of our interviewees, when asked if he treats women differently at work from men, assumed we were talking about him favoring women because they were good-looking. He went on to explain, "I've mentored many women and stayed in touch with them. They are very grateful to me."

We have also heard about men who hire only women, surrounding themselves with subordinates they believe are hard workers who will never challenge their authority. One business owner told us, "My former company had a deliberate policy to hire women because they work hard and will accept lower pay." Another company had a policy to encourage new hires to take the lowest possible salary, regardless of their background experience, even though that negatively affected women more than men. One of our interviewees, however, said he hired only men because he knew he treated women differently and felt he had to watch what he said around them.

Finally, let's talk about sexual harassment. Women we work with describe the feeling they get with some of their male colleagues: that they are only interested in one thing. It can be as subtle as a glance that considers her whole body or a handshake held a second too long. It can be a glitter in his eye or an overenthusiastic smile. Sometimes it's demonstrating feats of strength where two guys compete for her attention with exaggerated stories of weekend athletics or sales performance. One woman told us, "One of my colleagues went out of his way to drop by my office every morning for fifteen minutes of flirting. I would squirm under his scrutiny or avoid my office and try to hide in the restroom to avoid him. But he never seemed to get the hint." Other women have told us about the constant need to balance being positive, polite, and fun without sending guys the wrong message. One woman we worked with told us about a colleague who grabbed her behind at a client dinner, inviting her up to his room afterwards. When she declined, he followed her to the elevator, pleading with her to just give him a chance. He claimed she had been giving him a vibe for years, and he was merely following up on it.

Looking at harassment in light of bias and false assumptions can help us see why it happens. For some men, the need to attract women sexually is very strong. Being "the man" translates into "I am worthy and important when I get sexual attention." Even if they have no intention of following up on the spark, some seem to feel a strong pull to ignite one. And rejection, to them, doesn't just mean lack of interest; it means they are not worthy of sexual interest. It hits deep at the core of masculinity. This is why the response to rejection can be so retaliatory and why women fear rejecting them. If, for both parties, it was as simple as, "Hey, Sally, I know we work together but you are kind of cute and I'd like to take you out sometime," and "No, thank you, Tim," there would be no problem. Instead, it becomes a dance, where he is trying to arouse her interest, and she is doing everything she can to avoid the interaction altogether.

Of course, there are women who fall prey to this pattern of biased behavior too. As we discussed, women assume they need to look good—and often that means being sexually attractive. So she wears a low-cut top or bats her eyelashes to get attention. But there is a key difference: for men, the societal pressure is to be the aggressor, not just the recipient of the attention. Despite all the advances in women's empowerment, boys still feel pressure to ask girls to the school dance or to pay for dates. Men are still expected to propose marriage (and increasingly more elaborately). So, in addition to the pressure of having to be sexually appealing, some men also feel expected to do something about it. And at work, this can have dire consequences for both men and women.

The flawed assumptions that direct the behavior of so many men are based on unconscious biases both men and women have about unspoken gender rules. They get at the heart of what it means to be masculine, with implications for a man's self-worth. These biases can spark workplace behaviors that are limiting for everyone, especially as women have their own false assumptions to contend with.

BAD HABITS

These flawed assumptions for men and women—so widespread, so often unchallenged—have direct consequences for workplace behavior. And those behaviors, when repeated, form bad habits. We call them habits because they are behaviors, not permanent personality traits, and behaviors can be examined and changed. We also find that digging past these habits into their underlying roots can take the blame game out of the conversation in a way that focusing directly on behaviors does not. The underlying assumptions explain *why* the bad habits exist.

Let's summarize the habits that can flow from the flawed assumptions we've examined so you can recognize where they came from.

The bad workplace habits men can fall prey to include the tendency to:

- Question the technical competency of women, though not men;
- Talk over women during meetings and take credit for ideas women have expressed;
- Focus on the credentials of male colleagues but the clothing or looks of female colleagues;
- Assume that when mothers are out of the office, it is because of their kids, and question the commitment of mothers to the organization;
- Mansplain;

- Sexually harass women, including making sexist jokes;
- Use physical size and/or a loud voice to bully; and
- Brag or engage in risky behaviors at inappropriate times (such as in front of a group of women), exhibiting feats of strength.

Of course, these habits are merely symptoms of internal unconscious biases. They spring from men striving to be ideal.

And of course, women are equally prone to bad habits, including the tendency to:

- Do it themselves rather than delegating to others;
- Take on the lion's share of parenting chores at home and the "office housework" at work;
- Say yes to everything, and fail to draw boundaries;
- Feel entitled to work flexibility;
- Strive for perfection and thus obsess over minor details;
- Overcompensate for shortcomings or mistakes;
- Stay in their comfort zone rather than take risks;
- Think less strategically; and
- Fail to self-promote.

It doesn't take much analysis to see that men's habits can easily lead to intransigence and failure to support gender equity, and women's habits can have the same result, not to mention burnout. Combine the bad habits of men and women and you get real problems with organizational culture, which is the subject of the next chapter.

We have delivered training workshops to thousands of people over the past five years, and we consistently uncover these same bad habits over and over again, regardless of the industry, company size, or age group. And women in particular are fully *aware* of these habits, for the most part, and many have been working hard to stop doing them, telling us, "I know I'm a perfectionist, but I just can't help it!" But changing behaviors is difficult and can't be done without addressing the underlying assumptions. We can't just say, "Stop being a perfectionist!" That would be like telling someone who is struggling to lose weight to, "Just stop overeating!" It doesn't work. Rationalizing doesn't create behavioral change and neither does a laundry list of things someone should do. Men, women, and organizations have to look more deeply at their assumptions.

4
Organizational Bias

THE ASSUMPTIONS HELD BY MEN and women make it difficult for everyone—even well-meaning people—to overcome bias. But in the context of an organization—a company, an NGO, a school, or a government body—these unaddressed assumptions coalesce, become rigid, and embed gender bias in the organizational structure. Before describing what we can do to overcome bias, we want to show you how embedded organizational bias creates self-reinforcing barriers to women's progress.

Why do organizations need to change? Isn't the problem driven by how individuals behave? And aren't US and Western European companies already leading the world in terms of gender and inclusion? Won't change come as part of progress, especially if men and women address their own unconscious biases?

As we mentioned earlier, the pace of change has stagnated; it will be more than a hundred years before US organizations achieve gender equity.[93] Why? Because gender assumptions are codified in structural barriers and continue to exist in organizations, and even the best processes can often embed and reinforce them. So any solution must have three pillars: individuals, leadership, and the organization. All need to change.

In our workshops we are frequently encountering evidence of organizational bias. Here are a few examples:

- A beloved female manager at a firm stepped into more senior-level tasks when her director left the organization. For almost a year, she did the director-level job at her lower pay. Everyone thought she should be officially promoted. Instead, the company hired a director from the outside, one whom most people described as "a mediocre male, clueless about the job and highly ineffective." The passed-over woman was told, "While you're highly effective at the job, your sweet, giggly personality doesn't fit with our senior-leadership profile." At this company, leadership was defined as having a stereotypically male persona and this became a barrier to anyone who didn't conform, regardless of ability.

- A female HR director told us, "The problem with moving women from middle- to upper-management is that even when a candidate is identified as having met all of the requirements and checked all of the boxes, there's still often something intangible that they couldn't put their finger on that makes us hold back from promoting her." These intangibles were problematic for the leadership team, because they couldn't articulate them as feedback and thus the women couldn't strengthen themselves as candidates and were stuck. Here, the requirements for promotion were unclear and candidates were not getting the feedback they needed.

- Early in a manager's career, she was told that a male subordinate, who backfilled her old position when she was promoted, would be given the same salary as she now earned because "he is the breadwinner in his family and needs it more." She escalated this to HR and was told that was just how things are. The manager quickly realized that, in the company's eyes, she would never truly be this man's supervisor, and the opportunities to undermine her authority were too great for her to continue in the role. In this case, biases about gender pervaded the compensation structure.

In all these cases, the biases were not coming only from individuals, they were unchallenged and reinforced by the organization. Left unchecked, unconscious biases can compound quickly. A famous research simulation showcases how this happens. Researchers started with a situation where eight levels of workers, split 50/50 by gender, were given performance reviews where the women were graded out of 100 and the men graded out of 101. This simulated an ever-so-slight 1 percent bias for men. After running the simulation, where 15 percent of each level turned over each time, and the replacements were drawn from the highest score of the level below it, a high percentage (65) of the upper levels were filled by men and most of the lower levels were filled by women. All from a 1 percent bias advantage! In a world where the bias advantage held by white men is many times greater than 1 percent, it is no wonder organizations continue to look as they do, despite women's higher graduation rates and all the progress made in the past fifty years.[94]

ORGANIZATIONAL ASSUMPTIONS

Can organizations suffer from flawed assumptions as individuals do? Of course. Shared individual biases become entrenched in organizational processes, role models, and decision-making. So it is important to recognize flawed assumptions and their consequences. And if these assumptions sound familiar, it is because they have been around for a while.

Many organizations are suffused with the belief that the problem of gender equity will solve itself; that there has merely been insufficient time for gender equity to occur at all ranks since the organization began hiring women equally. This assumption is concerning because it suggests to leaders that, a) no one need to do anything, because the problem will go away on its own; and b) all is well because the world is slowly changing. Leaders can get away with ignoring bias (as long as it doesn't result in legal action) and keeping diversity initiatives at arm's length (don't really change anything, just make it look good) because eventually the situation will resolve itself.

Where is the evidence for this assumption? Let's look a little more closely at current gender and diversity initiatives. For starters, who is generally responsible for them? Usually, we find that organizations appoint one of four people to head up a program for women:

1. Someone in HR who manages workplace accommodations such as flextime policies and maternity leave;

2. Someone in learning and development who manages training;

3. Someone with a diversity and inclusion title; or

4. An enthusiastic champion volunteer, usually a woman from the business who takes this on in her spare time.

Rarely do these people run the business or have real power to change how business gets done. They all work from the periphery, usually without much of a budget or decision-making authority.

As we said in our introduction, gender equity is a business problem, not an HR problem. Many organizations have gender-focused HR policies and programs, compliance training around sexual harassment, maternity and flextime programs, and disabled access. They have affinity groups and special programs targeted at a range of different topics. Though these organizations believe they are doing a lot for gender equity, most programs are developed to meet accommodation requirements or to avoid litigation. Even something highly visible, like sending a contingent of women to an exciting conference for women, while initially motivating for attendees, does not make for lasting organizational change. Such initiatives are not designed by leaders to change anything; they are designed to accommodate, appease, and make the organization look good. Further, success is often measured in the negative (what didn't happen, a lawsuit, or bad publicity) rather than the positive (what did happen, getting closer to gender equity).

Many people view these programs as costly without an obvious return on investment (ROI). Compliance training can cause business leaders to fear HR intrusion and hold HR specialists at arm's length or pay lip service to the latest policy initiative. ("Here we go again. What do we have to do *now*?") Managers can become fearful and focus on being politically correct, rather than open to new, creative ways of doing business.

Even worse, some of these programs, especially those supporting maternity, may actually reinforce stereotypes in the process. If a maternity-leave policy is for women only, it risks reinforcing the idea that parenting is primarily a woman's job. And women are often penalized, financially or socially, for utilizing flexibility programs. They often see their compensation and responsibilities cut and promotional opportunities reduced. How is that helping women through the maternity barrier? Men are unconsciously socialized not to take advantage of such benefits and often get dinged if they do, so they shy away.[95] While companies try to check the never-ending list of boxes to appear gender-friendly, they avoid addressing the unique and very real structural issues that block inclusion across the organization. So the needle on progress doesn't move.

And here's the problem with many employee resources or affinity groups: First, they are usually run by volunteers in addition to their regular job who rarely get recognized for the extra work. Second, the volunteers tend to represent the very groups that have been excluded or marginalized, so they, by definition, tend not to have the power or influence to change anything in the core business. Third, it keeps critical conversations about barriers and biases in an echo chamber and out of the ears of mainstream leaders who need to hear them. It's an approach we define with this attitude: "Here's some catering money. Get together with your affinity group monthly and have a book club about empowering women." It creates an illusion that something is getting done when it isn't.

Some organizations keep the need for change at arm's length by intentionally not counting the numbers of women. They claim they don't like to use measurements because they seem too much like quotas. Organizations measure everything . . . except the number of women and where they work in the organization. As a result, people often assume there are a lot more women than there really are. Women walk the hallways and people think, "We already have gender equity!" even if those few women are mainly administrative assistants and accounting clerks. The lack of measurement hides the problem. And it's more difficult to generate an investment of time and resources to solve a problem that isn't visible.

All other strategic business problems are measured, tracked, and assessed. But because organizations assume that the problem of gender equity is going to fix itself, they avoid measuring gender and inclusion.

One of our key insights in the introduction to this book is that the meritocracy doesn't exist. Of course, the assumption that it does exist is a huge organizational barrier. We hear it all the time, especially about an organization's entry level: "We hire only the best people," "Anyone can get ahead here based on their ability," and "I don't see men and women treated differently here."

We will say it again: if the meritocracy did exist, there would be gender equity at the top of the organization. Since there is not, it means that those who believe in the meritocracy are suggesting that women are less capable. Otherwise, everyone would benefit. So which is it? That the meritocracy works and leaders are biased, or the system is biased and needs to be fixed? We believe it's *both*: leaders and the system need fixing.

Many assume that admitting bias attributes intent, and few of us want to think that women are deliberately held back. There is even fear that acknowledging bias opens the organization to conflict and blame. But ignoring bias and pretending the system works is what *creates* conflict and blame.

But don't take our word for it. Let's look at the data. There is bias all over the talent development pipeline, from how jobs are advertised to how hiring decisions are made; from how performance is measured to how it is rewarded; and from who gets mentored to who gets the plum assignments that are needed for growth. And the consequences for women are as tangible as you can get.

THE THREE PS: PAY, PERFORMANCE, AND PROMOTION

The first consequence—the most obvious one—is pay. Women's salaries are lower on average than their male peers. Pay is a very complicated and interconnected problem. If, for example, women gravitate towards administrative jobs, take time out of their career for family, and work reduced schedules, it can be difficult to attribute differences in pay to bias rather than to personal choice. That said, national government studies have found that women make 18 percent less pay for the same work, even after adjusting for all other factors, and that has to come from somewhere.[96] This discrepancy is much wider for women of color. For example, on average, black women receive 61 percent of the pay of white men for the same work.[97]

Nobody likes to talk about unequal pay for fear of opening Pandora's box. Here's the thought process: "If we look closely at our pay structure and find a gap, it is going to be expensive to fix and could open us up to litigation. And we will look like jerks." But it is not hard to identify some common biases that impact pay. For example, pay is often based on what a candidate made in their last job. So if the last place was biased, then the bias problem gets perpetuated. Another important influencer of pay is how well the candidate can negotiate.[98] That might be fine for someone whose job includes negotiating, but do we want to reward this skill so strongly in everyone? Especially when, as we have learned already, women are socialized to avoid negotiating rewards for themselves?

We find several areas in organizations where bias impacts pay:

1. There is a gap in pay for men and women at the same level. Usually, men negotiate better on the way in and compound the advantage by better negotiating successive raises and promotions. Either that, or the hiring managers all coincidentally found the women candidates less worthy, which also reflects bias. Intangible factors unrelated to actual results are recognized in pay and discretionary-bonus allocation, such as men's family status (breadwinners make more[99]), men's potential, and likability factors. We have encountered this bias consistently, and research has repeatedly shown that there is a fatherhood premium and a motherhood penalty.[100]

2. Women's pay is often lowered due to time off for maternity leave or reduced work hours, regardless of the results or quality of her work. We've met women who agree to a thirty-hour work week for a 25 percent pay cut and then work forty hours anyway, and the organization thinks it's fair because, "the rest of the people are working fifty-plus hours." But men who work forty hours or produce lower-quality work don't get docked for not working fifty. We have also heard stories from women who had their bonus cut for the quarter (or even the entire year) because they took six weeks maternity leave, and some who lost two

bonuses when their maternity leave straddled two quarters, even when they achieved their key performance indicators (KPIs) or financial targets.

3. Those who hold "women's jobs" are paid measurably less than those in equivalent "men's jobs." Jobs in HR and marketing often attract women while jobs in finance and IT are seen as the realm of men. So the stereotypically women's jobs are referred to as pink collar. And the problem is, those pay less, even if the workload or value of the role is the same. As we learned in the chapter on history, even jobs once held by men are assigned less pay once women reach a critical mass of representation in them.[101] Researchers suspect it's due to institutional inertia. [102]

4. Women in understaffed departments are unpaid for absorbing extra work. Often women describe doing double duty when employees leave, whereas men avoid picking up the extra slack. Remember the do-it-all rule? Women do this without compensation or recognition. Sometimes it results in slowing the employee-replacement process, so the women end up maintaining the extra workload for longer periods of time and this reduces their level of success with their own regular jobs.

Let's consider the second P—performance—and how's it's evaluated. It is common practice for organizations to ask their employees to provide self-assessments summarizing their performance and prospects for promotion. But self-assessments don't work out for women![103] As we've mentioned, women have an internalized cultural bias against self-promotion which holds them back from boasting about their accomplishments. Even when they do promote themselves and ask for more money or responsibilities— guess what—they are marked down for being too aggressive or pushy. But if a woman doesn't self-promote, her busy managers sometimes forget what she's done and neglect to give her credit.

Failing to self-promote is often interpreted as a lack of confidence, which can lead to confidence being over-weighted as a job skill. We've heard women describe the situation this way: "I started out the review with my boss talking about my project. I'm working on these tasks, documenting the steps, and letting him know I'm on track to finish by the deadline." Everything is positive. Then he asks the question, "What are the areas in which you'd like to see improvement?" She takes time to humbly document her developmental goals and agrees to the improvements she will make to earn a promotion down the line. She leaves the meeting and later finds out that one of her male peers who hasn't performed nearly as well but who also wasn't quite so low-key or developmental during his review, got promoted immediately. She is crushed, frustrated, and further loses confidence.

It begs a question—how much of the evaluation process should measure the skill of self-promotion versus the actual skills required to do the job? Men are consistently more likely to overrate their abilities compared with women.[104] And while confidence may be an important aspect of any job, over-weighting this factor continues to unfairly perpetuate a gender divide at senior levels. Some of the challenge is the self-promotion problem and some of it is the prove-it-again problem. Even women leaders expect women to perform better, or nearly perfectly, before promotion, whereas men are promoted for their potential to perform.[105] Though completely unconscious, this tendency is clear when we look at promotion velocity. We have worked with organizations where women spend twice as long at each level, or where new titles are created for women that represent half steps to the next level. (This is now becoming standard practice in law firms.[106]) It stands out when it is primarily women who have these extra hurdles or when the first person with a half step was a woman.

The way organizations share developmental feedback can exacerbate the bias. Informal feedback is an important tool, but it is also another intangible that unintentionally holds women back. Most of us can acknowledge how important informal feedback is to a career. Small nudges are needed to course correct and modify small behaviors that contribute to big results. But men and women experience informal feedback differently. Women tend to report receiving much more positive feedback than men do. But it is often vague and not tied to business outcomes, or it is full of conflicting statements. Women often tell us they do not receive enough developmental feedback, and when they do, it's very much, "You're doing great—keep going." These same women reported that they were surprised later when they were not promoted. Our concern here is that many people are culturally biased against giving women sufficient developmental feedback, particularly negative feedback, which hinders their ability to progress.[107]

We have also heard that managers are afraid to deliver negative feedback to women because they're worried that emotional reactions will be out of proportion to the feedback: women will cry, or argue, or retreat into themselves and stop taking risks. And while some women do express emotion (or even quit) in response to negative feedback (though remember it may be confirmation of their bias about not being "good enough"), that doesn't mean they don't need it. Both male and female leaders have reported how uncomfortable they find emotional responses from women and how impatient they become with their female charges. It can shut off the feedback loop. It's just bias: men can react emotionally too—by yelling, slamming doors, or even crying—but somehow when women cry, many object. Don't let that stop you from delivering the feedback women need.

The third P is promotion. Getting promoted is typically a factor of high prerequisite job performance as well as some above-and-beyond extras, such as amassing well-rounded divisional experience, challenging assignments, or people management experience; and a whole range of intangibles such as "being a team player," appearing "managerial," and "paying dues." Having the right mentor or sponsor also can play a big role in getting promoted, and women have traditionally fallen short in this area.

Okay, let's talk about well-rounded experience. Often, this means travel and/or working in satellite or foreign locations. It can also mean doing different types of jobs such as finance, IT, or sales. This is an area where women are often at a disadvantage. We hear statements embedded with bias about family obligations: "She can't travel for business; she's got little kids!" or "He needs to travel for business; he's got little kids!" These same biases can also keep a woman from moving readily to different locations as the job changes or taking jobs in male-dominated fields. And that's if they are even asked. Many male and female managers assume women won't want to do these things so they don't even ask. But when it comes to promotion, women are dinged for not having the right kind of experience. By the way, this also puts an unfair burden on the men to do all of the traveling.

Even if a woman bucks social convention and travels extensively for work, moves to a remote location for a job, or takes a job in sales, she often doesn't get the same credit as a man for the experience. She can be labeled as cold or someone who doesn't have her priorities straight despite doing a good job. And it's not only mothers who aren't supposed to be all-in for work; often an intense focus on work can alienate single women from friends, family, and coworkers as well, as her behavior can violate the well-entrenched rules of femininity.

Not having sufficiently challenging assignments can be another problem for women. First, the perfectionism bias keeps many women from proactively seeking risk at work. It is tempting to give full effort toward something achievable and delight everyone with the results rather than risk being less than perfect in a more challenging role. So women themselves may not raise their hands for more difficult assignments. But it gets worse when well-intentioned managers try to help women by giving them easier experiences intended to showcase them for promotion. More often than not, nobody is fooled, and women are easily dismissed for not having enough of what is needed compared to male counterparts.

People-management experience can become problematic if women give up management responsibility to cut back after maternity leave. It starts with the assumption that women need to step back from their career when they become a mother. It is reinforced by the assumption that only full-time employees can manage people. So women with children get stripped of management responsibility right in the middle of their career, when they need it most. Often, when they do come back to full-time work, their early management experience is forgotten or dismissed as not continuous or recent enough. So come promotion time, women are set back and skipped over.

When women take time off related to family, they are highly scrutinized and penalized for a perceived lack of commitment. Six weeks of maternity leave seems to be remembered as years out of the workforce rather than the half-quarter it really represents. Maternity leave is considered a fault or an irreversible mistake. Taking time off seems to signal a lack of commitment to career or company.

Research underscores the importance of sponsorship and mentorship and the traditional (though unintentional) exclusion of women from both formal and informal networks.[108] Many women see networking or meeting with mentors as selfish, career-focused activities that they are not entitled to, especially when they are supposed to be working. So they eat lunch at their desk and avoid wasting time at the water cooler.

Second, even when women do network, they often feel uncomfortable talking about money, which limits many networking conversations to the social realm. And women and organizations tend to pair women with women mentors, but since there tend to be so many fewer women in leadership, this limits the effectiveness of the sponsorship piece. And it burns out the few women mentors available. This challenge is exacerbated for women of color because there are so few mentors, placing undue burden on those who are in leadership.

Pay, performance, and promotion—these very tangible areas of business will continue to be more difficult for women to negotiate and secure as long as organizations believe that a meritocracy exists. Many organizations aren't aware of how biased they are, and even tout the strength of their merit-based system. But the emperor has no clothes.

THE PROBLEM OF HOMOGENEOUS LEADERSHIP

Another organizational problem that persists is the predominantly homogeneous make-up of most leadership teams. Today it's still white men at the top. Thought to be in the process of changing, the situation actually foments significant hidden barriers. First, it signals that leadership is naturally male, so good leaders need to have stereotypically male behaviors and traits. Earlier we examined how leadership characteristics, though readily attributable to both genders, remain the domain of white men in most organizations. In fact, because many people still define leadership as male, they also extrapolate other male characteristics as being good, even if these features are independent of leadership skills. Being competitive and confident, for example, are valued more heavily than being collaborative or connected.

A recent study documented that even in a situation where objective performance measures were identical for a group of men and women, the language—the actual words used—were very different.[109] Women were six times more likely to be described negatively. And even the words used to describe them positively were laced with stereotypical assumptions: women were compassionate and organized while men were analytical and competent. The most common negative words for women included inept, selfish, and excitable, and for men they were arrogant and irresponsible. Remember, it was for the same performance level!

This is both a language issue and a leadership issue. While a compassionate woman is nice to have around, the competent man is seen as able to get the job done. And while you might need to fire someone who is inept, you can somehow live with someone who is arrogant. This bias infects performance evaluations as well. Words reinforce stereotypes. When a woman prepares well for a presentation, she is labeled organized whereas a man is confident. People hear "organized" and subliminally think secretary. When they hear "confident," they think leader.

One of the ways we figure out if an organization is overly focused on superficial characteristics and under-focused on objective skills is to ask its leaders to define their ideal worker. The words they use can be very telling, especially if they describe themselves. (What a coincidence?) It's more problematic if the words are descriptive of characteristics, such as hard worker or detail-oriented, rather than values like responsibility, integrity, or commitment to lifelong learning. Company cultures with similar values are open to everyone with those values, but cultures where everyone shares the same superficial characteristics tend, by nature, to exclude women.

However, we also caution organizations to be careful about using meaningless descriptive words in performance reviews. What do organized and confident actually mean, and what role do they play in getting the job done? Performance evaluation should have nothing to do with personality traits and everything to do with observable actions that create a specific, quantifiable result. Too often descriptive words characterize *how* a person is doing the job, or how managers subjectively feel about them as people, not *what* they are doing or objectively how effective they are. We will talk more about leadership competencies in the tools section of this book, but for now it's important to recognize that the inability to discern good leadership from male leadership is a significant issue.

This language bias shows up in both hiring and performance evaluation processes when the conversation turns to the intangibles. Words like *style*, *fit*, *likability*, and *gravitas* mask more subjective factors and become excuses to favor men. Many women have described losing out to men who look the part—graying hair, deep voice, conservative clothing—despite out-qualifying the men. Being chatty, using too many words to communicate, giggling too much, and appearing too young are common reasons women have been given for not quite being ready for leadership. So women take longer to rise into leadership.

Substantial research suggests that women often feel the need to craft an image that is narrowly defined according to male standards, often exacerbated for women of color. This image creates "an impossible self"[110] where woman deny their own identity in order to conform to the external definition of success. It's the pantsuits-versus-dresses dilemma. It's an assumption that women "are more of a risk to bring on in a marketing situation [in a consulting company]. I have seen people talk about [how] 'too many women look weird.'"[111] The role becomes the standard and everyone must conform regardless of how narrowly it is defined.

Role modeling shows employees what is expected of future leaders in a company by looking at who is in positions of leadership today. It is critical because employees view the career paths of existing leaders as role models for their own careers and follow them closely. But many women don't see themselves reflected at the top, so they get a subliminal message that they aren't inherently right or need to change to make themselves fit. Many give up because they cannot reconcile themselves with the difference.

Having a men-only senior team (or even women who behave like men) signals to women that they don't fit into leadership roles. And it doesn't help to appoint a token woman: research into group dynamics has found that group norms will not be impacted by minority members until they make up 30 percent of the group; until then minority members are more likely to conform their behavior to the existing group state in order to fit in.[112]

The personal lives of senior leaders are also scrutinized to provide cues for the kind of life that supports those careers. When those leaders are mostly men with a stay-at-home wife, for example, and a few women without children, a skewed but influential message permeates the culture. This lack of background diversity tells us that the only family model available for successful leaders is one in which they are supported by someone who sacrifices their career. Employees with a different family situations are discouraged from striving for leadership. It is yet another reason why so many women ask for flexibility when they have children: they have not seen another option represented. It sends a subliminal message to women: "There is only one way to be successful here and if you don't want that life, then go elsewhere."

Even having a few women leaders doesn't always help increase the number of women leaders. What behaviors and stereotypes are the senior women role modeling to younger women? Since many senior women got to their role by emulating traditionally male behaviors and sacrificing family, they can be hard on younger women who may crave a different approach. "We paid our dues," some older women believe, "so the younger women need to as well." And young women look up and can't see a way forward for the life they want to live. Women have told us, "Look, those leaders don't spend any time with their family. I don't want that. That's why I changed companies."

Let's face it: until leadership contains more women, leadership is going to continue to be seen as masculine.

THE PROBLEM OF CULTURE

Organizations are unique and organic. Each has its own culture. Part of each culture is a mirror of the outside world and part of it is defined within. Organizational culture can determine who feels included and who feels like an outsider. Insiders get more done, get promoted, and receive recognition. They are more successful. A recent job advertisement for a CFO said, "To work here you need to work hard, play hard, love whiskey and beer, and live for this company." (Truly, you can't make this stuff up!) The vision this ad conjures up is an organization for young, single bros who want to hang out together. The odds of many women working there (or responding to that ad) are low.

The culture within an organization is rarely homogeneous; it usually varies from department to department, location to location, and team to team. As a result, it is prone to influence by unfettered unconscious bias. Given the flawed assumptions we have been examining, it's not surprising that many corporate cultures present challenges for women feeling comfortable in the working environment, knowing their voice will be heard, or feeling that their contribution is valued.

Imagine coming to work every day and being reminded that you are an outsider, altering yourself to fit in or remaining on the periphery of what's going on? It's like the shy kid in high school who attends classes, but isn't invited to parties, eats lunch alone, and spends all her time in the library. That student is not likely to be a spokesperson, recruiting students by touting how great the school experience has been. Nor is she likely to spend any extra time at school once the end-of-day bell rings. If a transfer opportunity arises, she is likely to take it. And she probably spends most of the day stressed, keeping her head down and hoping not to stand out.

Workplaces with a culture that celebrates and encourages extreme masculinity[113]—and there are a lot of them—usually occur when the majority of workers, especially leaders, are male. They usually arise when employees spend a lot of social time together inside and outside of work and where leadership has encouraged hyper-competitiveness. The tech industry has become famous for its flagrantly bro-culture moves, such as when Twitter (79 percent men[114]) hosted a frat party for one of its teams or when Uber sent executives to Las Vegas for a raucous week of partying that left embarrassment and sexual harassment claims in its wake.[115]

An organization's cultural narrative also can have external impacts, such as how customer service is delivered. Bias against women holds back employees *and* can impact sales. The bias can also show up in a company's external marketing or brand presence. Even products that aren't directly targeted to women can experience negative consequences from insulting or exclusionary practices. For example, an *X-Men* movie billboard in Los Angeles showed a large masculine character choking a smaller, feminized character. It received almost instantaneous and universal negative reaction from women and was quickly retracted.[116] Were there no women in the entire chain of people who conceived, created, printed, and erected the billboard? Or did women in the movie company's marketing department, creative team, advertising agency, printing service, and billboard installation team raise concerns only to have their opinions dismissed and overruled?

Think about the "booth babes" who continue to pervade trade show floors—even in those industries where women are often the key buyers.[117] And it's not only women who can feel out of place in a bro culture—many men describe feeling uncomfortable but feel unable to speak up for fear of appearing too soft or less masculine. It can be a serious, unspoken, hard-to-fix problem for companies that want to improve gender equity. In large tech companies, 40 percent of women report that it's difficult to succeed. Interestingly, in those same companies, the men think women don't succeed because they lack technical skills.[118] Can you imagine any other area of business where the problem affects so many employees and the organization not focusing on it? It makes no business sense!

Many organizations administer personality assessments or conduct other social experiments during the hiring process to gauge how a person will fit in or work with others in the organization. There can be a lot of weight given to a candidate's "cultural fit" in many companies' recruiting and promotional processes; far more than figuring out if the candidates share their values. From holding cocktail parties at the end of the interview process to teams socializing when working on projects together, getting along socially is an important way the organization reinforces fit. But fit really means *be like us*. And mostly, it means *be like men* or *be like white, privileged men*. Typically, even women who make it through the process often have to act similarly to the core group, further perpetuating the homogeneity and alienating anyone with a different background.

Social events and hanging out together outside of work can reinforce this sameness factor. Socializing is fun, and having a good social relationship with coworkers can enhance working relationships. But when it excludes others, either by design or accidentally, that exclusion can carry over to the workplace culture. We aren't saying avoid social events. We're asking you to look at how sometimes fun can limit who socializes.

We have worked with many organizations with employees who socialize together. When those organizations have a gender equity problem, we notice key patterns in the social network, namely that all the company social activities are skewed male or are segregated by gender. This becomes especially exclusive if senior leaders socialize by themselves.

Companies still routinely spend large sums of money on professional sporting events (mainly men's sports), golf club memberships, and large bar tabs, which they justify by entertaining employees and key clients. (Think of the messaging that sends to clients as well: we assume all clients are men!) Women may be welcome to attend, and plenty of women drink or like to go to professional sporting events, but these events are often very obviously designed to be enjoyed primarily by men.

When women don't conform, they get blamed for their own lack of progress. By shifting the blame for the leadership gap onto women, organizations reduce the need for anyone else to change. The message here:

be like us. This is why so many companies invest in training to shore up women's skills to the level of men's. There is no room for leadership to look any different.

Organizational barriers—from flawed assumptions, to the leadership gap, to the pervasiveness of hyper-masculine culture—arise primarily from unconscious bias. This bias hides behind myths, such as the ever-present ambition myth: women aren't interested in moving up, especially when they become mothers or they see the lifestyle of the top jobs. In fact, women *are* as interested as men, or start out that way, but interest decreases over time as they meet other barriers[119] or watch their male colleagues get rewarded for things like confidence rather than competence.[120] McKinsey has found that 69 percent of women want to move to the next level compared to 74 percent of men.[121] It's more likely they don't display ambition the same way, or just get fed up trying to live up to the male leadership ideal, and thus don't realize the fruits of their ambition in today's organizations.

•

Our flawed gender assumptions create an ugly reality. Women have them. Men have them. Leaders have them. And organizations have them. Unquestioned, these assumptions protect a system filled with bias that actively blocks women and keeps them outside. The system reinforces itself and thus isn't likely to change on its own. But it is ripe for a major disruption. So now it's time to see what can be done with these flawed assumptions to turn this reality around. Those who learn how can actually make change happen.

PART 2

THE SOLUTION: REFRAME AND RENEW

5

The Power of the Reframe

THANKS FOR STICKING WITH US so far. We know what the first part of this book must make you think: women, men, leaders, and organizations are all riddled with bias! If you're like many of the people who attend our workshops, you may feel discouraged at this point. You might think the cause is hopeless because bias is unconscious and automatic. Or that everyone is a jerk for perpetuating limiting biases. Women are impacted by these biases in daily interactions *all the time*. The anger, hopelessness, and guilt that women constantly feel as they deal with these barriers make it imperative that individuals and organizations do something about it. But in fact, many people who train organizations about the topic of unconscious bias stop at the definition! They leave the organization and its leaders feeling blamed, stuck, and fearful. But these behaviors are not inevitable. They are not natural and unchangeable. They are simply behaviors.

The good news is that we all can—and need to—do something about these barriers to individual and organizational fairness and success. There is a way. All these biases show up when our brains respond automatically to our own flawed underlying assumptions. That is, when we use System 1 thinking. What we assume is driving our actions. However, we do have control and we can switch to System 2 thinking. We can also consciously change the narrative of our biases. Because once we recognize flawed assumptions have been made, we can choose to change our assumptions and, in time and with practice, slow down our decision-making.

Remember the old saying about assumptions? When you assume you make an ASS out of U and ME. The idea behind that saying is true:

assumptions are subjective and can and should be challenged. Assumptions don't have to be unalterable—they can change.

Cognitive behavioral therapy methods suggest the same thing—that we need to examine our assumptions, figure out which ones are flawed, and then change them in our own minds before we can change our behaviors. Any behavior change we try to make will not take if the underlying assumption isn't tackled first. It's hard work to catch ourselves making mistakes all the time. We humans struggle to change bad habits, unless and until we shift the assumption underlying the ineffective behavior.

We call this shifting process "reframing assumptions." It's about identifying what rules are governing our behavior and then rewriting them so we can govern differently. We have to move beyond the symptoms (the behaviors and how we feel about them) and get down to the underlying condition (the assumptions that dictate *why* we behave a certain way). Then we change the underlying condition so we can change the resulting symptoms. Logic and desire for behavior change don't make it happen. But changing belief systems does. Reframing the assumption is changing the belief.

Here's an example: Sal often skips lunch and works steadily until mid-afternoon when he finds himself snacking at the vending machine. Sal knows he shouldn't eat chocolate and chips for lunch and that logically this is a behavior he needs to change. He wants to change. He may even penalize himself for doing it by skipping dinner. But Sal finds himself at the machine time and time again.

If he looks at his assumptions, he will see some underlying reasons for why he skips lunch. "I assume my work is more urgent than my health. I can survive chocolate and chips but not missing a deadline. Interrupting my work could cost me my job or reputation but delaying food will not. Or if I work through lunch, everyone will respect me as a hard worker." In Sal's mind, and at this moment, the work is more important than lunch. As long as Sal believes this to be true, he will prioritize his work over food. The behavior is not out of control; it is driven by these very real beliefs.

If Sal had diabetes, he would stop and eat lunch because it would be life or death. His belief or underlying assumption would be that his immediate health is more important than work today and every day. It would be simple. So clearly he *can* control the behavior. He might have to slow down, not respond automatically, but rather, think about his choice. But it can be done.

Sal needs to consciously decide which is more important for him, working without a lunch break or eating lunch. He needs to reframe his assumptions. If he decides, for example, that he can survive delaying work or that eating lunch is critical to his short-term performance, he will find a way to eat lunch. He can bring lunch. He can arrange for lunch to be delivered. He might even enlist other colleagues to join him for lunch. Sal has to slow down, reframe lunch as the higher priority in the moment, and believe he can consciously choose it if he wants to change.

Once you learn to look for them, it's easy to find hidden assumptions. In our work, we recommend that people ask "Why?" three times when they examine reasons behind a behavior. Why doesn't Sal stop working to eat? Work is more important than food right now. Why? Sal thinks interrupting work will stop his flow, and he could eat later. Why? Maybe Sal thinks continuing will produce better results than interrupting work. Ahhh.

Then we recommend asking, "Is that true?" If not, then what is true? That's the reframe. For example, Sal's reframe might be: "Taking a break and injecting fuel into my brain will improve the quality of my work." (And if he looked for it, he'd find research that makes this very point.) If Sal believes this new assumption is true, he will, as many successful leaders have, embrace breaks and healthy meals as a source of personal success, not a hindrance.

The ability to reframe is a powerful tool. But often people don't recognize that they have limited their options until they are frustrated with an impossible either/or choice. This causes emotional tension and guilt. "I know I should eat a healthy lunch, but the work is more important." We teach a five-step process for using emotion and impossible choices as clues that there may be a flawed assumption at work.

1. **Recognize the bad habit or behavior.** Acknowledge that every gut decision contains bias on some level. As we said earlier, it may help to get familiar with the types of bias out there if you are new to the bias conversation in order to recognize them in action. Pretending immunity almost guarantees biased decision-making. People can't help being biased but they can become conscious of when it plays a role.

2. **Notice resistance, anger, fear, guilt—whatever negative emotion arises.** Allow it to come forward so you can analyze it. What does the emotion suggest? If you are upset about a coworker who "always" leaves early, notice that. Then observe your go-to response. If you got upset with the coworker, was your instinct to lash out with a smart-ass comment about how nice it must be to leave early? Or did you gossip about it to others? Notice that. It's important to notice before acting. If you act, it'll be from the emotional place. Instead, simply observe and take notes.

3. **Uncover the underlying assumption and evaluate it.** Ask: What do I assume? Do I think she is less committed because I don't see her working as long? Or am I worried she isn't getting the work done? Are

these assumptions actually true? What is at the root of the emotion? Is the assessment fair? In our workshops, we teach that you will know when you've hit on the assumption because you suddenly feel an ah-ha moment. Ah, maybe I am reacting negatively because deep down I think her unwillingness to sacrifice her personal life to stay (like I do) makes her less committed to her job (than I am).

4. *Reframe* **flawed assumptions.** If the source of concern is about your coworker not being committed or getting the work done, these are facts that can be validated. So validate them! If your coworker gets her work done, then maybe she is efficient and should be held up as a model! If it is about jealousy, then maybe think about what it would take for you to leave early, too. The power of the reframe is that it opens up many new choices we hadn't been able to see because the flawed assumption dangling out there creates distraction.

5. From this place of increased choices, you can **consciously choose a response.** Instead of one limiting solution (avoid promoting her because she isn't committed), new opportunities abound (promote her because she models for others how to get more done in less time; use her example of leaving early to motivate others to work more efficiently).

Reframing flawed assumptions opens doors that bias closed. It moves from a rules-based, rigid outlook to one that opens up options. It allows you to view behaviors from other perspectives. The chapters that follow show you powerful ways we have used this to help women, men, leaders, and organizations.

Throughout any decision-making process, it's important to slow down. Slowing down means critically examining all the individual steps or personal milestones to ensure bias doesn't slip in unexpectedly. After any critical decision, for example, we recommend reviewing results, and whenever the outcome upholds group homogeneity, take it as a sign that System 1 thinking might have affected the process.

Developing this skill can take time. If someone is not an expert at recognizing or mitigating the effects of unconscious bias, it's important to give them time and space. Reframing is not an switch that can be flipped so System 2 thinking suddenly kicks in. It takes practice, awareness, self-reflection, and patience. Trying new things and then critically evaluating the results is a good way to learn these skills. There is no quick fix.

But it can happen! The inherent and unconscious bias that shapes our decision-making about hiring, promotion, and firing, with long-term negative impacts for women, can be altered by learning how to recognize flawed assumptions and reframe.

6
What Women Need to Do

IN OUR WORKSHOPS, WE HAVE helped thousands of women uncover and reframe their flawed assumptions. We begin by asking why. Why do they seek perfection, for example? When we dig deeper, we often find that in their core, women feel they are not good enough. Research professor Brené Brown has done a tremendous amount of work on this topic. She points out that when women feel unworthy and ashamed, they sometimes overcompensate by exerting too much control, perfecting low-value tasks, obsessing about details, and taking down other women.[122]

Millions of messages bombard women throughout their lives about how they aren't pretty enough, skinny enough, rich enough, motherly enough, good enough at math, and strong enough to lead. A Dove commercial, for example, shows an artist behind a curtain who draws pictures of individual women he hasn't seen based on their description of themselves. Then he draws pictures of the same women based on a description provided by another woman they just met. The women are surprised at how much less beautiful the pictures are based on their own descriptions; so much so that they realize how hard they are on themselves.[123] It is a powerful illustration of women's self-perception. It's hard for women to avoid assuming they are not worthy. And the fear of letting others see the truth is so insidious, it can cause over-compensation and the quest for perfection as a distraction.

The practice of examining underlying assumptions takes time to learn. For women, it means stepping away from autopilot situational responses (like saying yes to everything or waiting to be recognized for good work) and seeking understanding for the question, "Why do I behave this way?" Often, the underlying assumption has been unspoken and unchallenged for so long that it might even seem like an undisputed fact.

We have noticed that flawed assumptions for women often show up as guilt. When a woman feels bad because she didn't volunteer to take notes in the meeting, it should cause her to pause. Why do I feel guilty? Is it because a flawed assumption is at play? What *is* the assumption? If the guilt is based on her assuming that women aren't entitled to be fully present at the table or should be doing the office housekeeping, then she can pause and examine that assumption. "Do I agree? Is it true for me?" If not, then she gets to reject it and drop the guilt.

OPENING POSSIBILITIES

Most of the time, assumptions don't hold up under examination. Consider the assumption that women are primarily responsible for parenting duties. Let's reframe it: *Everyone* is responsible for home and family *and* earning a living. Or: *Everyone* is entitled to a rewarding career *and* a life.

Assumption	Reframe
Women are primarily responsible for the home and family.	We are *all* responsible for home and family *and* earning a living; or, We are *all* entitled to a rewarding career and a life.

The rigid rules that say women must do this and men must do that can now become flexible and open up new possibilities. Parents can work together as partners to solve career and family problems. Both partners can be part of arranging daycare; both partners can step more fully into fun and engaging work. Once enlightened, couples can work together on clever and creative options for managing career and family. One can manage school drop-offs so the other can go to work early, while the other manages pick-ups so the spouse can work late. If a baby wakes up before two in the morning, one can take that shift so the other can sleep—and then they can switch. Meal preparation kits can simplify shopping and meal planning, and there are businesses that provide safe, scheduled rides for kids.[124] Intelligent planning and collaboration can allow both partners to put in the focus needed at work to continue their career trajectories and have close relationships with their kids. The same can be done to coordinate business travel. Some couples manage childcare with an online calendar. Research tells us that couples that balance these career and family workloads equally are happier.[125]

You know who gets this? The divorced women and single moms we interview. They have no choice. They can't afford not to work, and their ex-spouses have no choice but to share in parenting. It is sad that they understand this strategy only after divorce. If they had worked together differently from the beginning, sharing responsibility more fully, perhaps they'd still be together. And research shows that some lesbian and gay parents already share workload more equitably.[126] So once we all learn to reframe the binary gender assumptions about work and family, the rules can change.

Here's another reframe for women. What if the assumption, "I'm not good enough" was reframed to, "I am a work in progress." I am doing really well for where I am in my development, *and* I'm still learning how to do better!

Assumption	Reframe
I am not good enough.	I am a work in progress *and* I'm still learning and growing.

After the reframe, she gets to make mistakes. She gets to learn and grow. She gets to acknowledge all the good she brings without minimizing it by worrying about not being perfect. Just like that, perfectionism isn't needed. This approach is incredibly empowering because the choice to reframe—the ability to rewrite the rules—is in the hands of the woman, not anyone else. Moreover, it's really hard, once a flawed assumption is acknowledged, to keep following it, basing behaviors and habits on what she knows is not true.

It's only socially unacceptable for women to reap the rewards of their hard work and to be able to ask for rewards because we've all bought into the bias. But women can turn this on its head. How about reframing the need to wait to be recognized to "I am entitled to the rewards for my hard work." Or "Money and power are fair trades for the value I bring." After all, a free market mandates trading work for fair compensation. And if a woman believes her work is valuable, then she may also want to think about ways of quantifying that.

Assumption	Reframe
I need to wait to be recognized.	I am entitled to and can enjoy the rewards for my hard work. Money and power are fair trades for the value I bring.

In our workshops, we help women do a math exercise called "quantify your value" to add up how much they bring to the company bottom line. It is often super challenging, because women aren't conditioned to think this way, but when they get there they often find they are adding far more value than they have ever given themselves credit for. And while they all may not run out and ask for raises, it certainly helps them navigate conversations about resources better when they come up.

ANTICIPATING AND OVERCOMING RESISTANCE

The reframe opens avenues our gendered society never thought possible. It also can be threatening to those who haven't done the work yet. When women push back against stereotypes, they often get resistance from both men and other women. It is important to anticipate this resistance so it doesn't come as a surprise or disappointment. But our experience is that this is one of the most powerful tools to free women from socialized assumptions.

We have worked with women who decide to step up at work only to find their colleagues push back apprehensively. They sometimes have friends or family members at home who chastise them for being so involved in work. And we've worked with men who decide to more actively engage in their non-work life, only to get pushback from their bosses, friends, and family, telling them they are risking their earning power. The temptation can be very strong to revert to the old rules and ways.

Consider that change impacts everyone—both those who have been included in the change process and those who have not yet learned that gender assumptions are all made up. Just because you've reframed your assumptions doesn't mean everyone has. And that's okay. They just haven't learned yet. Except it does mean some days are going to be a little harder.

So the key to managing resistance is to expect and even plan for it. Rather than being taken aback, we suggest giving it a nod, smile, and a little, "There it is." That gives you power. You can help other people dig for underlying assumptions, and you can help them reframe. But ultimately, you don't control how others will or won't support your growth. You can only control how you choose to respond.

We worked with one woman, let's call her Judy, who noticed that nearly every other senior leader had a dedicated administrative assistant, yet she was told she had to share one with a male peer. She found that he was highly disorganized and used significantly more of the administrative assistant's time than Judy, so Judy ended up investing a lot of time and energy in completing her own administrative tasks. It bothered her, especially when she found herself working late to get the job done.

Upon reflection, Judy realized that she hadn't insisted upon the dedicated resource because deep down she didn't feel she deserved it, particularly because she was organized and grateful to have been promoted to senior leadership. When she looked at her assumptions, she realized she and her team were entitled to support and sufficient administrative resources so they could do their best possible work. She acknowledged that she was actually harming the organization and her team by under-resourcing herself (something that research shows is very common—even men who work on teams led by women make less money than men on teams led by men![127]) So she reframed the assumption and changed her behavior. She calmly asked for a dedicated administrative assistant.

Of course, her boss pushed back, reminding her how organized she was (a common tactic, by the way, to get women to volunteer for administrative tasks) and telling her that the budget was too tight at the moment (another common tactic to guilt women into patiently waiting for compensation or resources). In fact, her boss was angry that she had asked (yet another common unconscious tactic to entice conflict-avoidant women to back down). Judy heard through the grapevine that her boss didn't think she needed support because she was naturally good at administrative tasks, and he was upset that she had the nerve to ask. But Judy, along with a supportive colleague, patiently persisted and appealed to a level above her boss who readily agreed with her arguments. Ultimately she got what she needed—a dedicated administrative assistant—*and* she signaled to others that she expected to be treated fairly.

Don't forget, like Judy's boss, someone who hasn't done this work yet may still be stuck with their own flawed assumptions. Judy can approach this challenge with empathy and understanding. It may require her to work on her own emotions first so that she can be respectful and assertive without aggression, anger, or emotion. And it will likely require perseverance. We work against others' assumptions too, even after we reframe ours. But it can help to be more empathetic when we see others struggle with flawed assumptions as we did.

Many women are fearful of asking for fair play, whether in the form of compensation, resources, or support. One of the false assumptions we explored in Part 1 was the idea that if women are perceived as too greedy, they risk punishment beyond rejection—a historically valid fear. Some women think even asking for anything could get them fired. But it's time to let go of this assumption. We haven't met anyone in our workshops who has been fired for asking.

Yes, someone might get angry, because their own flawed assumptions are at work, but they don't generally fire the person who triggered their anger. In fact, we have noticed the opposite. Even if a woman doesn't get what she asks for, asking often positions her higher in everyone's mind.

> **YEAH BUT . . .**
>
> Sometimes we get pushback about the very real external biases that still exist in the workplace, and that our approach is tantamount to blaming the victim. While that may be a tempting way to address the problem, let's not forget that bias comes from all directions, including inside us. What we are saying is that women must first get their own internal biases out of the way and then, with that new perspective, tackle the external bias problem with empathy and a new approach. Otherwise, the fix will be limited by blame, powerlessness, and the old way of thinking.

They respect her more. They also don't forget that she asked. Often, in the next promotion cycle, or when someone else asks for a similar benefit, the issue gets revisited and the woman benefits before anyone else because she is seen as next in line. We've noticed this phenomenon with speaker's fees. People ask us to speak for free. When we refuse and provide our fee structure, we get repositioned into a high-value bucket. The client either moves on to a different speaker who is willing to work for free (and thus has a less-valuable event), or they dig deeper, find resources, and approach us for a bigger, more visible speaking engagement. We remind women all the time that it is always no if you don't ask, and that doesn't hurt, it just means no. Generally, nothing worse will happen, and good things might happen now or down the road. And if there is a penalty, then you've learned something about the other person that can inform how you want to handle that relationship.

Notice here how empowering this approach can be. Obviously, there are external forces at play as well as a woman's own internal biases. And women need to know how to deal with the external forces. But all anyone can do about external forces is learn how to cope, teach others, and draw personal boundaries. Internal forces are a different matter. Everyone can do the work to understand the roots of behavior, reframe flawed assumptions, and consciously choose responses. You can do this anytime you want, in the middle of a meeting, or even in the middle of a conversation. (See Appendix G for a list of bad habits, hidden assumptions, and possible *reframes* for women.)

POSITIVE PRIMING

The extent to which a woman has bought in to a negative stereotype or flawed internal assumption can heighten its effect. Think about the last time you were introduced to a new technology. If you are south of thirty, you probably adopted it quite quickly. But if, like us, you are north of that age, you might have been tempted to hand it to your kids to figure out first. Is that because older people are less capable of using technology? That's certainly the stereotype. But more likely it is because older people *think* it will be harder and are thus impacted by subtle performance anxiety (especially if young coworkers are watching). And the older people get, the more they might buy in to this thinking.

If a woman is one of few women in a male-dominated group, for example, she can subconsciously internalize a greater amount of threat.[128] The underrepresentation itself serves to put more pressure on women to prove themselves, which reinforces stereotypes in their own minds.[129] And all it takes is a reminder: "Are you the assistant?" or "Can you take the notes?"

While stereotype threat can never be entirely removed, it can be mitigated. It helps to know how. As the results of the math test we talked about earlier hinted, priming can play a big role in reducing (or increasing) the threat. Reminding women they are smart, capable, and psychologically safe can make a big positive difference to performance. That's not hard, right?

Women can also train themselves to prime positively in preparation for challenging tasks. For example, performing affirmations like, "I am quite capable at this," or "Remember, I aced that last presentation!" can help a woman perform at her best. In our workshops, we help women positively prime themselves by reframing their negative assumptions right before a big meeting or potentially stereotyped interaction. This reframing technique brings strength to the positive affirmations because they are based on reality and logic, not empty words. These affirmations and reframes can also be customized to address each individual woman's deepest insecurities.

This affirmation technique, while it can be immensely successful for groups under stereotype threat, doesn't have the same positive performance effect for non-stereotyped groups.[130] So, in the workplace, it might be difficult for highly privileged groups, like white men, to empathize with or rationalize the practice. Maybe they'll even laugh. But that doesn't make the technique less important for women. Priming women with their own consciously chosen assumptions can insulate them from what is happening all around.

Try it next time you are in a meeting with a woman who looks nervous or insecure. Spend a moment reminding everyone of her credentials and a positive previous example of her work. See what a difference it makes on her confidence and performance for the rest of the meeting. It costs nothing!

Working in groups can help individuals perform better as well. Some research finds that Asian students tend to study and practice math in groups, allowing them to push past small, careless calculation errors that, if they were alone, might have derailed their confidence earlier in the process. Together they are able to get to the more challenging parts. The research finds that women and African American students who work individually tend to get bogged down by small calculation errors, causing them to over-effort and ruminate. This reinforces their internal stereotype threat about poor math performance. Workshops for women and black student groups that counter this lead to a positive improvement in math performance.[131] Grouping women on teams can, this research suggests, help reduce the amount of their stereotype threat.[132] It's also why we find such positive growth results from women in leadership programs in organizations that skew male—finally women come together with other women and realize their experiences as women are not unique. We often hear, "I had no idea other women experienced this and felt this way too."

Women can also recognize when others are unconsciously priming them for failure. A well-meaning person who says, "Oh, it's great to see you have a women engineer on the team," for example, may unconsciously subject the woman engineer to the influences of stereotype threat. By recognizing this, the woman can consciously reframe the situation in her own mind: "My team is stronger and more innovative than other teams because I am here providing a different cognitive perspective." The reframe tool can be extremely powerful for mitigating stereotype threat and dealing with internal unconscious bias.

Remember: Most bias is based on assumptions that are made up. Things are only true because people keep believing them to be true without challenging them. Buying into the social conditioning women receive from birth and going along with it happens because it seems easier. But long term, it is far better for women to do the deeper work of finding their own truth and living it freely.

DEALING WITH EXTERNAL BIAS: DIRECT SPEAK

With the reframe technique, women can control their own behaviors and uncover their own biases. But let's face it—they are still going to come up against a lot of external biases and gender stereotypes. And while they can't control if and when that will happen, they still have the power to control how to respond. It starts with understanding that, consciously or unconsciously, other people have biases. As much as people might wish the world was a pure meritocracy and that everyone could all be evaluated fairly, the reality is that it isn't and people aren't. The unexpected often has more impact and more power to derail or hurt than the expected. Also, the right response can set the stage for making further interactions more positive.

A woman, Jillian, overheard a male colleague telling a sexist joke at work that involved a stereotypical divorced women taking her ex-husband to the cleaners and now living a life of luxury. Jillian was outraged. She had just recently been through a divorce, and her ex-husband, who hadn't chosen to invest in a retirement account through his own work, was now getting half her retirement account, which she had diligently saved. What's more, the joke assumed that women are less worthy and undeserving of alimony and are just out to take down men. The whole joke was outrageously stereotypical, wrong, and insulting to women.[133]

When Jillian's male colleagues laughed at the joke, she was faced with a problem. Speaking up against it was risky. At best, she would elicit nodding, knowing looks of empathy and a mental note not to tell the joke again in her presence. At worst, she would be labeled a screecher—a word used to describe women who call out men for sexist behavior, but who, because of their approach, are said to take things too seriously and need to lighten up. Such a label would guarantee that she wouldn't be heard or taken seriously in future if she raised another issue like this.

Women find themselves in this kind of situation every day. Sometimes a joke or sexist comment is made to put a woman in her place, usually downhill from the teller of the joke. Sometimes, though, it can be part of decision-making, such as putting a woman in charge of ordering food and taking notes in the meeting thus diminishing her power and credibility with her peers. At its worst, it can be a veiled sexual advance or unwanted attention, made by the guy who hangs over the cubicle complimenting a woman on her outfit while visibly ogling her. When caught off guard, many women provide a common response: the nervous giggle. Faced with a no-win situation, the choice is to "screech" and be called out, or ignore the situation and almost guarantee it happens again. Calling someone out almost always will be met with pushback, though, because the perpetrator becomes embarrassed, defensive, and closed to learning.

We recommend a different approach. It is a technique we call the Direct Speak Model.[134] It helps give structure to a woman's response so she can keep the issue and desired behavior change in the forefront while removing the emotion behind the situation. This can help open the recipient of the feedback to learn because they don't have to fight defensiveness and blame. We encourage our clients to practice this technique often so it becomes second nature. Here is how it works:

1. **Bring in your perspective of the situation.** Show the other person how you heard or experienced the situation. It is not about arguing facts but rather displaying the facts from your perspective in a way that can't really be argued. Your experience of a situation is simply that—your experience. So, you state it. I noticed X. I saw Y. I heard Z.

2. **Describe how you feel without blame.** Clarify what assumptions you made about the situation. Again, it is not about arguing what assumptions the other party made (you can't know that for sure), but rather showing the other person the assumptions you understood from the situation, right or wrong. It gives the other party the opportunity to correct the assumption, or at least recognize how you could have jumped to the conclusion you did. I felt X. I assumed you thought Y. I wondered if that meant Z. If you add, "Maybe I'm wrong but this is what I thought you meant," you show humility and open the door for the other person to clarify.

3. **State your wants clearly.** Dispassionately state what you would like going forward. It is not about changing or revisiting the past, but rather about making sure that the future is one you can live with. I would like X. Next time, let's do Y. I recommend Z.

Here are some examples:

What I want/need	How to express it
For Jillian's situation	The joke about the divorced woman made me feel uncomfortable. I am divorced and my ex-husband received half of my retirement. Did you know that most divorces leave women significantly worse off financially? Would you be willing to not joke about such a difficult situation?
For my ideas to be heard and considered in meetings	I notice I am often cut off mid-sentence and my ideas are dismissed without consideration. It seems that then when others express the same thing, they are sometimes adopted. I feel that I am not being heard or taken seriously. I would like to be allowed to finish my thoughts without interruption and for my ideas to be fully and fairly considered.
To renegotiate responsibility for a task	I have been responsible for running the efficiency report for the past few years. I feel that while I have done a good job at this task, it is taking time and energy away from me doing more strategic work. I would like to have someone else take a turn at this task for a while.
For creepy guy to stop ogling me over my cube	I find you spend a lot of time complimenting my looks but you have not mentioned my work contributions. It makes me feel undervalued and uncomfortable. Would you be willing to shift your feedback to my work so I might learn and grow?

The key to changing the mindset of others is not to shoot the messenger. The blame game will never open a mindset for learning. Don't forget, just because a man or woman has not learned how to reframe, or doesn't know anything about the effects of biases some women experience daily, doesn't mean they can't learn or will always be this way. It can help lower frustration and the emotional tax for women to extend empathy to those who are learning, or who have just made a big mistake. "It's okay, they just haven't learned it yet." Humans have a big capacity to learn and grow. Besides, nobody can force someone to change if they don't want to. The only person you can control is yourself.

How Women Can Engage with Men

When women find themselves stereotyped in the workplace, there is a tendency to group with other women. That can mean migrating to jobs or departments where there are more women employees (pink-collar careers) or socializing primarily with other women at work. It can mean seeking out only female mentors and building a primarily female network. And it can mean managing only female clients. When seeking investment capital, this can mean tapping only female investors.

The problem with this tendency is threefold:

1. The majority of the power, wealth, capital, and influence in organizations is not held by women. So women further entrench the problem by cutting themselves out of the equation;

2. Women don't build skills for connecting with men or leveraging male allyship;

3. It keeps men from having the experience of working with professional women, further reinforcing negative stereotypes. How can they learn that women can do more than take notes and order food if the only professional women they experience are their female secretaries?

The social pressure for girls and women to stick together can begin as early as middle school when teachers devalue girls' skills in math and science.[135] But flexible social networks can reduce bias. Ensuring that men and women get many opportunities to work and socialize together as peers goes a long way to reducing the negative stereotypes each has about the other.

Of course, these interactions should be supported by safe contexts. We aren't talking about joining the men at a strip club or a bar. Even team-building events where physical strength is overemphasized can cause stereotyped behavior as men may feel pressured to compete with each other to impress women, rather than engaging with women (and of course this model also excludes those men who don't have these attributes). Instead, women should seek opportunities to work with men on cross-company projects, socialize in safe situations such as group lunches, and connect with male allies for mentorship. It is not always easy or comfortable for women to insert themselves into male-only groups, but our experience says it usually has positive consequences for everyone.

We will talk about how men can help be allies to women in the next chapter. But women can help by being open to allyship. And by choosing allies carefully. While many men might offer to help, sometimes the help can be less than, well . . . helpful.

First there is the man who seeks out women to mentor because he likes to feel benevolent but winds up patronizing because his underlying assumption is that women need mentorship because they are less capable. Women need to screen this man by assessing whether or not the mentor would be happy if the result was equity or even that his mentee surpassed his achievements. Those men do exist, and it is critical for women to find them.

One of our clients fell into a trap when a man she worked with offered to help her with a complex project. The man gave her all kinds of advice and peered over her shoulder while she plodded away. It was extremely helpful, until, as the project was coming together, he began to attend her project meetings and step in whenever she spoke to provide nitpicky corrections and finish her sentences so everyone would know he was helping her. She felt she was more than ready to cut the cord, but this man persisted and even communicated widely how she still needed more of his counseling before she could step up. It ultimately slowed her progress through this stage, the exact opposite effect she had sought from the mentorship process.

Then there is the guy who is afraid to work with a woman for fear she will make a false sexual harassment claim against him. This one is tough because he may make himself inaccessible or fail to personally engage at the level needed to advance the woman's progress. What's important here is to help him feel comfortable as we would want a man to do for us. Meet in open spaces, address the fear openly, explain intentions, clearly set out expectations. Ask him what would make him feel comfortable. This is about creating a safe environment for both parties.

So how can women be open to male allies but make sure they find the right ones? We recommend a few tactics:

1. If possible, look at who successfully helps other women be successful;

2. Interview male candidates objectively; and

3. Follow your gut. If you get a bad vibe at any point, use the Direct Speak Model to draw boundaries. Set respectful expectations so everyone's intentions are clear.

How Women Can Help Other Women

It may seem counterintuitive to suggest that part of what will help women rise is helping other women rise. But struggling against each other is a major problem, particularly the higher up women get in an organization. Women versus women conflicts can be a major unspoken barrier to women.[136] Why? Many women buy into the old assumptions about femininity and feel the need to socially correct those who don't.

Think about the stereotypical senior woman leader who gave up having children for a power career, working day and night and pushing back against male egos. She may be less than supportive of an up-and-coming mother of three who thinks she can one day take her place. She may even push a subordinate's career towards the mother track by giving her extra time off and work flexibility, only to state how she obviously isn't ready for promotion because she hasn't been as committed to her job. Other women may ostracize the imperfect—pointing out typos in emails and obsessing over mistakes women make (and strangely let their male peers off the hook for the same details). Such behavior further reinforces feminine stereotypes.

We have examined the assumptions underneath women vs. women conflict and summarized them in the following diagram, presented by level:

Senior Managers

Too Few Spots
Competitive, feeling that there can only be one of us so it needs to be me.

New Generation
They don't appreciate what we know.

Support Staff
Guilt. Why would a woman need admin support?

Struggle
It was hard to get here so everyone should have it hard, **or,** I didn't struggle so why do you?

Middle Managers

Mutual Limits
I will help as long as you don't surpass me, take my job, or knock me down.

Mommy Wars
Conflict about what is the right way to be a woman.

Gatekeeping
I can aggregate power if I am the only one who can do something.

Entry-level Associates

New World
Resent suggestions from older generation about what to wear, how to act, pitfalls to avoid.

Beauty Pageant
Compete for attention of male leaders.

Women v. Women Conflict Assumptions

At the senior-manager level, there is often the impression of a limited number of token positions available to women, so women need to compete with each other, and only with each other, for single spots. Researcher Robin Ely documented this issue in the late 1980s,[137] yet women are still grappling with it today.

But research has taken this concept to a new level. Tokenism has a multiplier effect because it is self-reinforcing: token women don't hire other women. "When a woman is the only female (a 'token' female) in a high-prestige work group, she is unlikely to recruit another woman to her team for fear of being either outperformed or undervalued. . . . Women in high-prestige groups are concerned that, on the one hand, a highly qualified female candidate will be viewed as more competent and valuable than they are, thus diminishing their value in the group. On the other hand, a moderately qualified female candidate could reinforce negative stereotypes about women, thus adversely affecting others' impressions of them due to gender stereotyping."[138]

The research found that the phenomenon occurred only if women were the minority in the group. Instead of competing for the top, if women were to actively recruit more women to join them, they could neutralize this effect. When women become the majority, they tend to recruit women half the time.[139]

Generational conflict, with a special gender component, can also be an issue. For many senior women leaders, there has been a single career path. The time it took to rise through organizations was relatively fixed. Motherhood was not an option without a stay-at-home partner; dual senior-leader families were (and still are) rare. But today, outside of the C-suite, there are up-and-coming senior leaders of organizations of almost every age. Some tech startups that made it big have leaders in their twenties. Some are run by telecommuters balancing babies on their hips. This can be very hard for a traditional leader to handle.

But women can make a difference for each other. Instead of dwelling on what experiences the different generations might be lacking or how differently they communicate, women can embrace this diversity and leverage it to their advantage. Because the same diversity advantages women bring to teams is also what different generations and different models for leadership bring to support innovation. And by inviting different role models to the team, they can create many more varied career path opportunities for women. Remember, in the same way that having only one career path nets fewer women leaders, having many role models can shift the balance.

Sometimes women leaders struggle with having and utilizing support staff. And their support staff, who are usually female, often struggle with having to support women leaders, reducing the effectiveness of both parties and erupting in passive-aggressive conflict. Mostly it is based upon internal biases women have about needing or deserving support. If both parties can recognize these flawed assumptions and reframe, they can help support each other's success. It is also critical that women leaders make sure to compensate their support staff equally to others' support staff. This can help ensure loyalty and prevent under-resourcing their own success.

Sometimes female middle managers, on the other hand, can be a barrier to women moving through the organization's mid-level. Whether it is out of fear of being surpassed, fear of having their version of working women or working moms threatened by a better way, or fear of giving up power gained by gatekeeping, women can undermine other women. Recognizing why this is happening and using empathy can help.

One of our clients, Frida, found that her female manager nitpicked her performance in ways her male peers didn't seem to experience. Frida suspected that, even though her manager was passed by several men on the way up in the organization, she excused it because she had taken time off to have a baby. But if a woman, especially another mother, passed her, Frida's manager worried it might mean she wasn't good enough at her job. So Frida took her manager for lunch one day and asked her about her career goals. Frida suggested to her manager that they work together to demonstrate how effective their team was, cross-promoting each other whenever possible, in the hopes that Frida's manager would get promoted and Frida could backfill her position. After that, the two were a dynamic duo, powerful allies who moved up together through the organization.

Surprisingly, women at the entry level of organizations seem to have conflict with each other as well. Sometimes they are competing for the attention of male leaders—and not always in the most professional way. Based in insecurity and a need to "be picked," this behavior is destructive for relationships as well as overall credibility for women in the workplace.

Tension between entry-level women, who are seeking to pave a new path or do things differently, and more senior women, who want to prevent them from self-destructing or reinventing the wheel, also has the potential to disrupt. We knew of a senior aerospace executive who volunteered to mentor young college graduates at the office. Her advice about what to wear, how to speak, and what behaviors to avoid often came across as rigid and outdated. Her mentees found her annoying, particularly when she called them out for what she considered inappropriate attire like short skirts, low-cut blouses, or bare legs. The executive only wanted to help and had the young people's best interest at heart, but the young women couldn't see how clothing posed a problem.

In all of these cases, instead of joining the battle, we again recommend reframing—"It's not her fault she thinks this way, she just hasn't learned yet." This approach takes the blame and emotion out of the situation. Remaining relentlessly accepting[140] and consistently even-keeled, women should use the Direct Speak Model to express their needs calmly and stay the course. Certainly when each side hears the other perspective and takes the time to evaluate underlying assumptions, a mutual reframe can be constructed that meets everyone's shared goals.

Women banding together instead of engaging in conflict is extremely powerful. So is seeking allyship from other women. Finding others who are going through the same transformation can be especially helpful— that's why we invented accountability partners in our workshops, so each woman would have a peer who is going through the same thing, someone who won't let her slide backwards and provides the support to help her push through resistance. In our research, we found that the higher-level women almost all had a strong supportive women's network behind them: women who would challenge them to realize their potential and speak up for themselves.

7
What Men Need to Do

ATTEMPTING TO CHANGE A HABIT is very difficult on its own. It can feel like an endless list of shoulds and shouldn'ts, rules that have to be memorized and followed diligently. So over the years we have worked with many women to recognize their own bad habits as nothing more than symptoms of internal biases or flawed assumptions so they can reframe.

It's no different for men. The rules can sound negative and intimidating. "I shouldn't mansplain"; "I should let women finish their sentences"; or "I shouldn't compliment her on her looks." So instead, we encourage men to examine these behaviors more closely to identify *why* they happen. What is the underlying belief? On what assumption does it rely? How can we tell? If working with a partner or coach, we use the same method we do with women and encourage the coach to ask "Why?" three times.

> Coach: "Why didn't you speak up when Joe told a sexist joke?"
> Man: "Well, I wasn't sure I was allowed."
> Coach: "Why?"
> Man: "I thought he might laugh at me."
> Coach: "Why?"
> Man: "I thought he might think I'm less of a man."
> Coach: "Why?"
> Man: "I thought he might think I'm not man enough. Oh. I get it."

Remember that this type of conversation can be had with yourself, too. Once the assumption has been uncovered, we suggest closer inspection. We ask our audiences to think of the assumption as an object with many sides, an object they can pick up, turn over, and look at from all angles. If they agree with the assumption and the rule, then great, they can carry on, but with more consciousness. But we've found that most people don't agree and see the problem with these rules.

RELIEVING PRESSURE, OPENING POSSIBILITY

Let's apply the reframe technique to some of the male assumptions we raised in Part 1. Remember the assumption "I must be the provider"? Well, how about reframing as: "Everyone is responsible for career and family."

Assumption	Reframe
I must be the provider.	Everyone is responsible for career and family.

With the reframe, the pressure to earn it all is off. His wife doesn't have the right to stay home while he runs the rat race alone. They both have a responsibility to provide and care for their family. This belief system also enables men to understand that truly providing is not only about money—it's also about caring about and for people, something often socially penalized for men. They are also able to choose work they enjoy rather than worry so much about their paycheck. In a qualitative study we conducted with men from a variety of industries, many we interviewed[141] spoke about this issue. One said that he went into sales because he didn't want to manage people. He wanted "less stress, to be able to relax, have fun, and be with the kids more." His wife also worked and managed her schedule so they could complement each other, with him dropping the kids off in the morning and her picking them up.

This reframe relieves men of the stress of solely carrying the family financial burden or planning a career focused on money. Or feeling obligated to have an incredible career trajectory to brag about to parents and friends. Jack told us, "I thanked my wife for working when I got laid off because it relieved the pressure and gave me more flexibility to find the right job." Ted said, "I am glad we have had two incomes; it has paid off for our family."

Others took time off on a regular basis. Lew said, "I didn't tell anyone I was taking a break in the middle of the day, I just took it because I needed it. It made me more productive later and allowed me to grab lunch with my kids." Some men had the luxury of being higher up in their organization, so they were able to leverage power to get the flexibility they wanted. But by role modeling this behavior, they opened the door for others below them to do the same. Many men we interviewed identified strongly with the provider assumption and tended to diminish their wives' careers, but other more balanced breadsharers (those with working spouses) tended to support and promote their wife's career.[142]

This reframe opens up possibilities for everyone. Abandoning the old rules generates creativity. One woman we interviewed[143] swapped the primary career role with her spouse every three years. *Wall Street Journal* work-life columnist Sue Shellenbarger writes about dual working couples hiring au pairs, making mid-career switches, and in general living much more flexible lives.[144] A range of services has emerged to support dual working couples, like meal delivery and door-to-door dry cleaning. More creative solutions are likely to develop as more couples embrace the "we are *all* responsible" reframe.

In our research,[145] we found a large proportion of men sought better work-life balance. And those who found it were unwilling to give it up. One man got to spend a lot of time at home with his younger kids when he was between jobs and realized what he had missed with his older ones. When he took a new job, he insisted on better flexibility and more time off. The "everyone is responsible" reframe allows men and women to work together so that both get to design an optimal work and life plan.

We have seen how many men assume they need to look successful and important. We combat that assumption with the reframe: "I am happiest when I can be myself." What if the pressure to look the part just evaporated and a man could be his authentic self? How much would this confidence open up new possibilities? Instead of fearing what others think, that energy could be spent on being more productive. Instead of thinking about only himself, what he can achieve or accumulate, this reframe gives men permission to reach outward to help others be successful. Research shows that even men "have the 'disease to please'—always trying to do or say things that we think will make others like us and think we're 'good.' We hide our true selves."[146] Instead, we can work to understand our vulnerabilities and shame about who we are and work to be more authentic.[147] We can seek to understand what this mask is trying to hide so people can bring their more authentic selves to bear.[148] It's good advice.

Assumption	Reframe
I need to look successful and important.	I can be myself.

One young man, early in his career, felt pressure to conform to a very hardened view of manhood. So he escaped and became a snowboarding instructor for a couple of years. But there he "felt pressure to get a real job." The pressure continued until he explored his thinking and realized that what he needed was to question the assumption. "I realized I needed to give myself a break and let up on the pressure." Now he is several years into exploring what that means and discovering himself in depth in a way that he wouldn't allow before. He says now, "I had no idea who I was or what I wanted. Now I have a depth of contentment that wasn't possible before." He also found meaningful work in a whole new field. He's not rich, but he has what he needs and is happy.

A Gallup poll found that only 15 percent of people are engaged at work.[149] Think about that: 85 percent of people work at jobs they don't like! How many men are working to look important, rather than to strive for happiness? What could work look like if they simply reframed?

As women assume they must be perfect, men assume they must be strong. Both assumptions can be debilitating. What a relief it could be for a man to reframe the strength assumption with the acceptance of vulnerability.

Assumption	Reframe
I must demonstrate strength.	Vulnerability is acceptable, even desirable.

The online men's apparel company Bonobos takes a somewhat fresh look at masculinity in a commercial available on YouTube. The video captures the reactions of a variety of men to the textbook definition of masculine. There are smiles, nervous laughs, and questioning glances as the guys consider adjectives like strong, aggressive, macho, well-built, red-blooded, and so on. The men decide this definition doesn't fit them and challenge the viewer to think differently.[150] The video recommends that men "be able to be brave enough to be who" they are, and "be able to cry, to smile, to love." Some of our interviewees told us about coming to terms with vulnerability in their own way. Thomas found it "liberating to say I don't know—I am vulnerable."

How can this reframe affect the workplace? Professor Jennifer Berdahl and others have written about how an energy company changed the way masculinity was defined on an oil rig—where we might assume traditional norms abound. The company found that masculinity contests ("may the best man win") were costly in terms of safety, poor decision-making, and legal risk. Instead, the company rewarded a speak-up culture where decisions could be questioned, listening was valued, and where cooperation and even caring for each other resulted in significant cost savings.[151]

Another researcher, Avivah Wittenberg-Cox, has written about a workshop she led where participants were split up by gender. The women had no trouble discussing the leadership development topic and where failures in leadership occurred. The men did.[152] Their strength assumption was so powerful they couldn't see past it. A workshop we conducted recently yielded the same results. The male participants seemed to find it much harder to shed the strong veneer and admit weakness. We get it. It's hard to explore emotion when you haven't been allowed to do so by society.

But it is extremely difficult to do self-development work when hiding behind an emotional shield. We once worked with a group of bankers and found there were small opportunities for these men to open themselves up. When they did, they were able to see their self-limiting assumptions about not wanting to ask questions or admitting they didn't know something. They were worried that violating the strength stereotype would undermine their credibility. They expected community pushback. What they found was the opposite. By asking questions, they made themselves more accessible and uncovered information that they had not known before. And when they said, "I don't know," their colleagues had the chance to speak up and get some airtime for their perspectives.

Fearing a negative reaction likely stops many men from experimenting with vulnerability. Knowing that, we can all help. When we notice a man trying to walk his own path, instead of pointing out how different he is, or seeing it as weakness, we should give him the space to explore bringing his authentic self to the table. (See Appendix H for a list of bad habits, hidden assumptions, and possible reframes for men.)

DOING MORE . . . TOGETHER

Boys are typically raised to protect their sisters or younger siblings. It's a tough habit to break. But that advice assumes that the protected person is physically weaker and more vulnerable. In the workplace, unless colleagues are under threat of physical attack, physical weakness plays a much smaller role, if at all. Work colleagues don't need protection, they need support to learn and grow. They need development, challenge, and a safe environment to practice without fear of being undermined, all of which can be provided through mentorship.

But as we saw in Part 1, men can often choose to mentor women not out of a sense of support but as a way of earning gratitude or indebtedness—another form of protection. By reframing protection as the challenge to learn and grow, men can earn respect from female colleagues rather than suspicion.

Assumption	Reframe
Protect the weak.	Challenge others to learn and grow.

Sabrina recently worked with someone whose mentorship was extremely patronizing. In fact, she hadn't even asked him to mentor her; he took the appointment upon himself. He focused his feedback on rudimentary elements of her work and kept telling her she could work on higher-level projects once she could handle those first steps. It seemed he was intentionally holding her back by making her reach a level of mastery that nobody else had nor was needed. What's more, he communicated to others how much he had to help her, reinforcing this with constant widespread commentary about her mistakes. She was extremely frustrated. Through his actions, he inadvertently communicated to her and others that she was weak and in need of his protection.

Luckily, she reached out to another colleague whose approach was very different. He challenged her to jump right in to some higher-level work and he stood beside with encouragement and cheerleading while she struggled through. He also gave her honest, critical and developmental feedback so she could make the necessary course corrections along the way. When she completed the assignment successfully, he showcased her results to others. Sabrina didn't need protection, she needed to be challenged, and the second man was the effective leader who made that happen. Women at work need support, not protection.

Assumption	Reframe
Women are a threat.	Together we can do more.

On a more micro level, there is no evidence to suggest promoting women means they will take jobs away from men. At its core, the supposition that the jobs were men's to begin with is inherently flawed! On the other hand, teams with a balance of women on them perform better so their leaders perform better. When men help women by hiring, promoting, and including them, those men get better results. It's a win-win situation.

There is overwhelming evidence that women in the workplace don't take the proverbial pie from others, they grow the pie. And yet so much of the gender debate seems to be concerned about what men give up when women rise. The addition of women added between 1.4 and 1.9 percent to East Asian GDP between 1965–1990.[153] In North America, the economic growth benefit of advancing women's equality is expected to be $11.8 trillion by 2025.[154] Nicholas Kristof of the *New York Times* argues that when women got the vote, they voted for things like women's maternity health which meant more babies were born alive, including boy babies.[155]

A long-standing, culturally reinforced assumption that many men unconsciously perpetuate is that women are less competent. Many women hold this assumption, too. So here's an obvious reframe: competence has nothing to do with gender. Learning to recognize it, discerning the difference, and challenging it are skills that won't come overnight. But the rewards are significant, especially for leaders, because this reframe unlocks the skill of discernment. Discernment is recognizing competence behind the layers of bias that it tends to hide.

Assumption	Reframe
Women are less competent at work than men.	Competence has nothing to do with gender.

It helps to practice starting from a place of high expectation. Expect competence, and it will be easier to notice. When we start with the expectation of less competence, we are surprised when it occurs and note every flaw as proof that we were right to begin with. And we note every success as lucky. When we start from high expectation, small, inconsequential flaws are easily dismissed as being, well . . . small and inconsequential—a normal part of the learning process.

Women leaders who work in male-dominated industries such as tech or finance often have their technology credentials questioned by clients. But male managers can support their female teammates by saying things like, "Juanita is our strongest manager. We are giving you the best," or "We are lucky; Cindy is the one of best coders we have." Helping others with this reframe can pave the way for women to be more successful.

How Am I Worthy?

As we have seen, sexual attention as a validator of a man's worth can be a source of disruption in the workplace. Focusing on objective contributions as a basis for worth can free men to bring their more authentic self to the workplace and exhibit true respect for women. This is how we reframe the sexual prowess assumption. It helps decouple gender and sexual attraction from the conversation. It has to be a requirement. Said one expert, "Never entertain the possibility of sex (with a female mentee). No amount of attraction, bonding, or emotional intimacy *ever* gives you clearance to sexualize a relationship with a woman you mentor, particularly when you hold any sort of power relative to her. No exceptions. Deal with it."[156]

No matter how tempting it may seem, this energy should be redirected to something similar to a sibling relationship, what psychologist Robert Sternberg calls "companionate love."[157] Ironically, the return on this type of emotional attachment is much more intimate and lasting in the long run.

Assumption	Reframe
I am worthy and important when I get sexual attention.	I am worthy for my contributions.

An important component of this reframe is to recognize conditions that may lead someone of any gender to feel the need for sexual validation, such as low self-esteem. Marital problems or getting passed over for a promotion might make a man vulnerable, thinking that sexual validation would make him feel better (of course, this can happen with women too). Self-awareness is an important tool to prevent this misperception. It is everyone's individual responsibility to get their own internal house in order and work on building their feelings of self-worth so they can maintain healthy relationships with others.

One of our workshop attendees, Peter, was having a tough time. His brother was going through a nasty divorce, and his father had recently been diagnosed with Alzheimer's disease. Though his marriage was fine, he found himself flirting more and more often at work. When he went out after work with the guys, he flirted at the bar. It was part of his happy, friendly nature.

When a new colleague, Cheryl, joined his team, he flirted with her. At first, Cheryl seemed to enjoy the attention, bantering back and engaging in personal and even sexual jibes with him. Peter convinced himself it was all harmless, and the thought of Cheryl seeing him as sexy was very appealing. He didn't tell his wife about it because he didn't think there was anything to tell.

One day, Cheryl sent him a particularly forward text on a Saturday. His wife intercepted it and became angry. They talked it through, and Peter realized that this was not how he wanted his life and work persona to be. He wanted Cheryl to respect him for his work and not see him as a potential sexual encounter. He took Cheryl aside at work on Monday, apologized for his behavior, explained that he had crossed a line, and committed to removing flirting from his work behaviors. He made it clear he had no sexual interest in her and he had been wrong to insinuate that. Instead, he switched to a positive, more brotherly persona with all women he came across inside and outside of work. He was still happy and cheerful, now without the sexual edge. He also committed to engaging a therapist to work through his anguish about his brother and father.

Peter had a crucible moment where his life could have been destroyed by his behavior, but by recognizing and reframing the basis of his worthiness, he moved to a much more secure and happy place.

THE IMPORTANCE OF ALLYSHIP

We define male allyship as men recognizing how unchallenged assumptions have given them advantages in the workplace and disadvantaged women, and actively helping women enjoy fair and equal access to the power, rewards, and engagement of work. Male allyship is crucial for women, of course, but equally importantly it does no harm to men. In fact, it helps them too, since it moves toward developing twenty-first-century leadership skills and creating a true meritocracy.

The path to allyship can start in a number of different places. The continuum below shows the various levels of understanding and bias awareness individuals may have. Each has the potential to develop towards allyship, but it is important to acknowledge the current state. Ask yourself honestly where you are on this continuum. Even women may be in denial or have their heads in the sand about the effectiveness of the meritocracy. But with knowledge and experience, people can grow and become better allies.

Denier	Gendered	Ostrich	Acknowledger	Ally	Sponsor
No problem here, we've got a meritocracy.	Men and women are different.	I know there is bias but I am not biased. I treat each gender the same.	I am learning about gender bias and actively working on it.	I am mostly aware of gender bias and am helping others learn, too.	I actively champion diverse candidates for promotion into leadership.

Allyship Continuum

The first stage of becoming an ally is working on self. For men to help women, they first need to recognize, shift, and reframe any limiting assumptions. One false assumption is the meaning of allyship itself. Many men think being an ally is only about coming to women's events and learning about women's issues. That's a great start. But allyship is also about being willing to take risks, admit mistakes, and change things when it is obvious change needs to happen.

We knew of one CEO who was keen to be an ally for women. He made big, public announcements about how important women were to the organization. Then his six-person, all-white, all-male leadership team added two more white men. When the CEO was called out, he couldn't see a problem and was unwilling to change. His assumption was that allyship meant nothing more than making ceremonial gestures. Had he been willing to use his power to make a difference, he may have been ready for allyship.

In conjunction with Brandon Hall Group,[158] we conducted a male allyship survey and found overwhelming support for the need for allyship and the desire to be an ally. Let's consider some of the concrete ways in which men can be meaningful allies to women at work.

MAKE SPACE FOR WOMEN TO BELONG

Belonging is a key ingredient of effective teams and cultures. When men are on a leadership team that is predominantly male, they automatically feel like they belong. They feel good. Everyone knows the rules and there is a strong sense of camaraderie. And so when we ask them to give this up, it can feel quite threatening. Give up belonging? Whew.

But what if there was a sense of belonging at a level beyond gender? We just belong. Not because it's an all-male team but because we've created a system, a team structure, and process flow that enable us all to belong. That is something to strive for.

One way an enhanced sense of belonging is reached is when a team finds a common enemy outside of the team or a cause that rallies team members to combat it.[159] The challenge of the cause, if high enough, can serve as a stimulus to bring fresh ideas and talent to the table and help the team overlook trivial differences. This happens with sports teams. Common cause can erase gender status as the unspoken us versus them and focus this natural tendency *outside* the team.

We've taught teams of diverse MBA students made up of men and women from a variety of socioeconomic backgrounds who speak four to five different languages (in a team of five to six). The overarching goal is to develop and deliver a high-stakes solution to a real client challenge after three months of research. The pressure is intense, but the common outside goal enables these students to bridge and then leverage their diversity gaps. The output often exceeds the output of many MBA student teams that aren't so diverse. And students regularly report that it is one of their most effective and enjoyable teaming experiences.

Such an approach requires a process of creating group norms that rise above differences, but it also requires that women aren't alone on the team. One woman on a team tends to go along with team decisions and get stuck doing most of the legwork. We've heard an undergraduate on an all-male team say, "We didn't do well because we didn't have a girl on our team to help us organize the work." But when there are two or more women, gender barriers tend to begin to disappear. When there is a sense of belonging within the team for women, the team can focus more readily on the external challenge.

MENTOR AND SPONSOR WOMEN

Mentorship "matters because it [leverages the experiences of leaders and] teaches people the skills required to be successful in an organization or industry."[160] It helps people outside traditional power demographics to overcome the barriers built within in.[161] And having multiple mentors enables more connections.[162] Women who want to be leaders need mentors. The challenge has been that everyone assumes women need to be mentored by women. And since there are so few women in leadership . . . well, it can be a self-fulfilling prophecy. So the message for men is: we need you to mentor women.

And we get it. Male mentors sometimes unconsciously reinforce the organization's flawed assumptions—that leadership looks male and that women aren't as technical, for example. Mentors need to be clearly aware that sometimes mentorship can assimilate mentees into the dominant culture, and of the implications to individuals of full assimilation, such as succumbing to unconscious bias. They need to be clear about what skills and experiences are truly required for progression (such as the ability to do business development) and which are more assimilative, be-like-me attributes (such as golfing).

Mentorship is only one part of the solution. Research consistently shows that sponsorship is how people are consciously plucked upwards into power roles. Women need not only advice, but also investment. Someone in the room needs to take a risk and be women's advocate when decisions are made. "Let's give Paula a chance at that role. I think she would be great."

Social capital is the grease that helps this process. And though having a robust network of connections at the peer level is critical early in a career, as people move upward it's the more senior and connected relationships that make a difference.[163] That's what gets people sponsored.

Here again, men need to step up. Often sponsorship can be more a result of informal interactions such as socializing after work or golfing together, and these activities often exclude women. And because women spend time trying to dispel negative stereotypes about themselves, rather than promoting their work,[164] male allies can help by consciously seeking to sponsor women based solely on potential and outcomes.

We have noticed that many clients have the tendency to have men mentor or sponsor men and women mentor or sponsor women. In our view, this is a big mistake. First, since there are fewer women in power, it puts a lot of pressure on those who are there and contributes to burnout. Second, it assumes that the only way for women to work is to emulate other women, and this leads to very narrow role-model examples. Finally, it excludes women (and men) from cross-gender experiences and reinforces gender lines and the whole gender-equals-capability divide. Women need mentors of all genders and so do men.

Upstand

As women become more vocal about harassment and aggression, gender conflict and microaggressions against women have increased.[165] There has also been an increase in hostility and mistrust in the workplace. Now more than ever, men need to upstand and speak out against the male behaviors that have pushed women to protest. Fueling a gender war and reinforcing gender biases sets everyone back.

We define upstanding as men recognizing when other men's flawed assumptions create a limiting barrier for women. Note that we do not mean protecting women because they are weak. We mean instead the understanding that while many men have done the hard work of uncovering and reframing their assumptions, others haven't. With compassion, these folks need to be coached. This is not about catching people, calling them out, or making them feel stupid. It is about helping them learn. That way, we can work together to create more enlightenment instead of more division.

We learned about Floyd, who had noticed that Jeff was dominating meetings, cutting women off, dismissing contributions, and rolling his eyes whenever a woman would speak. It was clear Jeff didn't think the women in the room were making a valuable contribution and resented their presence. Floyd took Jeff aside after a meeting to hear him out. Using Direct Speak, Floyd asked, "Hey Jeff, I'm noticing that you often cut women off mid-sentence or roll your eyes if a woman speaks. It's causing women to shut down in the meetings. What's going on?"

Jeff eventually admitted, "Hey, I really don't think women should be doing this work. They just aren't as capable." Floyd didn't rise to it (although he had a knot in his stomach) but continued asking "Why?" questions and found out that Jeff hadn't really worked much with professional women. Lack of skills and experience made Jeff feel uncomfortable. So Floyd helped Jeff reframe by patiently bringing in data and objective information. Jeff was particularly swayed by the idea that being able to discern performance was an important developmental leadership skill—so instead of having to buy in that *all* women are as capable as he is, he can evaluate them individually and critically. Floyd's willingness to mentor Jeff was received positively as well.

Upstanding at work is important, but if nothing changes at home, it's harder at work for everyone. We interviewed a senior manager who challenged her female employees to step up at work and her male employees to step up at home. She had noticed that only her female employees would ask for time off for a doctor's appointment or similar. So she started asking her male employees who were parents when they were taking time to do these types of family responsibilities. And when her female employees asked for time off, she asked if their spouses were matching that effort as well. She refused to buy into outdated assumptions about gender assumptions.

Men need to learn to do this too. One interviewee, Jay, told us "I didn't want to do laundry, so I purposely shrunk my wife's sweaters." Another colleague told us his wife does everything at home (cooking, cleaning, organizing), and she loves it. It's her choice. But women do 3.3 hours per day of housework on average compared to 2 hours per day for men. And if given a fair choice—between doing housework and resting up for work—most women would prefer the latter. When men display flawed assumptions, allies can help them reframe: everyone is responsible for taking care of the home and family and earning a living. Or: If everyone works together they can get the housework done *and* get some needed rest.

FIX THE SYSTEM

The workplace barriers that protect privileged groups and inadvertently entrench their power in an organization are not easy to fix. We've shown you what individuals—men and women—need to do. We've shown how the power of the reframe can begin the process of disabling the flawed assumptions that underpin unconscious bias and perpetuate workplace barriers. The individual reframe strategies will, in turn, enable the organization to remove those barriers. Male allyship is a great step toward fixing the system by helping the whole institution recognize barriers, acknowledge their impact, and work visibly to remove them.

To do so, male allyship needs to move beyond the meso-level of symbolic gestures and onward to the micro-level (fighting microaggressions or speaking up in a meeting) and the macro-level (mentoring, career support, and identifying organizational barriers women face and helping remove them). The "more positive interaction men have with women in professional settings, the less prejudice and exclusion they tend to demonstrate."[166] We get that change like this is not easy. But we also hope we've shown how much power we all have as individuals. By changing our perspective and embarking on this journey, everyone benefits. This is about creating a bigger pie. And a better organization.

8

What Organizations Need to Do

OKAY—SO WE'VE SHOWN YOU what men and women, in their different but overlapping ways, need to do to upend false assumptions, overcome unconscious bias, and promote gender equity in the workplace. And it is important for everyone, as individuals, to examine attitudes and behaviors and commit to reframing. But as we mentioned earlier, even though organizations are made up of individuals, they have unique, organic identities, and it is up to everyone within an organization—particularly its leadership—to commit to principles that can move individual change up to organizational level.

Earlier we discussed some flawed organizational assumptions that persist within companies. It is common to believe in the validity of an existing meritocracy (despite a lack of women) and think the problem will solve itself. And many organizations define leadership—as demonstrated by mainly white men in the past—as male. That is why most solutions to the problem of including women in the workplace have been to train them to fit in—work like men and lead like men—and accommodate their additional roles as women. Few have recognized that the underlying assumptions are invalid. A system that is designed and sustained by a single group is inherently biased against others.

But businesses don't change because of lofty shoulds, just as individuals don't change because of guilt. So it is critical for leaders of organizations to acknowledge that their organizational assumptions are flawed by reframing these main assumptions. The meritocracy is flawed due to bias, which needs to be removed before it can work correctly. The problem won't solve itself; it needs proactive help. And leadership needs to be redefined. You can't solve tomorrow's problems with yesterday's skills. The sooner that reframe happens, the easier it will be for organizations to move forward and develop creative options that will allow true equity to emerge.

This reframe exercise will help move the gender equity conversation from a peripheral HR project to a central operating principle of an organization. All parts of the talent pipeline must be involved in building and fixing the meritocracy. All leaders are required to have new competencies.

That may sound intimidating, and for many of our clients, this realization has been met with an emotional response. Because it is big. Like when women are confronted with flawed assumptions and can't go back—they can't pretend they no longer know why they skipped a networking lunch to organize their desk—leaders can't pretend that the reason they have no women in leadership is because women aren't qualified enough. Understanding that unfair obstacles are hidden all over the organization, which derail great talent and create business vulnerability, can cause a good deal of anxiety. It can seem like a big management challenge. And there are no clear roadmaps for how to tackle this problem.

Until now.

Coming as we do from operational roles, we recommend an operational solution. Instead of thinking about this change as part of a massive, complex, and ethereal social movement, we challenge company leaders to approach it from a process perspective: it's no different from any another business operations problem. Think of the steps any operations consultant would tell you to take: create a vision, motivate people to engage, assess where the organization is, compare where it needs to go (gap analysis), create an implementation strategy, and develop a post-implementation feedback loop.

CREATING A VISION

We've already talked about how important it is for leaders to visualize what a diverse and inclusive environment could look like. It isn't about dreaming up social recognition but truly envisioning the work environment in 360 degrees. What does the organization look like? How do different people get along? How do they interact with customers? How does work get done? What kind of social life will the organization have? Who does well in this environment and who flounders? What skills do leaders need and how will we know when they have acquired them? What can we all achieve as a result?

This vision needs to be documented—translated into words—so it can be communicated by leaders to the organization. Write it down! It needs to be as concrete as possible. Giving the context of the equation illustrates why it is the right vision as well as how it benefits members of the organization as individuals. Defining context signals that the change is important enough for everyone to invest time. It's tempting to limit the vision conversation to logical arguments for diversity, but rational arguments don't really work. It comes down to the emotional connection people feel. Can they imagine themselves in the new way of working? Is it fun? Do they want to be there? What does the experience feel like for suppliers and customers? This emotional context is essential for people to have enough information and feel connected to the outcomes so they will consciously buy in.[167]

Of course, this vision can't be imposed from the sidelines. Even if the initial push comes from a task force or HR, accountability for the vision needs to be held at the top. It can be tempting to assign gender equity to a high-profile woman champion in the organization as her side project, or to assign diversity and inclusion to a dedicated diversity specialist in HR. Both these people lack the ultimate authority or resources to make change. And such an assignment signals the goal is not important enough for the people at the top to spend time on it. Wait and it'll go away. As with all change effort, senior leader ownership and accountability signals that the change really matters.

We usually start our consulting process by facilitating a visioning session with senior leaders or a core task-force committee that has been given resources—including time. This ensures buy-in and sponsorship for the project but also signals that senior leaders are aligned on the shared future. Often this process unearths some important issues with diversity and inclusion goal setting. Leaders are often fine with diversity and inclusion (or any other change process) as long

VALUES IN ACTION

Stating and then demonstrating values around equity sometimes requires a tough conversation. One international organization struggled with gender inequity in some of its global locations. But gender equity was a core value. So one of the managers said, "This is what it looks like here. Everyone's voice matters. Men, you may work for a woman, and women, you may have men on your team. And we are all in this together as equal contributors. And we will help get you the skills—and create the forum for the conversations—so you can learn how. If you can't work with this, then you can't work here."

as they don't have to do anything differently. "It's everyone else that needs to change, not me." Remember where we started our discussion—with individual leadership skills. Until leaders change, nobody will change.

A visioning session is critical and should ideally be professionally facilitated. We often find that the process unearths the real motivation for undertaking a gender or diversity initiative, and usually it has less to do with a quest for equity and more to do with looking good. And that's fine, because often many of the changes needed to look good will actually improve an organization for its women. But honestly visioning and agreeing on what success looks like can set the stage for a workable plan with results that can be objectively measured. It helps move initiatives from nice-to-have dabbling to more formal and defined projects.

Here are some steps to the visioning process:

1. Paint a picture of what change could mean for the senior team. One mostly male team we worked with was interested in gender balance but unwilling to consider changing senior leadership meetings from weekend golf events. They adamantly wanted the women to learn golf instead. They invited the women to join the golf club—that's inclusion, right? They didn't think about the fact that many women, and even some of the younger generation of men, aren't all that interested in golf.

2. Understand the longer-term impacts of adding diversity. It's not a one-and-done project (Great! Now we are diverse!), but an ongoing cultural change to maintain and foster diversity. It requires recognizing when a diverse-looking team has become insular and stagnant. Yes, this is a commitment. But commitment indicates seriousness.

3. Come to agreement about what happens when uncomfortable insights show up in the discovery process. For example, what if a highly visible, richly rewarded, favorite team leader creates a not-so-inclusive team and we recommend remediation? Or we uncover a potential harassment situation? Or what if a client doesn't want a woman sales representative? Are leaders willing to follow through and address these situations? If action aligns with words, buy-in will begin. If actions are misaligned, it'll be a much longer road.

4. Set goals! Companies have goals for every other type of initiative and for measuring business progress/success. They also need goals and metrics for inclusion. Yes, goals. Concrete, tangible, and measurable. Some common goals include the following:

Strategic Goal	Possible Measures
Increase the diversity of our workforce for the next five years	• Percent increase in group representation per year
Increase our managers' diversity management competency	• Skills, defined capabilities • Individual team diversity
Remove structural barriers to inclusion in our organization	• Demographics throughout the pipeline at each level, e.g. promotions, velocity of promotions, turnover • Use of benefits by gender
Ensure the communities of our suppliers, customers, and other stakeholders reflect our diversity goals	• Demographics of suppliers, customers, and other stakeholders including board of directors • Gender impact on products and services

MOTIVATING ENGAGEMENT BY LEADERS AND THEIR EMPLOYEES

Motivation matters? Yes, in all change initiatives. At first, this step may feel like the most challenging. Resistance to these types of initiatives is often hidden, showing up in watercooler conversations and general apathy. You may hear questions like, "But really, is she an effective project manager? We don't want to hire her just because she's a woman." (Note: Try flipping this. Would anyone ever ask if a man is effective? We don't hire a man just because he's a man.) People who make fun of or scoff at these efforts or roll their eyes or cross their arms when the subject is brought up can influence others. People may gossip negatively about it in social situations, making it uncool to participate. Low levels of resistance add up. Framing initiatives as essential, the way forward, and what you're going to do—it matters.

Everyone comes from a different starting point. They bring their past experiences, good and bad. Some have had a lot of positive experience working with professional women and may be easier to motivate. Some have been burned for an honest misunderstanding and may not. And some who feel threatened by the process or resent the intrusion of women into their comfortable homogeneous workplace may actively work against the process. We have seen an unwilling male employee use his considerable size to intimidate female colleagues by standing too close to them to emphasize his point of view. He would also raise his voice and shout over women who spoke in meetings. He escalated his attempts at subtle intimidation even after management intervened. Ultimately, he was encouraged to leave the organization because he was unwilling to adopt the vision.

Three key factors help with motivating leaders and employees to embrace the vision and work to make change in the organization: a growth mindset, an improved skill set, and a supportive learning environment.

DON'T BE AFRAID TO MEASURE

It's become fashionable to resist measuring gender and diversity efforts for fear of the political backlash against quotas. "We don't do quotas." But quotas are different from metrics. Quotas are blunt and rigid mandates that leave little room for learning, flexibility, or changing conditions. They can encourage negative behaviors such as tokenism. Metrics, on the other hand, measure changes that demonstrate development. It's okay to set a target for improvement, such as increasing the number of female level-three engineers by 10 percent over time, because this goal recognizes improvement while leaving flexibility for individual choices. It also enables analysis of why a target was met or not. Abandoning measurement entirely is a big mistake. Set a target performance goal similar to one that exists for any business challenge. Nothing in business gets done without targets and measurement of results. Why would this be any different?

IT STARTS WITH AN OPEN MIND

Mindset is critical to how people learn and grow. Improving the team means its members need to be open and ready and willing to learn. A closed mindset rarely leads to learning or change. A fixed mindset makes people believe that their personal traits, the situation, and their skill set are based on an unalterable situation. They assume these attributes are fixed.[168] So you might hear a woman say, "I'm no good at math. A budget? Yikes!" Or a man say, "I don't do well with change." This doesn't mean they can't learn to budget or participate in a change project, but simply that they have closed their mind to it.

A growth mindset is the opposite. With a growth mindset, situations, skill sets, and attitudes are all malleable. Growth-mindset people are more

WHAT?	HOW DO THEY FEEL?
Concrete	**Emotional**
What behavior was observed?	How do the others involved feel?
A confident teammate suddenly stops participating in a robust discussion.	She appears frustrated and disengaged. She's mad. She's upset. She's a drama queen.

WHAT DO YOU SEE, HEAR?	WHY?
Observational	**Understanding**
What are you noticing?	What is her assumption/point of view? (Hint: Try to unearth a fundamental need for her.)
She got quiet and folded her arms and legs across her body. She started looking at her phone. The group facilitator spoke over her several times and didn't write any of her ideas on the board.	She shares that she doesn't want to waste her ideas or energy on a group that isn't listening. She feels disrespected. Her need to be respected and of value has been violated.

self-aware—they know where they are starting from and have the self-efficacy to believe they can learn. They are also naturally curious, so new challenges are seen as opportunities to learn. Humans have an amazing ability to change and learn new skills at any age as long as their mindset allows them to believe they can.

And the good news: people can be taught to shift their mindset. Language is really important. As with reframing, people can recognize a fixed mindset when they hear their inner voice say, "I don't need to learn this," or, "If I don't try, I won't make mistakes." If you catch yourself negative self-talking, you can shift your language. "You know, I can learn this. It'll help me," or "If I try, I might be able to achieve something new!"

A useful tool for shifting mindset is to use empathy to understand what is happening.[169] An empathy map deconstructs how someone else might experience a situation differently and help you understand why. Let's say a usually confident woman teammate suddenly stops participating in a robust discussion. The group can move on, ignore her, and miss out on her contribution. Or an observant participant can walk through an empathy map, thinking through each section of the chart above. Note that the idea here is to unearth insights about why she shut down. Once the map is prepared, asking questions can verify the assumptions made.

Another tool is to walk in someone else's shoes. We encourage people to sample a different context to see what might happen and how people react. Here's how it works: First imagine what the other person thinks, feels, hears, sees, says, and does, as well as where they experience pain or gain. Then take on that new experience.

Consider a senior male leader whose wife stays at home with their kids. What if for one week he took the kids to school and picked them up, prepared three meals, and did whatever other chores had to be done? Plus he still worked. After that week, the leader knows more about what it's like to be a dual-working or single parent. The result? A more open mindset from new-found empathy.

Sometimes it is enough for people to know that the organization believes them capable of building necessary skills. One way to do this is to carefully select a special team of early adopters to be first to go through training. Tell them they were selected because of the organization's confidence in their self-awareness and leadership ability. This confidence can rub off on them so they commit to the change process. Even recognizing small steps helps confidence. For example, leaders can notice when an aggressive male colleague keeps himself from interrupting a female colleague and thanks him for his patience. Here's a new role model of behavior that showcases what the organization believes in. It also recognizes that employees are trying to learn and grow. People will feel it and—guess what—they tend to open up more as a result.

You Can't Solve Tomorrow's Problems with Yesterday's Skills

It is really important for leaders to agree upon and clearly articulate the skill set required and expected from people. Fostering or managing inclusion sounds great but what does that really mean? In Part 3, we'll outline specific competencies that you can develop to help everyone build the right skill set. For example, leaders can role model how to recognize and eliminate bias from decision-making. They can show what it looks like to effectively work with differences to become more collaborative and creative. Can team leaders foster diversity of thought and positive disagreement? Can everyone on the team maintain a safe place where alternative viewpoints and experiences are valued? Do people feel valued and are allowed to participate? Are bullying and other exclusionary behaviors shunned? These are all competencies that organizations need to codify so they can be recognized and rewarded.

A critical question is, "How can we tell?" Agreeing how to evaluate and measure this skill set is essential. It's tough, because it's tempting to hide behind politically correct language and superficial gestures. Instead, one way to measure skill sets objectively is to look closely at people's teams. Is the team diverse? And is it truly diverse—not with token representation but with people who have truly different backgrounds, experiences, and perspectives? What about this person's previous teams? Is there positive conflict or just groupthink happening when they get together? Are their teams becoming more diverse over time, indicating that the leader is learning? Are they leveraging diverse perspectives in their team processes? Are employees moving through this team on the way to greater things?

Leaders who get this know: you have to measure skill set growth as you do any other business change. Evaluation needs to be made as objective as possible by aligning key performance indicators and the actual numbers behind measuring these skills. Bringing in an outside coach or consultant can help take some of the internal politics out of evaluating colleagues on this potentially touchy subject. And identified gaps should be seen as training opportunities rather than character flaws. Individuals can then be trained, given opportunities for practice, and re-evaluated until they develop proficiency with understanding and mitigating bias.

REDUCING BIASES IS A SKILL

Good bias-awareness training is different from standard diversity training because it gives people the skills to facilitate conversations between groups and integrates awareness by incorporating action. If the problem is a poor attitude (that is, there is no interest in learning more about unconscious biases), then seriously question that person's long-term leadership potential at the organization. It's okay to have been unaware of bias previously, but it's not okay to think someone can recruit, promote, or manage people in the twenty-first century without self-awareness in this area.

AN ENVIRONMENT OF GROWTH

Finally, motivating engagement depends on leaders creating a positive learning environment so people are encouraged and supported while they develop. We all need a safe, positive space to learn, which creates a sense of psychological safety. We will talk more about how to establish this safety in Part 3, but it is important to know that the environment needs to be free of the negative consequences of interpersonal risk-taking for people who are learning something new.[170] And before you dismiss this idea, consider this: Google studied fifty years of data, conducted an internal study, and found that psychological safety was the key ingredient to team success.[171, 172] The goal is to create that psychological safety at an organizational-culture level.

One way to do this is to make clear that bias does not equate to intent. Blame needs to be eliminated from the conversation. As we've discussed, unconscious bias is exactly that, unconscious. People can work from their starting point through all of the learning levels without being blamed for the negative impacts of things in the past when they were unaware. Sometimes this can be hard because there can be a lot of emotion from those who are injured by bias. So everyone needs to put blame aside for the sake of learning.

Here's the essence of a psychologically safe team: When people speak up and share something that runs counter to the group, they aren't shut down, dismissed out of hand, or bullied. Instead, the group (usually through what's called "ways of working" or "group norms") develops standards that create a "blend of trust, respect for each other's competence, and caring about each other as people."[173] Teams with strong psychological safety learn more, and as a result, perform better. Think about that—*they learn more* and that positively impacts performance.

And it is more than just voice. Psychological safety means enabling people to bring their whole selves

HOW TO HELP PEOPLE HARMED BY BIAS

Just as it is important for people learning about bias to have space for making mistakes, it is important for victims of bias to be given an outlet for their emotions while they work through anger. It is also helpful to recognize when they formerly would have expressed emotion but have clearly progressed to a more neutral place of acceptance. Having honest and open conversations can help with healing when there have been negative impacts of past behavior or even to discuss bias overall. There are many facilitation approaches, including nonviolent communication* and the "Engaging in Conversations" worksheet provided by the global nonprofit Catalyst, both of which provide concrete tools to help. †

to work. When people are psychologically safe, and when they bring everything to the table, the entirety of their experiences and skills can be utilized. This means that Jolene doesn't have to change her hair, and Wanda doesn't have to lower her voice. It means that Lewis doesn't have

---

* "Nonviolent Communication Skills in the Workplace," PuddleDancer Press (2009), https://www. nonviolentcommunication.com/learn-nonviolent-communication/nvc-workplace/
† "Infographic: Conversation Ground Rules," Catalyst (October 17, 2016).

to compete to speak all the time. And Jiacam can get angry on occasion without kicking off a stereotyped response.

It doesn't eliminate debate over content. We want that! In fact, it's quite the opposite—psychological safety can encourage people who normally would be hesitant to speak. It just means people don't get bogged down in disputes over style.

So when people speak up and share something that is counter to the group, it is important they are not immediately shut down. It means that people generally feel safe to share and explore alternative ideas.

If leaders want a learning organization (and we are saying that it *really* matters), think about how mistakes are handled. When learning is the goal rather than perfection, people learn from their mistakes much more quickly than if they think that they always have to get everything right. Mistakes become learning opportunities. Punishments, especially by labeling, can close down mindsets. Ignoring mistakes, however, can perpetuate them. There needs to be an appropriate response. If a man calls the women in the office "girls," someone can politely and lightheartedly reply, "You mean *women*." It's a casual, gentle reminder, not a punishment. If a male colleague makes an unwanted pass at a woman at work, however, the conversation might involve a more direct, boundary-setting conversation. And then if he does it again, it gets escalated because it is no longer an honest mistake. If leaders, or those on the receiving end of bias, spend too much time punishing minor mistakes, nobody will learn.

In our experience, many women are fearful at work that they must contain themselves to workplace norms. Many experience impostor syndrome: they don't feel they are good enough for their role. This is especially true if they have been burned before. Maybe they did something bold or confident and got labeled arrogant or aggressive, or they admitted having a personal problem that required time out of the office and had that used against them, or they were accused of being too emotional whenever they expressed passion or compassion.

It's easier to shut down, take fewer risks, and emulate the rest of the group. When one of our clients was breastfeeding, she found herself stuck in a four-hour meeting feeling increasingly distressed because she needed to take a break to express milk. She feared that speaking up in the otherwise all-male room would draw attention to her femininity and what she considered a weakness. Instead she became increasingly distracted and less focused. Suddenly, one of the men interrupted the meeting to request a food break, stating that he was diabetic and couldn't continue the meeting until he brought his blood sugar back up. Everyone immediately agreed and the meeting broke for lunch. Problem solved. His honesty and comfort expressing his personal situation and needs were in stark contrast to our client's hidden distress. And nobody felt he was weak; they merely expressed empathy for his human situation. After lunch the meeting resumed with much more energy and focus than the hour just before lunch. And of course, everyone was more productive as a result.

Can you imagine a workplace where, instead of women hiding themselves or working under fear, they fully and authentically brought their whole selves to the table? Just imagine! Teams could actually break down groupthink, capture the resulting ideas, and create innovative solutions! Yes, it will be different, and sometimes the group might have to break for its members to take a personal moment, but wow, it could be positively transformative.

Once an organization has established a sense of psychological safety, the next step in creating a positive learning environment is to actively facilitate learning opportunities so they can be studied and debriefed. Hand-selecting diverse teams for certain projects by purposely putting different people together works well. Holding roundtable discussions to allow departments to talk to each other about bias and how it impacts them personally is also effective. And structuring social events, such as scavenger hunts with preselected teams, can purposefully mingle disparate groups.

Now remember, diverse teams sometimes (and often at first) foster more conflict. But with effort, teams can move through conflict to performance.[174] Teams need practice getting past their superficial traits so they understand that at their core they share many of the same values. Then they can jointly design a process for negotiating conflicting values.[175] This process enables shared values that provide a sound basis for discussion of the areas of conflict so the team can resolve differences, learn, and include each other's perspectives more fully.

The three areas of motivation are interconnected and interdependent, and individuals need all three to garner the needed engagement for change: the right mindset and a safe learning environment to truly learn the skill set. But without the skill set, mindset and learning environment won't move the needle. So it is really important that leaders spend time to work through this motivation framework in advance of, and in preparation for, implementing change.

GAP ANALYSIS

Your organization has a vision. Great. It understands the need for motivation. Even better. But where are the inequities? How can leadership reveal them? This challenge needs to be addressed like any other business change: assess the organization's current state, compare it to the vision, and identify the gaps. Organizations need to evaluate their gender equity and inclusion status and uncover the drivers responsible for any inequity. Why automatically invest in a daycare program as a solution for women's advancement issues at your company, for example, if it turns out that the majority of the women in the company don't need it, especially if it then reinforces the attitude that daycare is a woman's problem instead of all parents' problem? Understanding the problem at a deeper level gives leaders the ability to prioritize the right solution.

We've created a gender-equity assessment and scorecard process that helps organizations answer the question about where and why inequity exists and identify opportunities to improve the organization's competitive advantage as it relates to attracting, retaining, and engaging talented women.

But before using these tools, it is critical to get a baseline count of women in the organization at every level. We continue to be amazed at how many organizations invest time and money in women's leadership development programs without really quantifying the situation. Anecdotally, leaders tend to believe that equity exists, even when it doesn't. Research tells us that if leadership is just 10 percent women, half of male leaders and a third of female leaders think there's equity.[176] The only way to know for sure is to count.

This is often an eye-opening experience. What seems like lots of women often turns out to be less than 40 percent of the organization, often congregated in marketing, customer service, and HR, mostly at entry or mid-levels. Counting by department and by level illuminates issues and opportunities and raises key questions. Why does the northwest region have fewer female sales leads, for example? Why are all the accounting clerks women while all of the financial analysts are men? Is the only woman on the senior team the vice president of HR? How many female engineers are team leads? Counting also allows an organization to set concrete, measurable, specific goals for improvement.

In our approach, we evaluate organizations at three levels—entry, mid-level, and senior—on twelve gender-scorecard dimensions (see the figure on page 123). We send out surveys, conduct individual interviews, review data, and research comparative statistics during the evaluation. We look at processes such as recruiting and intangibles such as how mentoring happens (or doesn't). We also look at how companies show up to their external constituencies, as evidenced in their brand presentation and media instances. The details of this process will be covered in depth in Part 3.

After our analysis is completed, we compile individual ratings for each dimension and provide a letter-grade score that enables organizations to see how they rate compared to other organizations in their industry and what areas need improvement. This gap analysis is an essential starting point to setting goals, recognizing where there are gaps, and prioritizing which efforts will produce the biggest impact.

Scoring Gender Equity

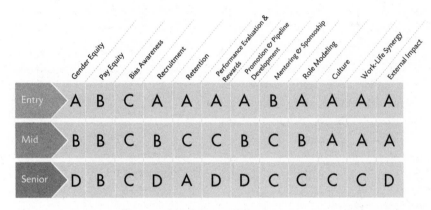

	Gender Equity	Pay Equity	Bias Awareness	Recruitment	Retention	Performance Evaluation & Rewards	Promotion & Pipeline Development	Mentoring & Sponsorship	Role Modeling	Culture	Work-Life Synergy	External Impact
Entry	A	B	C	A	A	A	A	B	A	A	A	A
Mid	B	B	C	B	C	C	B	C	B	A	A	A
Senior	D	B	C	D	A	D	D	C	C	C	C	D

Gender Scorecard

CREATE AN IMPLEMENTATION STRATEGY

Change happens through developing a realistic implementation plan with pre-agreed milestones. Enlist an action committee drawing from key influencers—not just senior leaders, but employees from across the organization who have a lot to say and tend to sway others' opinions. As influencers, they will be the loudest voices for change, and even if they don't agree with the plan, dissenter voices will be a valuable asset to have in the conversation.

It is essential that the gender scorecard and implementation plan be shared across the organization so that everyone who participates in the evaluation process, even only responding to the survey, can see the impact of their involvement.

Once the plan has been developed and agreed upon, we recommend using the implementation process below. It will require some patience, but the results will help develop a sustainably diverse organization that can compete for decades to come. Of course, it is not a one-time fix but an ongoing development process that requires testing and retesting, because every step of the way the organization will evolve.

Here's an example: A client of ours decided that it was time to change the gender paradigm of their organization. The leaders made many ceremonial declarations and appointments, including putting one of their best performers in charge of the initiative—full-time. They held a visioning session to align expectations and set goals. We then conducted a gap analysis for their organization where we uncovered many opportunities for improvement, including an opportunity to recruit more broadly for key roles. They communicated their commitment to the organization and enlisted all line managers to the task. They obtained training in unconscious bias and diversity hiring. Leaders committed to an aggressive target to expand their talent pool and elicit four times the number of women candidates. They

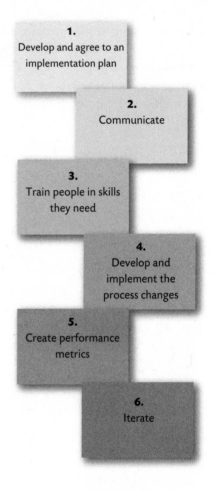

1.
Develop and agree to an implementation plan

2.
Communicate

3.
Train people in skills they need

4.
Develop and implement the process changes

5.
Create performance metrics

6.
Iterate

The Six-Step Implementation Process

attended recruiting events at schools they previously overlooked. When at first they still attracted only a small number of women candidates, they regrouped to figure out why. They hired a more specialized recruiter who documented feedback from female candidates about the "bro culture" they sensed at the company. This caused the leadership to rewrite their job descriptions and job marketing materials in a whole new way. And guess what—more women suddenly found this company and applied.

You may recognize this process as a common approach to how organizational change is made. If you decide to embark on a project like this, it is only through implementation that you will learn what works and what doesn't. Where change makes an impact. How people can start showing up. Regularly go back to your vision—where you are headed. Of course, this process assumes your organization really wants to make change. Because we promise, if your organization is committed to implementation success, change will indeed happen.

PART 3

MAKING GENDER EQUITY HAPPEN: TOOLS AND TECHNIQUES

9
Promoting Leadership

In Part 1, we described some barriers that women face as they pursue equal opportunities in the workplace. Part of that description was the acknowledgment that much of the bias that makes it challenging for women to secure fair treatment is unconscious—unintentional, culturally ingrained, and without malice.

In one sense, that unconsciousness is a further challenge—if people don't know they are part of a problem, they don't believe they have anything to fix. But in another way it is encouraging—if people don't intend to build barriers, it should be easier to convince them to help take them down.

We're optimists, so we look at the second part of that last paragraph, the encouraging part, as the basis for finding solutions. And in Part 2 we did just that—showed you what women and men can do to uncover the false assumptions that underpin unconscious bias, and then reverse bias's consequences via the power of the reframe.

But in the last chapter, we began the discussion of how individual responsibility and positive, empowering attitudes and behaviors—as great as they are—still need to flow upward and outward within an organization, so the workplace becomes a place where pursuing gender equity is the default, and best practices are standard. This is a leadership issue, but we don't mean that only executives need take it on board. Everyone within an organization is a leader or potential leader, so our tools and techniques are aimed at everyone with the goal of creating an organization that is mindful of, committed to, and prepared for the process of building gender equity.

The relationship among individuals, leaders, and the organization is critical for a company striving for gender equity and holistic change. Our three-pillared approach allows us to lay out how an organization can pursue a successful inclusion strategy by:

1. Identifying and removing barriers and biased processes within the organization that stand in the way of inclusion;

2. Including critical missing diversity and inclusion elements to leadership competencies so leaders can more effectively manage inclusive teams; and

3. Training individuals to recognize their own unconscious biases that may limit themselves and others from full workplace participation and reframing them.

Before we show you how to embark on an organizational assessment process, let's take a closer look at what inclusive leadership really means.

THE LEADERSHIP GAP

The effects of bad leadership can be devastating. Many organizational leaders, often in good faith, promote practices that restrict diversity and inclusion. Yet leadership gaps can be tough to spot. Organizations are often poor at understanding the skills, competencies, and capabilities of inclusive leadership, which is critical for aspiring leaders and organizations.

Let's compare two leaders we have come across in our work.

Tom is a mid-level manager who is seeking promotion to senior leadership. He has an impeccable record with the company. His career story is shared with new hires. He started in the Portland, Maine, office right out of college (a private liberal arts school in the northeast). He worked evenings and weekends, out-producing those around him. Soon he was running the Portland office and then the Maine region. He treated clients well, often taking them on golf outings and to sporting events, and cemented his extensive relationships and status within the industry. Tom has recruited many bright stars to the organization, many from his own school, and is a mentor for many up-and-coming employees. His region's sales growth has always been consistent. The company considers him a model employee.

The employees in Tom's region are mostly white and mostly male, except for the administrative and maintenance staff. Most of Tom's customers are white men. Tom has always happily taken the firm's diversity and inclusion training as well as the required sexual-harassment classes. He has never been accused of harassment, and most people would agree that he has never done anything that could be considered sexist.

He feels he treats everyone exactly the same. On his annual review, there is a section for human rights that is meant to reflect Tom's treatment of women, among others. Tom routinely gets an A grade in this section.

The company promotes Tom to run the Northeastern region, which includes Boston and New York City. He inherits a staff (and customer base) that includes women, people of color, LGBTQ members, and millennials. Now Tom starts to struggle. A woman manager complains to her colleagues because he asks her to make copies and take notes in meetings. An African American man skips critical mentorship opportunities because Tom holds most events at his golf club, which up until recently didn't allow people of color as members. A Chinese American customer quietly moves their business to a competitor because of a light joke Tom made one night at dinner about fortune cookies. Over several years, Tom's team demographics shift back to a team of all white men, through turnover and attrition, so the complaints about his leadership cease. In fact, his team routinely rates him highly because of his ability to connect with them and meet their needs on a social level. His customer demographics are similarly reflective of his team demographics and many of his customers become personal friends.

Nobody ever complains to HR about Tom or even has an conversation about diversity on Tom's team. Tom swears he fosters a meritocracy and says he hires and promotes only the best. The guys on his team are all hard-working and dynamic people. When sales drop, most people attribute the loss to a new, dynamic competitor, rather than to Tom's team. So when an even more senior level role opens up, the company considers Tom as one of the very few candidates qualified for the role because of the size of the region he runs and his years of experience with the company.

You've stuck with us this far into the book, so no doubt you see the problem. Tom clearly lacks the ability to build, foster, and sustain a diverse team, but his weaknesses are hidden to the organization and their impact on his performance is hard to measure. In addition to his lack of experience with building and managing diversity, Tom has no understanding of bias and culture and does not have the motivation to do anything about it. He probably doesn't understand the benefits of having a diverse team. And he has never had to.

His management style is one-dimensional: be like me and you will succeed. This style has a significant impact on the team's ability to innovate and attract diverse customers. But not only has he gotten away with it, he appears to flourish without those skills. And is rewarded. His influence has now spilled to another part of the organization, touching other managers. As Tom rises higher and higher, and his influence further masculinizes and homogenizes the culture, the organization has no idea it is fostering a monochromatic workplace. So it is no surprise the organization has become vulnerable to competitors: those with managers better equipped to manage an increasingly diverse workforce and customer base.

Organizations with Tom's approach to leadership exist because inclusivity hasn't been recognized as a critical leadership competency. It hasn't been effectively measured, cultivated, or rewarded. The ability to lead inclusively is not included in most workforce-scorecard metrics, and if it is, it is usually a small bullet or subjective checkmark (human rights), which is somehow supposed to represent the necessary skills. Also, few leaders have enough confidence with the topic to effectively rate or coach others. And let's face it—it doesn't get measured or critiqued: Who wants to give someone a lower-than-perfect score in a category called "human rights"?

Complicating this lack of understanding and competency is the sensitivity around being accused of sexism. Defensiveness can stymie growth. So nobody wants to go there. But wait a minute. If someone lacks experience working with professional women, how could they have these skills? And how will they ever learn if nobody will talk about it?

People need honest evaluation and feedback in order to learn. They also need space to make mistakes in the process. Mistakes help us learn, after all. If we evaluate inclusive leadership skills only in a category like human rights or diversity, we risk creating a potentially explosive context most people want to avoid. Maybe this is why most companies seem to measure diversity and inclusion in terms of how much training has been delivered or received, not how much knowledge someone has about a topic or how effectively they implement it. That way, they avoid the emotional risk.

Yes, getting trained about unconscious bias matters—but it is only one stage in the capability development process. You also have to be able to do something positive with the information. As a leader, that means helping people overcome bias, reframe flawed assumptions, and remove barriers so everyone can succeed. It also means getting the very best out of people in the process. Today, few companies link their diversity and inclusion progress to a demonstrable impact on the bottom line. And they don't measure whether there has been any action or execution on the ground or whether a promoted leader has the full complement of skills to build diverse and inclusive teams so she can leverage the best talent and be innovative.

To get a sense of how to start this critical process, let's consider a second example.

We worked with an organization that sought to create a new service product. They pulled together a stakeholder team to address serious market issues the company faced. Sales had been declining. The product offering had become unfocused. They offered many interesting services but they lacked a cohesive narrative or point of view. Also, local and national online competition was increasing, not only from established companies but also from rising upstarts. This competition meant that the price point for the program needed to be lower. The team was taxed with delivering more, better, and for less money. Sound familiar?

Working with company leadership, the product manager, Maya, assembled a diverse team to get new perspectives. They purposely selected people across the organization from different departments, backgrounds, and ethnicities.

The process took longer than expected and was fraught with tension. Meetings were filled with argumentative debate and often uncomfortable levels of conflict. Conversations about topics thought to be resolved were revisited. Frustration mounted but was never allowed to become personal. The entire basis of the program was challenged—why are we here, what do our customers need, what does the marketplace demand? Fortunately, Maya was a skilled facilitator and knew how to structure team meetings creatively, often using fun and games to draw out new ideas from team members. The whole time, she kept the team focused on the broader goal—how do we compete—while exploring different perspectives.

Ultimately, the resulting program was incredible. It differentiated the company in the marketplace, brought new innovative tools to the services, and supported clients in new ways. Further, the team built in an ongoing learning and development component to the program to ensure it didn't drift in the marketplace again.

Maya's work is an example of something we call "synthesis." She was able to build a diverse team and leverage its diverse perspectives to produce a game-changing result for the organization. As in science, Maya's synthesis combined simple elements to make something new—a compound. And compounds can do things that individual elements cannot.

When teams operate at the synthesis level, they combine unique aspects of their individual members to generate something truly better than what the elements could do on their own. Now, we recognize that there is plenty of research to say that teams by themselves do not always net better results than individuals,[177] but in our definition of synthesis, teams are built and supported precisely to deliver superior performance. The diverse nature of the elements as well as the team's leadership and supportive environment create the magic needed for synthesis-level execution.

Synthesis allows an employee's perspectives to be incorporated into the processes an organization uses to get work done.[178] Consider a situation where the views of a woman in the group were leveraged to change how a product was delivered for their client, such as when a female stockbroker creates a portfolio specifically for divorced women starting over.[179] But the potential for synthesis, we think, is even bigger. We envision revolutionary changes to the way we work when leaders learn to truly leverage the different perspectives, experiences, and skills of diverse individuals on their teams.

And like synthesis in the chemistry lab, it can be messy. Teams have to identify "tension points"[180] so they uncover underlying assumptions. Team leaders need to facilitate—even foster!—sufficient conflict to overcome inertia without team members undermining each other (or breaking up the team) in the process.[181]

In diverse teams, cultural differences can trigger tension. It's why global leaders need to develop intercultural skills and learn how to recognize talent.[182] Yet again, we come down to an essential skill set of leadership. In our model, managing diversity is needed for all leadership because cross-cultural tension doesn't happen only in an international business context, it also happens between employees with different backgrounds who live in the same city and function in the same environment.

We do not treat inclusive leadership as a separate leadership skill. Our integration process recognizes that inclusivity is integral to twenty-first-century leadership. Leadership without inclusion is no longer effective for organizations. For this reason, we have developed a unique taxonomy, examined in the next chapter, which we apply to an organization's leadership competencies. This taxonomy will help you and other leaders move, via a series of increasingly complex levels, from becoming inspired to embracing diversity to leveraging diverse teams that generate better business outcomes.

10
Building Gender Equity from Vision to Reality

YOU BUILD A HOUSE FROM the ground up on a solid foundation. The beautiful views on the third floor are wonderful, but they aren't possible without careful construction below.

Building organizational leadership that is capable of turning gender equity from a vision into a reality requires the same painstaking attention to a well-founded base and an integrated process. Our view is that *every* leadership capability must contain a commitment to diversity and inclusion skills. *All of them.* So we've developed a taxonomy to organize leadership capabilities and show how they can move from a robust foundation of supporting diversity to a comprehensive synthesis of skills that will produce impact to an organization's bottom line. Our taxonomy allows leaders to evaluate where people are, how well their skills are developing, and what more needs to be done.

THE TAXONOMY: A LADDER TO INCLUSIVE LEADERSHIP

Our inclusive leadership model has four principal levels.

Diversity is where leadership starts to notice, understand, and realize that there are significant benefits to a diverse workforce. It's where awareness happens and intent begins. It is an essential first step. Belonging starts to be built at the *inclusion* level, where the fundamental skill set of how to foster and build a diverse workforce gets developed. At the third level, *engagement and voice*, diverse perspectives become integrated and heard. People begin to notice a changing environment and new insights. *Synthesis* is where it all comes together, where diversity generates positive strategic

Diversity	Inclusion	Voice/ Engagement	Synthesis
Diverse inspiration	Diversity intelligence and experience	Building talent with voice, empowering influence, engaged direction	Competitive edge, collaboration, agile execution, inclusive business judgement

Level of Difficulty & Commitment →

Level of Strategic Impact →

outcomes for the organization. It's at this capstone level that organizations achieve the true innovation benefits of diversity. It's also where diversity becomes integral to the business and essential to its core strategy.

Because most leaders haven't yet fully built these synthesis capabilities, they fail to leverage diversity to its full potential. Have you? Are you stuck wishing that you had more diversity in your organization? Well, desire is a good start. Once you are aware of what you need, you can learn and progress through the taxonomy, moving from the implementation of tactics that attract diverse candidates to leveraging strategic gains from diversity at the synthesis level.

Moving up the taxonomy expands your skill set and has an increasingly positive impact on the organization, but it is also a progressively more difficult climb. It requires commitment to stay on track. As a team becomes more diverse and complex, cultivating and leading it and its outcomes become more difficult. But difficult does not mean impossible. The leadership task just gets harder. And remember: teams require certain conditions of tension for optimal performance. Creating—and effectively nurturing—these conditions requires more advanced skills.

We see this challenge all the time. Mastering diversity intelligence is not as simple as appointing a token woman to a team or setting up an employee resource group. It requires investment. These capabilities take time, and resistance abounds. It is important to not let the level of difficulty discourage learners from embarking upon the process. We will talk more about how to develop the right mindset and put in place the right processes to support this development in a moment. For now, let's define the capabilities and how to measure them in individual leaders.

Our clients typically determine their own specific desired leadership competencies and codify them in their performance management system.

So for the purposes of this discussion, we find it useful to use a leadership capability matrix such as the one developed by the professional-services firm Deloitte.[183] Deloitte argues that the exhaustive competency lists most organizations develop can be condensed into the following general capabilities of effective leadership: inspiration, direction, influence, building talent, execution, collaboration, business judgment, and competitive edge. We've adapted these to highlight how diversity and inclusion competencies impact them. We also add one: diversity intelligence and experience. Using this modified matrix, let's look at how leadership capabilities can be built to get to the synthesis level.

DIVERSITY

If you picked up this book, you probably already have the leadership capability of inspiration. It means inspiring others to take action. [184] *Diverse inspiration*, on the other hand, means you are intellectually curious, morally motivated, and feel genuine concern for women and want to help with change. For example, you may hire someone extremely different from the usual group profile or do business with a women-owned vendor.

Note the word *curious*. Being curious means wanting to understand what someone else's experience is like. Being curious means wanting to know what the barriers are and seeing how they need to be removed. An uncurious person might think, "This is *so* frustrating, why do they do things that way?" or "Why are they like that?" or "It's so much easier to work with Chuck." When these thoughts arise, it is important to fire up your curiosity. "Hmm, why do I get triggered here? What can I learn from it?"

Intellectual curiosity can help make sense of the notion that there is a level playing field. Many people have been taught that they are entitled to earn a living, that they will be respected and compensated for the work they do, and that the amount of input and hard work can be directly tied to results. Fundamentally, many believe this must also be true for everyone. But earlier we showed you how that is usually a false assumption. The playing field is not level and not every person's experience or opportunity is the same.

Curiosity prompts you to test what is true for others. Maybe Joelle doesn't enjoy this same reality and feels that she has been left out. Being curious means seeking to understand her perspective. To leverage the talent of those who haven't benefited from a "fair" system, openness to diversity is critical. In essence, curiosity enables you to seek to understand others' experiences and to become a role model for change as you inspire others to join you on this journey.

Leaders with diverse inspiration believe in the social cause of diversity, gender balance, and fairness. They respect Equal Employment Opportunity (EEO) guidelines for their underlying intent and provide fair access to all groups. [185] For Tom, it could mean deciding to deepen the hiring pool for his next team member, consciously choosing to interview female candidates or hire a woman. It may also mean motivating others to take up a cause, such as voicing concerns about group or vendor homogeneity.

You can't move up the taxonomy without starting with diverse inspiration. We applaud all of you who are inspired to help women. But that is just step one. You can't stop there. Consider organizations like Warner Brothers, which was criticized for their all-male leadership team. The CEO decided to make gender diversity a strategic priority in the wake of a sex scandal with their former studio leader, so they hired a diversity manager to ensure all casting decisions going forward be reviewed with a more balanced gender lens. They also plan to put in place processes to eliminate gender bias in the future.[186] The company leaders show they are inspired to change, but we argue that this solution—hire someone to fix other people—is not going to address the demographics of current leaders.

Unfortunately, we see this situation far too often. Companies get inspired to change, so they hire a head of diversity and the box gets checked. The head of diversity is in charge of making sure the company addresses diversity (assuming they have been given power and resources, which often isn't the case). Check. But this approach relieves everyone else of having to do anything to change. The leadership team itself was the problem. Are they just going to fix the bottom of the leadership pipeline so that one day in the distant future the leadership team will be more representative?

Think about this. Why are leaders so afraid to make their leadership team diverse that instead they make up a diversity role and call *that* the diversity hire? It's a step, yes, but a long way from truly capitalizing on what diversity can offer organizations. Here's a radical thought—hire some women to the leadership team. Put them in charge of the actual business!

In a different example, think about what Canadian prime minister, Justin Trudeau, did. Inspired to help make a difference with gender equity, he appointed women leaders to 50 percent of his cabinet "because it's 2015."[187] This was an excellent, inspiring start to advancing gender equity in government. However, as we will discuss below, this gesture remains a great first start at the diversity level because without supporting competencies in the inclusion, engagement, and synthesis levels, the benefits of gender equity cannot be fully leveraged.

INCLUSION

Once you are inspired to build diversity into your business, the next step is to foster the ability within yourself to create inclusiveness. For this, you need *diversity intelligence and experience*, which requires a demonstrated knowledge of gender, culture, and the impact of bias. It focuses on building knowledge about gender and intersectional* differences, and how those differences affect the treatment of women.

This critical ability is missing from many popular leadership models. Deloitte omits it except for leaders in international contexts.[188] The Balanced Scorecard, a common management performance tool, doesn't include it either.[189] It is not considered a key leadership competency. If it appears at all, it tends to fall under HR leaders' metrics for legal compliance and understanding of discrimination laws, not understanding actual people, their cultural contexts, and how to work together.

Demonstrating knowledge of different genders, cultures, background experiences, and contexts helps leaders and individuals build bridges with others and improve empathy for different perspectives. It also builds respect among different communities. Failing to understand where someone is coming from can damage relationships. A mid-level woman who points out that her company's leadership is all men often risks provoking defensiveness. But if male leaders seek to understand why she raised the point and why she sees it as a problem, they can view it through her lens.

We believe that diversity intelligence and experience is foundational for all leaders so they are able to create inclusive teams and organizations.

Consider this example, which we came across in a Facebook group discussion:

A black woman is walking along pushing her twin babies in a stroller in a predominately white neighborhood. While she is walking, a police car does a sudden U-turn in front of her and a white officer jumps out and walks up to her. The officer asks if she lives around here and then asks about her kids, where they go to school, and how old they are. The woman, of course, feels extremely uncomfortable and mistrusts the policeman. She does her best to end the conversation quickly and walks away.

Once safely home, the woman asks her friends what they thought of the situation. Many of her black friends understood her discomfort, agreed that the situation seemed odd, and suspected she was being profiled. Her

---

* "Intersectional" describes the confluence of ways people define themselves. For example, someone can be a woman, a lesbian, and Latina. Each of these areas could be a different aspect of her identity.

white friends, other the other hand, felt the officer was connecting with his community—part of his job. One of her female friends raised the possibility that the officer was hitting on her, though a male friend said that he thought the officer was just being friendly.

As it happens, the police officer had recently adopted twin African American babies and was hoping to meet another parent of similarly aged kids. However, because he was not as sensitive as he could be to a black woman's perspective (mistrust of police because of unwarranted traffic stops, mistrust of men approaching without being asked), he left her with the wrong impression. Of course, her white friends and her male friends brought their own biases to their interpretation of the situation, which was complicated and nuanced, with multiple perspectives of the same behavior.

The full story came to light after the woman complained to the police department. The officer, required to explain himself to management, revealed his perspective. And he learned that if he had been more aware of the woman's perspective—if he had developed diversity intelligence—he would have approached the woman differently. He could have introduced himself and explained from the beginning why he was asking her questions. He could have explained the U-turn and apologized if the abruptness of it made her ill at ease. His lack of cultural intelligence, or his willingness to dismiss it as unimportant in the situation, got him in trouble.

Knowledge of bias, especially unconscious bias, is a prerequisite for understanding different cultures and contexts. Most experts agree that people can't begin to mitigate bias if they don't know what it looks like and how it manifests itself in the stereotypes they have about people.

We like to say that "the cure for ignorance is travel." Why? Because experiencing different cultures and contexts gives people new perspectives. It humanizes others and provides explanations for otherwise unexplained actions. Of course, diversity intelligence on its own isn't enough, and it can be insufficient without associated experience. When people travel, for example, they see a new culture merely from a convenient and somewhat privileged outsider's perspective. No matter how difficult it gets, or how unpleasant,

A WORD ABOUT BEING QUALIFIED

Here's a question we hear a lot about specific hires: "Are women as qualified as men?" People rarely ask if white men are qualified. In our approach, qualification is table stakes. Candidates have to be qualified to be in the running. Of course. So let's take this question off the table and assume that, *yes*, everyone is qualified.

they ultimately have the choice to leave. They can examine and even partake, but not live in that space forever. What is required is intelligence *and* experience. Practice walking in a different set of shoes, intentionally putting yourself in different settings and experiencing discomfort. That is where experience will pay off with new insights and revelations.

This is why it is so important for so-called strong diversity leaders to actually have diverse teams, not just lots of diversity training. They need more than information—they need experience. They must demonstrate they can build, manage through conflict, promote, dismiss, and perform with a diverse team. They need to succeed as well as fail. And the proof is that they literally have a diverse team. If it hasn't been clear before, let's say this again a little more directly: no leader in the twenty-first century should be recognized, rewarded, or promoted if the people on their team are all white men. Period.

When male leaders ask us for guidelines to inclusivity, here is what we recommend:

- Hire women for their differences, not because they resemble or act like the white men you already have; and

- Be inclusive by learning about the women you work with—discover how they bring a different perspective and do things differently.

Learning to follow these guidelines—and follow them consistently— will show everyone on a team that the leader means for the women to be truly included, rather than treated as token hires who sit quietly in the corner. Inclusion is a step toward understanding that diversity should not be assimilated or neutralized but brought to bear on the business.

Whistleblowing and upstanding on behalf of women are good examples of inclusion. Instead of laughing at a sexist joke or encouraging a woman to lighten up, an inclusive male leader will point out the situation's inappropriateness in a way that makes everyone on the team feel equally valued. One leader we worked with shut down bullying of women by meeting individually with each man in a nonconfrontational interview. He discovered that most of the men didn't support the main aggressor and were uncomfortable—yet they didn't speak up. They claimed they, "didn't know what to say." The leader turned that situation into an empowering moment for everyone.

When you role-model speaking out, others feel they can too.[190] Some companies have created tools for their intranets that help people understand how to speak up safely.[191] Yes, sometimes egregious situations require severe action, but for dealing with many—even most—

behaviors, upstanding is enough. You can use your coolness factor, credibility, and influence to role-model and make upstanding cool for others as well. The goal is to eliminate situations where someone is excluded, especially due to a lack of understanding or awareness about their diverse perspective.

Diversity intelligence and experience is an inclusion-level capability. Working to build a diverse team and being aware of cultural differences so women aren't excluded is a big step, but there is even more to be done to give women an engaged voice in the process and to synthesize what they can offer into productive output.

ENGAGEMENT/VOICE

Leaders really start to reap rewards at the next stage of taxonomy. Using their diversity inspiration and intelligence, leaders can move the gender equity process further by *building talent*—giving women (and others) a voice to express their perspective. This is a very active step. It requires fostering an environment where women impact the business by meaningfully representing the company and becoming part of its future direction, set by the organization's leaders.

At this stage, some organizations match "the demographics of the organization to those of critical consumer or constituent groups."[192] Because there are now more women in leadership, for example, there is a demand for more female financial planners.[193] An organization should see this demand as an opportunity. Perhaps a company hires a Latina sales leader to figure out how to attract more Latinx customers. These operating choices show engagement by giving diverse groups a voice. Leveraging the skills and background experience of women and others enables an organization to gain credibility and a competitive edge in critical markets.

Diversity and gender inclusion are part of a successful organization's direction only if they are included in the company's vision—what our taxonomy calls *engaged direction*. We are always surprised when we work with organizations by how little thought they have given to what their organization would look like with women represented equally at all levels. Or how decision-making would get done and how that might look different from how it gets done now. Or what the new culture would look like. It most certainly won't be business as usual—which was the whole point of attracting diversity to begin with—and yet somehow this reality gets overlooked.

We have seen many times in our work what happens when leaders claim to be committed to gender equity but then don't include it in their actual plan. Sidelining commitment to add-on HR initiatives almost guarantees that true equity won't happen and signals that it isn't really important—leaders are only saying it is important so they can look good. But compliance is not engagement.

And just because a company already has female customers doesn't mean that gender equity shouldn't be included in its strategy. Up until recently, car airbags were tested on crash-test dummies with primarily male characteristics. The addition of female crash-test dummies in 2011 was in response to a study that showed women sustained significantly more injuries and death than men in auto accidents.[194] How did it never occur to anyone, in forty years of crash testing, that perhaps dummies representing only half the population would put the other half in physical peril? It wasn't done by design. It was done by default. It was assumed that women would be included by default in the safety strategy, but they weren't. This mistake is repeated across many industries and products, including medicines[195] and even spacesuits.[196] To avoid this kind of default error, leaders must make their engagement overt, visible, and real.

Another critical capability is *empowering influence*. True engagement and voice come when women are empowered to influence. What does this mean? For leaders, it means leveraging power and credibility with respect to gender and diversity. It means transcending what we will call "old boy" power—conforming with and exemplifying majority group norms—and empowering less-popular ideas or perspectives. It means hearing—and responding—when a woman says, "Are you sure that's a good idea?" Now that is real organizational power. Imagine the impact of actually being heard!

One simple technique well supported by research for ensuring equal voice for all team members is to have stakeholders write down their ideas on a piece of paper. Then go around the table, giving each person a chance to speak, noting their thoughts on a larger chart (depending on the decision). Only after everyone has spoken does the analysis begin.[197] This simple facilitation tool can ensure that influence is shared across the team, not influenced by the first (or loudest) speaker.

As we saw with Tom, recognizing who hires and gets the best out of all people and who doesn't is essential for the twenty-first-century workplace. Many modern leadership experts agree that management style, like teaching, should ideally be adapted for each employee or situation rather than a one-size-fits-all approach. This requires knowing where each employee is coming from, how they learn, and what stimulates their best performance. It also requires the ability to discern poor performance from style.

Let's look more closely at this discernment skill. Discernment of performance is challenging because it is often laced with bias. Have you fallen into the trap of believing the best of the people you like and the worst of people you don't (in-group/out-group bias[198])? Or do you negatively evaluate a result because the person who delivered it used a different process or approach than you would have? It's an easy trap to fall into, and we all have to work to avoid it.

It can be hard to hear through the noise. Organizational psychologist Tomas Chamorro-Premuzic argues that companies have a discernment problem in general. He thinks they promote incompetent men based on factors such as overconfidence—which is taken for competence—narcissism, and arrogance. "Companies should actively work to keep incompetent men out of leadership," he says, and he advocates for "eliminating charisma and charm as criteria for promotion."[199]

We often ask: "Why is asking for a raise a key criterion in getting one? Are they related?" Asking signals that the person feels they deserve a raise and of course believes they deserve it. Perhaps they do. But does that mean those who didn't ask aren't? It should be an objective review for everyone, not just rewarding someone's personal belief and willingness to ask.

We get it. This sounds simple but it is really hard. We've tried, in our own business, to exemplify hiring and leading a diverse team. Our practitioners come from many different walks of life, ages, cultural backgrounds, and work experiences. We spend a lot of time considering what difference each hire will bring to the team and how we can leverage their experience. But this approach can result in a cacophony of raucous management interactions, from robust team meetings to daily drama as we integrate these voices and approaches. Sometimes performance isn't any better; sometimes a different approach is not the ideal way. When we get it right, though, it's brilliant. And overall, we think it's worth the struggle.

For Tom, reaching the engagement level would mean doing more than making women feel comfortable and welcome on his team. He needs to leverage their strengths and their representation of important stakeholder communities. He needs to ask questions and hear their input into the team's direction. The women on his team need to play a strategic role in how he grows his business with female clients. They need to be considered part of a built-in focus group and their input truly considered in his go-forward plan, even if it is quite different from how things were usually done in the past. Tom may need to advocate for the women on his team in other parts of the organization where male-dominated teams may not respond favorably to the voice he's given to these minority groups. Yes, it will take time and patience for Tom to spread his level of influence beyond his own team, but it is so worth it.

SYNTHESIS

The final stage of our gender equity taxonomy is where it all comes together. At the synthesis level, leaders need to be able to leverage the diverse teams they've built and included, and ensure all members are given a voice so they can achieve great, measurable results. It is not enough to assemble teams of strong individuals and ask them to participate. The trick, the real magic, is getting them to work together to innovate and integrate their talent and experience so they can produce great results.

Such a goal is challenging. It requires the ability to facilitate teamwork at a high level, to collaborate broadly and effectively, and to foster the right culture so a team can maximize diversity's potential. Often it means letting the team determine how it will do the work, not just the work it will do. It means allowing different approaches to steer. This can be very disconcerting to a leader! In Chapter 8 we talked about the importance of establishing an environment of psychological safety on teams and within organizations; building such an environment is

OUR HERO, MATT

Matt leads a diverse team at a tech company. He's committed to creating a psychologically safe environment. One of his team members, Molly, highlighted a problem she found with one of the systems. At first, the group glossed over it as insignificant. She got quite heated and gave an impassioned speech about why she felt this was such a big issue. Her passion got the team's attention. They saw that her emotion signified importance, so they investigated. It turned out she had uncovered a problem related to a significant opportunity for revenue. They put Molly in charge of the fix, which diverted from the traditional approach and ultimately revolutionized how the business worked going forward. If Molly had worked for a more traditional, less psychologically safe team, it is likely her emotional presentation would have been dismissed and possibly ridiculed as "too feminine" for the workplace. Synthesis is the difference between women conforming—behaving like men and bringing nothing different or diverse to the table (and being rewarded for it)—and women engaging their voice and the voices around them to change the way things get done.

complex and challenging, but it helps any organization operate more efficiently and effectively—a capability we call *agile execution.*

Once there is a safe environment, then leaders need to establish a high, healthy bar of performance expectation. Note the word *healthy* here. We are not talking about impossible standards or perfectionism, but an expectation of high performance. In our taxonomy, performance still matters. We do not advocate a feel-good gathering that ignores poor performance so nobody's feelings get hurt. A diverse team must discern the difference between performance and compliance, and its leadership must offer a high degree of nurturance. That is, providing employees an environment where they are seen, heard, and valued; where it is safe to disagree and speak the truth; and where there is compassion and empathy for everyone's humanity.[200]

Because a safe environment fosters conflict, leaders also need to be comfortable with that, both emotional and constructive. Emotional conflict is inevitable—it's an important part of group work—and effective leaders allow some conflict. But they nurture positive results from it before it becomes long-lasting or damaging. We learned about a group working on succession planning, in which one leader allowed conflict to fester for two months. If he had stopped the tension by deciding within the first few days of the conflict, it would've had gone away. Instead, it grew to the point where people left, the team had to be reorganized, and morale suffered.

The ability to manage emotions effectively is also necessary in a psychologically safe environment. When someone says something that triggers someone else—saying that all pregnant women have a foggy brain, for example—leaders need to pause, take a breath, and decide how to help the person see the challenge in the statement. This can be very difficult and will require practice. But there is no learning when emotions are too hot. Even waiting and coming back later in the day when there's been a chance to reflect is better than reacting in the moment. Safe places help people understand each other's perspectives and experiences.

Remember our Direct Speak Model from Chapter 6? A good leader can use this method to encourage a woman to articulate her unique perspective and needs in a three-sentence, dispassionate way. For example: "It seems you thought I was behaving in a forgetful way. Attributing that to gender makes me feel discounted. I would like for you to help me remember instead."

The skills we have suggested, up through the synthesis level, are merely good facilitation skills that leverage the inherent skills and knowledge of team members. Listening, participation, curiosity, and healthy discussion, though critical, are often overlooked in leadership models.[201] Diverse teams of men and women, all enabled to contribute and produce collaborative results that are bigger than any individual idea, stand a good chance of growing and becoming more productive. But leaders must ensure that women are not isolated in team dynamics. If there are only a few women in an entire department, research shows that grouping them together on a single team, rather than scattering them, is surprisingly more effective. Being isolated increases the likelihood of a woman being subjected to stereotypes or harassment, or of adapting her behavior to the in-group culture and suppressing her unique strengths. By grouping women, you give them more power and confidence to perform and be authentic.[202] But remember, we are not suggesting that you create groups of all women; we are suggesting that women are not the "only" woman on the team.

Creating psychological safety is an ongoing job. It requires not only recognizing what elements can create threats for different communities, but also holding people accountable for behaving appropriately and nudging everyone towards positive group behavior. But it takes two sides and two equal forces: a leader who provides a safe context and an employee who brings her authentic self to the team. If the team leader thinks he has created psychological safety but the employee still holds herself back, then there is more work to be done, likely on both sides.

Remember that your ability to adapt, reinvent yourself, and be willing to learn can help synthesize your positive assumptions and make gender equity work. Leaders who accept feedback and feel comfortable as a work in progress, testing and experimenting as they go, will ultimately get better long-term results. As with any other leadership strategy for staying competitive, this means being open to a changing level of empowerment, understanding, and discourse. Yesterday it may have been okay to call someone "she," for example, who today needs to be called "they." But we can ask! Effective leaders are those who are open and willing to change as needed. After all, something that seems small to you but that means something big to someone else matters.

Now let's consider the *collaboration* capability—the skills required for leaders to be strong collaborators, including the ability to seek out, hold, and analyze multiple viewpoints of the same challenge, or idea.

First, strong collaborators know how to identify and engage stakeholders. This isn't new: you already know who the team's stakeholders are. But how often do you actually do something productive with this information? You need to do more than check the box or superficially acknowledge various communities without engaging them. We want you to take it to the next level. Consider the difference between the organization that merely translates English-market advertisements into Spanish versus the one that creates a custom product and pricing plan to address specific Latinx client needs. The first knows the stakeholder is there; the second engages.

Secondly, collaboration requires that you understand the perspective and experience of all team members to synthesize it into an ultimate solution. Every stakeholder has a viewpoint and underlying reasons for it. What are those reasons? Highlighting where there are synergies and common ground and understanding why there may be conflict gives you a fantastic opportunity to create win-win solutions.

Finally, collaboration enables you to create new and bigger solutions. This is where all the hard work of the previous stages comes to fruition, creating forums to enable creativity. There are a variety of facilitation tools to help at this stage, including Agile Project Management[203] and Design Thinking,[204] but effective meeting facilitation,[205] with practice, should become the team default. A synthesized, gender-balanced team, department, or group has a great chance of coming up with an organization's most innovative ideas and getting them implemented.

We worked with an HR officer, Jamika, who was tasked with developing a new maternity-leave policy. She worked hard to understand the perspectives of the various stakeholders: mothers, fathers, immediate supervisors, and others whose workload would be impacted by the initiative. She learned that new fathers wanted time off too but were concerned that their performance would be criticized. New mothers had the same concern but didn't think they had a choice—they *had* to take time off. Managers were worried that they wouldn't be able to get all the work done—and also wanted to know that new mothers would eventually be coming back. Finally, peers wanted assurances that extra work wouldn't fall to them.

Instead of creating a rigid policy that dictated a fixed amount of time off after having a baby, Jamika created some new work standards

A WORD OF WARNING

As we discussed earlier, many people use background credentials as a proxy for capability, and people on peer teams can defer to the experienced member rather than question them or exploring their own perspective. Linda has a doctorate or Bob has seniority, so their solutions are silently accepted. Background credentials and other things that create power imbalance can disrupt diverse teams unless care is taken to neutralize the effects on decision-making. And good facilitation can make that care happen.

for everyone, which included flexible parental leave. She created a support structure so managers got their workload needs met, including consigning some temporary help and co-opting some assistance from other departments. She designed a new off-boarding and on-boarding process for long-term leave, so roles and responsibilities were clear throughout. And she ensured that managers who encouraged employees to take leave were rewarded publicly, so everyone could see how much the company invested in employees for the long term. In essence, Jamika created a program that managed challenges and still met the goals and varied interests of the stakeholders. In other words, she created a new and bigger solution.

When a group is truly diverse, it is important to balance different and often conflicting opinions that may all be correct. A situation that may seem gender-related to a woman—a man always interrupting her, for example—may be seen by another man in the group as simply a bad habit. The differing perspectives could trigger a set of unfortunate responses, so it is important for the group's leader to develop the ability to synthesize both perspectives as part of the collaborative decision-making process.[206] This skill is called perspective-taking and allows for the possibility that people who have opposite viewpoints are both right.

The comprehensive skills required to synthesize diversity and gender make an organization more successful and give it a *competitive edge*. Recognition of, and commitment to, gender and diversity are essential to understanding diverse markets and the ability to innovate and stay ahead. Both the labor market and customer markets, especially in the United States, are becoming increasingly diverse and have been for quite some time. It is no longer effective to treat customers as a monolithic group without alienating large segments of the market and labor force.

Barbie used to be a leading toy for girls around the world. Increasingly, Barbie's market share has been eroded by innovative products such as Bratz (brown-skinned dolls with Latina and African American features), L.O.L. Surprise! (multiracial dolls), and Disney Princess (multiethnic dolls each with a cultural background story), all of which reflect more diverse appeal. Instead of synthesizing something completely new to address an increasingly diverse customer set, Mattel has merely made superficial changes to the original Barbie product—first by adding different skin colors (and only more recently body types), and then adding wheelchairs, glasses, and other accessories to represent diversity. Customers weren't fooled; they understood that skinny, white Barbie was the real Barbie and even African American girls bought them—until competitors came along and made a doll that actually looked like them. Which approach does your company want to take to addressing diverse customers' needs and wants?

In another example, having so few women engineers in Silicon Valley has had an alarming impact on emerging technologies. A hiring algorithm at Amazon that uses artificial intelligence [207] skewed male and was biased against women. The AI was taught sexist bias through past data inputs, which went unchecked by the men doing the programming. What will that mean for how computers think in the future? Our guess is they will more deeply entrench sexism, and possibly even compound these forces.

By adding and measuring a diversity component to a leader's competitive edge capability, organizations are able to reflect a more appropriate definition of the entire market. In doing so, it is no longer acceptable for a leader to manage an all-white, heterosexual male team or customer base, regardless of how well they know it and how well they appear to manage it. Or for women to be excluded from teams that develop future technologies. Or for products to be optimized for only half of the market.

Demonstrating a commitment to developing the skills for creating diverse and inclusive teams and considering customer diversity across the spectrum supports the development of competitive strategies for sustainable marketing leadership. Diversity is integral to the product development process.

Finally, the most significant capability at the synthesis level is *inclusive business judgment*: using judgment to ensure the best possible outcomes for the business. Does that seem obvious? Well, the benefits of gender and diversity that we have spent so much time discussing may never happen if leaders don't see how they will help the business. So many diversity initiatives fail to realize their goals. Sound business judgment enables these benefits to be appreciated and realized.

Let's go back to Tom. For him, synthesis would open a whole new way of operating his team and his business. Once he builds a team of diverse perspectives, learns about the cultural norms of its members, involves them in direction-setting, and engages their insights, he will have a team that can change the business. It may open him to new product ideas, new ways of delivering services, and even new ways his team operates so they can develop new opportunities. He will need to be willing to take risks, make space for his colleagues to germinate new thinking, and have their backs if they get flak from the outside. He will have to stand up to tradition in the organization, difficult given his long history there, but it would be worth it.

Pixar showed us synthesis. They created an animated video starring a pink ball of yarn named Purl who joins a company full of good ole boys and tries to participate. At first Purl the yarn doesn't fit in, and she thinks about leaving. Then she modifies her style to mimic the men, and things look up for her. But when another ball of yarn is hired, Purl is faced with a choice: ostracize the new employee and stick with the in-group, or reach out and include the new yarn. The inclusive choice she makes ends up changing the culture of the entire organization.[208]

The ultimate goal of the synthesis level of leadership is better performance and better results. But no one achieves all the levels all at once. It is an iterative cycle. You get better at synthesis by getting better at diversity, which makes you better at inclusion and engagement. Once you are skilled at synthesis, you realize how you can be more inclusive and so it goes. So don't be discouraged—this is a learning process. The key is to keep practicing.

11
Making and Measuring Progress

IN THE LAST CHAPTER WE DEMONSTRATED how our taxonomy of leadership capabilities can be used to guide leaders and potential leaders through a structured journey from a vision of gender equity to the reality of an inclusive organization that leverages gender equity and diversity to become a fairer and more successful twenty-first-century company. Using our taxonomy, your organization's leadership can develop the critical skills that have too often been omitted in many leadership models. But now comes the next challenge: How do you know you have been successful? How do you know you are sustaining gender equity going forward? To answer those questions, you must be able to measure.

At the highest level, gender and diversity performance can be measured in sheer numbers and by looking at the faces and backgrounds of team members. While this may only address one aspect of diversity, it is a great place to start. Also, since we've shown the depth of bias that exists based on demography, improving numbers also indicates that you've been able to learn how to better overcome bias. Teams with token or no women are likely led by people with few diversity capabilities, if any. A team with 50 percent women and a demographic balance that reflects the current marketplace is likely led by someone who has achieved at least the basic taxonomy level of diversity. That metric should be relatively simple to calculate.

It should be noted that teams with more than 60 percent women should also be seen as non-diverse. Let's face it, we cannot argue on the one hand that too few women is a problem only to end up with too few men. It also means that women leaders who are not inclusive should also be coached accordingly. What good does it do to have someone without these important capabilities in a leadership role just because of their demography? The key to diversity is having representation of all perspectives and that means diverse leaders need to have diverse teams as well.

Diversity of thought, or cognitive diversity, is the real goal, and racial and gender diversity on its own is not empirical evidence of its presence. There are plenty of examples of women in the workplace who behave no differently from traditional white men. This is particularly common when a pool is made up of women from the same socioeconomic background, who have attended the same small group of schools, and have a similar family situation (such as a female executive with a stay-at-home husband). Many companies start their quest for diversity by inadvertently hiring women and members of other demographic groups who are remarkably similar to their existing personnel. It looks good on paper, but doesn't achieve the goal. Special care should be given to look behind the faces to ensure that a team or organizational structure is sufficiently cognitively diverse. That said, this is not an excuse to reward a leader with a team of only white men. A demographically diverse team with members from various backgrounds is a better predictor of diversity of thought than one that isn't, as those diverse members likely had very different experiences growing up.

We put together a rubric for assessing leadership capabilities against our taxonomy and created a sample—both are in Appendix F. This rubric can be a great tool for measuring whether leaders have included diversity in their vision, direction, or execution. Those capabilities or competencies that do not measure up can then be addressed with additional training and development. Leaders who are assessed should be provided with specific examples of their shortcomings to illustrate what needs to improve. For example, if a leader has an adequate number of women on his team but has not made a significant effort to include their perspectives in what the group produces, then he needs to improve his direction-setting. And let's move beyond the lens of diversity or diversity skills being relegated to the "keep us from getting sued" territory. Think performance, not compliance.

So let's return once again to our old friend Tom and apply the performance measurement standard to his situation. Tom needs work on all his leadership capabilities because he has not gained sufficient experience with a truly diverse team to exercise any of them. We would recommend his organization start this work by discussing the benefits of diversity with Tom and moving him toward inspiration. We would hope he experiences an ah-ha moment where he engages and wants to learn more. If he can't rise to the challenge, then maybe it's time for Tom to leave. Leaders like Tom will hold the organization back from all the benefits diversity can provide, if unmediated. Luckily, you now have the tools to identify which leaders have these important diversity capabilities and can lead your organization to greater success.

If Tom is ready to improve his skill set, then the next step would be to train him about unconscious bias. It would also be helpful for him to work with an executive coach to ensure an open mindset and that Tom has a safe place to experiment where he can make mistakes. Once it is certain he can navigate diversity respectfully, then he needs to practice. Maybe he gets inserted onto a highly diverse team. Or is encouraged to transform his own team's diversity. He should again be closely supervised through this experience, and an executive coach should regularly curate and give him feedback.

The rubric we suggest, along with the taxonomy, can be used for individual assessments. But as we have said many times, though made up of individuals, organizations have their own organic identities, and assessing the organization is a more complicated process. So now let's explore how to assess and adapt organizational processes, culture, and practices to enable the benefits of the diverse talent we keep highlighting.

THE GENDER ASSESSMENT PROCESS

We're going to let you in on a little secret. One of our primary organizational assessment techniques is simple: we listen to gossip. Yes, that's right, gossip. When assessing an organization, we learn many things from the stories employees tell us—stories about their daily interactions with the organization. We conduct personal interviews and surveys, comb through comments on chat boards and websites, and unearth real-life drama. We have found gold in these stories.

Of course, gossip has to be compared to quantifiable facts. But the gossip tells us where to look. Let's consider two fictional but representative employees within the same organization: Chen and Joe. We want you to see how their experiences differ because of their gender and what barriers they face. Also note that their experiences are not confined to one process or level, but extend throughout the organization and developmental pipeline. Maybe you'll recognize some of these details from your own organization.

After we introduce Chen and Joe, we'll build on their story to help explain how you can use our gender assessment scorecard to comprehensively measure how well your organization is doing in its pursuit of gender equity, where the risks lie, and how those risks can be mitigated.

Chen is a highly qualified and experienced tech leader. She applied for a vice president role at an up-and-coming midsize tech company. The company website featured stock photography of men and women of various races and ages who looked happy working there.

When Chen walked through the office for her interview, she saw plenty of friendly looking men and women sitting in cubicles. However, the panel of interviewers (senior leaders) was all older white men. She wondered what jobs women did. She later found out that most employees were men, particularly the senior leadership team, sales, engineering, and finance. There were a few women in marketing, human resources, and administrative functions, but none in leadership roles. Until Chen. She was a little worried about being an only, but thought it might be fun to pave the way for other women in the company.

On her second day after starting in her new position, Chen met a colleague, Joe. He ran another division. He went out of his way to welcome her and showed her around, introducing her to people. Joe was kind and playful with Chen, teasing her in a friendly way about being one of the guys. It seemed important to him that he talk about what they all liked to do after work, such as drinking beer, playing pool, and going to the gym. He showed her where the locker room was, although she noticed that the shower room was unisex and there was no separate locker area for women. He asked her if she had seen the game last night. Chen realized pretty quickly that to fit in, she was going to have to act more like her peers. This didn't seem to be a "white wine with Mozart" kind of place.

This is the beginning of the story. Yet you can see that even within a few days of Chen's hire, the lack of gender equity is exerting influence over her expectations and behaviors. She senses the culture and already feels abnormal. Largely because of her interactions with Joe, she is already contemplating adopting a different persona, which may also mean holding back parts of her authentic self.

To measure the organizational success of Chen and Joe's company (or any other), our gender assessment scorecard uses twelve categories, which are grouped into three sections: gender landscape, processes, and the supporting environment. We'll break down those categories for you in a moment, but first we want to describe the five types of gender risk that can occur within those categories if a company fails to measure up. We define these risks to help quantify the extent of any barriers we might find. It is the cost your company will face without gender equity. Quantifying this risk can also help your organization understand the financial impact of improving gender equity.

The five types of risk appear throughout this chapter as each category is explored. Noting the types of risk will help you appreciate how valuable it would be to your organization to measure up in all areas of gender equity.

1. Turnover risk is the risk someone will leave. It has been well-documented to cost companies anywhere from half a salary for entry level employees to twice a salary for senior level employees.[209]

2. Legal risk is the risk of legal liability. Legal risk can cost hundreds of thousands of dollars per incident.[210]

3. Productivity risk is how we quantify work lost in salary hours or output.

4. Stagnation risk is the impact gendered solutions have on reinforcing the status quo and preventing systemic change. It can be measured in the number of years it adds to the change process.

5. Opportunity risk is the risk that a potential business opportunity will not be realized. It is measured in lost sales or cost savings.

As you consider the experiences of Chen and Joe and their organization, take note of the risks involved and do some back-of-the-napkin math to see how quickly the cost of gender risk can add up for an organization. (Appendix D includes a worksheet to help track risk and score your organization for each of the twelve categories.) And note that often there are assumptions in your organization that may inhibit you from assessing each of these twelve categories. We offer a reframe to help you overcome those false assumptions.

THE GENDER LANDSCAPE

Gender landscape measures how equitably power and influence is distributed in the company. It helps people understand the organization's baseline and how it is doing compared to peers. Its categories include gender equity, pay equity, and bias awareness.

Note that Chen's initial impression was that there were plenty of women in the company. It was only after she joined that she realized the women were all concentrated in administrative level or pink-collar jobs, and that 70 percent of employees were men. For most of the meetings she attended, she was the only woman present. She spent a lot of time and energy trying not to stand out due to her gender, and if someone called it out, she cringed. She felt she had no choice but to act like a guy to fit in.

How many women work at your organization? In what departments and at what level do they work? To score an organization on gender equity, we start by counting how many men and women are in the organization at each level. There's usually more equity in the lower levels, but the balance slips significantly through the mid and senior levels. Or certain departments or roles have equity but others do not.

You need to count so there's a quantified starting point, not just an impression. We count the numbers of women at each level, in each business area and show the discrepancies. Often we find that some departments are much more equitable than others. If the information is available, we also look at the velocity of promotions (how long it takes women to move through an organization via promotions compared with men) and we look at retention rates. Together these numbers give an initial baseline against which improvement can be measured. As we've discussed, this also allows us to open some eyes and set realistic goals for transformation.

We like to create helpful buckets for this count: entry level, mid-level, senior level, as well as departments, teams, and regions or geographies. These buckets allow us to pinpoint whether or not a problem is widespread (and thus likely process or policy-related) or the fault of a lone individual leader who needs further skills development. What do you find when you count women at your organization? Is there even distribution or are some departments doing better than others? Are there departments with few women? How does this compare to the marketplace? College graduation rates? What improvement goals can you set from this information?

Make sure to compare to recent statistics, not just perceptions, to ensure accuracy. We find clients are often surprised by how many more women are graduating with degrees in traditionally male-dominated fields. Data is available: use it.

The risks of lacking gender equity? Considerable:

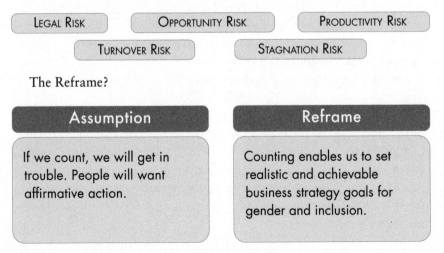

| LEGAL RISK | OPPORTUNITY RISK | PRODUCTIVITY RISK |
| TURNOVER RISK | STAGNATION RISK |

The Reframe?

Assumption	Reframe
If we count, we will get in trouble. People will want affirmative action.	Counting enables us to set realistic and achievable business strategy goals for gender and inclusion.

Okay. You counted the gender numbers. Now consider pay equity.

Chen was hired to run a division of the company and is the only woman on the senior leadership team. When she was hired, Chen negotiated a bump in compensation from her previous role at a different company and was happy her new company agreed to it until she found out that Joe makes $15,000 more. She justified it to herself because she was newer to the company and perhaps her division was smaller or less profitable than Joe's. But it stuck in her mind as unfair and left her feeling like the least valued executive on the team. It sucked away a little of her enthusiasm for the job and played in her mind every time she attended a meeting with peers, realizing they make more for the same work.

Most organizations struggle with the fear of pay inequity, yet there is almost always a structural reason somewhere in the organization that is fixable. To get started, organizations can take small samples in representative areas and look for the signs of inequity. The chart on page 159 summarizes bad habits that plague organizations and how they can be combated.

Perception matters. So it's important that employees perceive pay to be equal and fair or at least that the company is working on it. We all know how distracted people get when they think something is wrong with their pay. Perfectly happy employees one minute can become agitators the next when they find out their overtime check was miscalculated or they make less than their peers. Organizations often keep pay scales or pay gaps hidden, because they think employees will get mad if they find out someone else is making more than they do. But it is not true—what people get upset about is finding out someone else is *undeservedly* making more than they do. Or that the pay gap they suspect (let's face it, they have heard national studies) is being covered up by the company.

Equity theory[211] tells us that when people feel that they are contributing more than someone else for less money or rewards, they will reduce their contributions. There's so little value in underpaying one person! Fairness matters—it literally impacts productivity. Why would it be in any company's interest to intentionally demotivate people with salary? If we all truly want fairness, then there should be nothing to hide.

Transparency is the best way forward. Being honest when problems are found allows the organization an opportunity to work together to address it. It also gives the company credit for the time spent studying, creating narrow salary bands and job grades, and engaging in ongoing analysis of its pay systems, bonus structures, and performance measures. And if a pay gap still exists after all this work, then transparency invites more input into the process of fixing it.

Bad Habit	What To Do
Women's starting salaries are lower than average than their peers.	Do not ask candidates for salary history. (In some states, this is now illegal anyway.) Avoid seeking short-term cost savings by offering a lower salary. This will end up costing you much more over time. Stick to a narrow, predefined salary range based on job qualifications, especially at the entry level.
There is a gap in pay for men and women at the same level.	Add more structure to pay conversations so they are about actual requirements, not negotiation ability. Stick to a narrow, predefined salary range based on job qualifications, especially at the entry levels. If employees leave the organization due to pay, review salary bands and adjust accordingly. On an annual basis, conduct post-review gaps between men and women of the same level to identify pay discrepancies, making it routine.
Women's pay is reduced due to maternity leave.	Ensure pay is always based on results, such as meeting targets, rather than face time. Take special care not to penalize women for maternity leave (or men for paternity leave).
Men's bonuses are higher than women's at the same level.	Eliminate intangible considerations from bonus allocation. Stick to measurable targets.
Pink-collar jobs are paid less than equivalent men's jobs.	When salary grading, compare workload and impact. Consider anonymizing the jobs in some way to take gender out of the equation. Also, look at men in jobs traditionally held by women or women in jobs traditionally held by men. Are the women paid less in those situations?
Women in understaffed departments are unpaid for absorbing extra work.	Look at open job requisitions and pay attention to who backfills while the role remains open. Consider allocating the open job salary to those people as a bonus for as long as the requisition is open. This will also help motivate hiring managers to fill the jobs faster. Track volunteers and recognize them—even with pay.

Is there a perception in your organization that a pay gap exists? If so, we recommend a more comprehensive compensation review. Look at the data. Are there red flag areas, such as gender clustering in pay ranges and bonus payments? Are women starting out behind? Are women earning smaller bonuses? Why? Are the reasons valid? Who has had salary or bonuses pro-rated because of time off? Compare this to who has taken time off and why. Are women paying a higher compensation price for taking time off than men?

If a pay gap is suspected and studied, the organization should communicate the results and advertise to employees that the company has a goal to improve the situation. Additionally, we recommend conducting a regular review and reporting the results to signal to employees that the situation is being measured and reviewed and discrepancies managed on an ongoing basis.

The risks of poor pay equity?

| LEGAL RISK | TURNOVER RISK | PRODUCTIVITY RISK |

The Reframe?

Assumption	Reframe
We don't need a pay equity assessment. We already pay fairly based on performance.	There are often many hidden biases in pay and performance. We can evaluate our pay annually so that we can track any differences. We can understand that pay can both motivate and demotivate.

The last gender landscape category is bias awareness.

Chen attended a session on bias awareness given by a man in the HR department. She noticed that while he used politically correct terminology for various communities, he seemed to miss that some of his examples were biased. For example, he put up some photos of different faces and asked people to describe whether they felt each face was friendly or not. As he was describing the faces, Chen noticed that both times a young, male, Indian face was displayed, the HR bias expert noted that he looked like an engineer. And when a woman's face came up, he said she looked like she was in marketing.

Chen felt that the HR man was exacerbating gender stereotypes. He also joked that an older guy in a suit who came in for an interview wouldn't fit in at the company because he wasn't wearing jeans. She looked down at her own suit and wondered if he was trying to tell her something. She wondered how much more damaging it was for the company to have its bias expert reinforce stereotypes and gendered roles than if they didn't bother with the bias training to begin with. It also made her feel like the company wasn't really committed to ferreting out bias, particularly when she witnessed several senior leaders making jokes about the training in the hallway afterward.

The risk of this mistaken understanding of bias awareness?

TURNOVER RISK	OPPORTUNITY RISK

We've already described the myriad ways that bias can show up in decision-making. Our assessment measures it. We recommend looking for the telltale signs that unconscious bias is alive and well: comments that show a lack of awareness or that suggest that someone is above bias. It is also important to look for cases where men and women or people of color are treated differently because of their demographics. This is a sign that some of the organization's leaders need more skills development.

Learning how people perceive bias in decisions and behaviors that affect them can point to where the bigger issues are and where you can intervene more precisely to shift people's perceptions of each other. It shows up in other ways as well.

When Chen overheard some of her male colleagues talking about the #metoo movement, she was dismayed at how much they doubted the validity of women's accusations, even in those cases with multiple corroborating victims. Further, these guys had a loud conversation about how they suspect women in general of making things up to trap men or get them in trouble. They worried out loud about what would happen to them if they complimented a woman's looks—how she might think they were coming on to her.

These were some of the same men who Chen had gone out with to a bar after work, men she routinely had to keep at arm's length because they tended to get flirty after a few drinks. Chen wondered how they could so willingly disregard the facts of #metoo cases and turn women into perpetrators. It reinforced her belief that anything short of a public assault against a woman would likely not be penalized with these guys; a real concern for every woman who works in the company.

She no longer felt comfortable around them, and she felt like some of the men were keeping her at arm's distance. The risk to the company in this case?

| LEGAL RISK | TURNOVER RISK |

Bias is perception, and usually there's a perception gap between men and women. Men and younger people tend to believe women are generally respected and treated professionally[212] in cases where women, especially at senior levels, disagree. The same holds true for sexual harassment experiences. We usually find that the more senior the woman, the more likely they are to share that they have had a harassment experience. This doesn't mean that younger women or even men are not experiencing harassment; they are just less likely to report it.

Have you heard rumblings of #metoo in your organization? What has been the response? Are the concerns easily dismissed or could there be something going on? We have seen organizations ignore harassment claims to their peril. Often there were many signs—reports of small problematic interactions, jokes, and disrespectful comments—long before a harassment claim was filed. If you smell smoke, we encourage you to dig deeper because there is also likely a fire.

Chen was often asked to speak on behalf of her team to other departments or locations, particularly on the topic of bringing more women into leadership. She was a confident public speaker and loved to engage a crowd. Usually the people who gathered to hear her speak were mostly women. What she found interesting was that the interactive discussions she fostered and encouraged were mostly dominated by the few men in the audience. When she broke the group into teams, a man on a team usually became the spokesperson.

These men assumed they knew what women needed and threw out simplistic solutions. She was fascinated by how men had such strong opinions about the problems women faced in the organization and what it would take to get more women in leadership. They were so sure that they spoke on behalf of the women. Further, she wondered what insights were missing from the conversation because the women's opinions about their own situation were simply not heard. The risks were clear:

| TURNOVER RISK | OPPORTUNITY RISK |

Many men and women in organizations get it—they are open to learning about gender bias, aware there are issues, and are supportive in the quest to uncover it. Unfortunately, we also find some who *think* they know, and set women back by speaking on behalf of others instead of listening.

Or offering simplistic solutions that do little more than check a box. We identify and encourage recognition of the good ones who are truly bias-aware, especially if they are in leadership or influential positions, so that they can be used as positive role model examples to others.

Try to incorporate processes that detect and reframe bias, such as identifying underlying assumptions in decision-making. Or remember the flip-it technique—replace the statement about a woman with a man. For example, "Charlie, you should smile more; people really like positivity." Once flipped, it's pretty easy to spot the bias.[213]

You've seen the risks. The Reframe?

Assumption	Reframe
We've had bias training already so we are not biased.	We all have room to learn about bias and this learning is ongoing.

PROCESSES

The second section of our gender scorecard includes the categories recruiting, retention, performance evaluation, promotion and pipeline development, and mentoring. These processes all have to do with evaluating the systems where bias often lurks, so measuring them helps leaders focus on making small operational adjustments that can have a big impact. A recent survey identified a lack of management of the leadership pipeline as one of the biggest barriers for women in the workplace.[214] Lack of management can allow too much subjectivity into critical functions such as recruiting, performance measurement, and promotions. Many change initiatives can feel like throwing spaghetti at the wall and hoping something sticks, so a methodical approach to these processes will help understand what is working and what is not.

A few months after Chen was hired, the CEO revealed that her boss, the president, hadn't wanted to hire Chen, preferring a male candidate who the rest of the board felt was significantly less qualified. The CEO wondered if it was because the president had been a member of the same fraternity as the candidate. This emerged after Chen noticed that the president seemed to disagree with pretty much anything she said or did and subtly undermined her authority. She wondered why, in a company that touted hiring only the best, her boss had fought so hard to hire a less-qualified candidate and then expended effort tanking the candidate they did hire. Since they used a recruiter to find Chen, she thought it a potentially expensive risk the president was taking by subverting her efforts. Why wouldn't he instead try to make her successful?

Research suggests recruitment is an area with a large potential for bias, so it's really important to look closely at recruiting processes.[215] Most organizational recruitment processes begin with identifying a need and end with successful employee onboarding. We look for problems at every step in the hiring process (the full recruitment process is outlined in Appendix I).

Groupthink can disrupt recruiting—the loudest or most senior voice in the room can dissuade dissenting voices from contributing. Having multiple interviewers allows the recruitment process to obtain different perspectives and make sure they are heard and seriously considered. It can be helpful to make a list of pros and cons about each candidate and then review these lists as a group to see if any obvious bias markers jump out. Another technique is to create a survey that everyone answers individually and then discusses as a group. Comparing survey results enables a more equitable and measured discussion.

Hiring decisions require accountability—documenting the justification for the hire (matching it back to the criteria set in the very beginning) and providing follow-up reflection on the process and outcomes. For example, if the team decides to hire someone because they realized that social skills were more important than they originally thought, this should be documented so that the next hire includes a more tangible measurement and weight for social skills, and if the candidate ultimately fails to perform in the organization, there is some learning for the decision-making team about where their process went wrong. Enlisting the help of an external-bias expert to observe the process can help identify how selection may be biased. It is almost impossible for teams to see bias themselves. An external observer, brought in initially to review the process and then on occasionally for spot checks, enables bias to be detected.

Standardizing the process by implementing a consistent, structured interview process including pre-set questions ensures consistency.

When we grade organizations on hiring, we track how many candidates go through each hiring stage and the demographic makeup of each pool. It is tough to have 50 percent women candidates end up in the decision stage if there weren't at least 50 percent to start. Many HR systems can track this type of information, though many organizations sub-optimize their HR systems by leaving most of the tracking fields blank. If your system doesn't track it, it can be helpful to use a spreadsheet to conduct a small sample study for a specific period of time. That way, you get the data you need without overly taxing HR employees. We encourage organizations to think of this like any other operational project—collect data, observe the impact, and note where outcomes fall short. This is a good indication of where in the process hidden bias has an impact.

The risk of failing to recruit without bias is:

TURNOVER RISK

The Reframe?

Assumption	Reframe
Few women apply or are interested. Those who want the job ask for it.	There are many unseen barriers to women applying. We can be more proactive and unbiased in seeking out the best talent to join our team.

What about retention?

Chen sometimes felt invisible and unheard in group settings at the company. She noticed on multiple occasions that her contributions in meetings were either ignored or attributed to someone else. Once she made a breakthrough point that moved a conversation forward, but when her male colleague summarized the meeting, he omitted it. She raised it again to many nodding heads, which drew more extensive conversation, and then her male colleague concluded the meeting with a summary that again omitted her point. She didn't think it was intentional but thought it odd nonetheless. Did he not hear her? Did he disagree with the point? Did he not see that the point was integral to the conversation and go-forward plan?

Another time, Chen started to make a series of three points, and a male colleague cut her off after the first one to explain why what she said was wrong. He led the group in an extensive conversation about what he thought the point should be, summarizing at the end with what amounted to a nearly perfect paraphrase of her original point. She watched, bemused, as he struggled unsuccessfully for the remainder of the meeting to come up with points two and three, which should have naturally flowed from the first point.

And it wasn't only Chen—she noticed that other women were similarly treated. One woman from customer service, Sue, brought up an important point from her experience that questioned a fundamental market assumption. Everyone listened and nodded as she spoke, but minutes later one of the guys plunged in deep with how to move forward with the plan based on the flawed assumption. Chen politely stopped the conversation and pointed to the woman, asking, "What about what Sue just said?" and got blank stares around the table. Had they even been listening when Sue spoke? Chen wondered why she bothered to waste her talent in this organization.

Everyone wants to retain good employees, and those who are engaged, satisfied with their job, and feel utilized by the company are more likely to stay. Many organizations experience more turnover with women than men (e.g. 45 percent of women leave tech[216]), and measuring employee happiness can reveal risks long before the turnover statistics. We recommend conducting an annual engagement survey. We also suggest measures for net promoter scoring in our survey tools, broken down by gender and race. This score helps understand the difference between employees who haven't complained and employees who are actively promoting the organization as a good place to work. A large number of detractors can highlight areas for further study and potential future turnover trends. Some companies also include employee engagement measures in their existing survey tools—we look at the data by gender and level to see if there are any notable trends.

USING A NET PROMOTER SCORE

Net promoter score is a tool used by organizations to assess how customers feel about their products and services by asking about how likely they are to recommend to someone else. It was designed to go beyond just satisfaction to how people talk about the brand to others. It is calculated using a scale of one to ten, where ten is most likely to promote, nines and tens are considered promoters, sevens and eights are considered passives, and zeroes to sixes are considered detractors because they are more likely to hurt the brand when talking to others than help. The score is calculated by subtracting the detractors from the promoters. You can imagine how this can be a much higher hurdle than a simple satisfaction score and how it could help unearth valuable feedback. For this reason, we use it to assess how employees feel about working for the organization and specifically if they would recommend the organization to women as a good place to work.

Exit interviews also help prevent retention challenges. If the HR system doesn't track them, we take a sample of recent vacancies and follow up. We ask: Why are women leaving? Are the reasons different from men? Was a sufficient effort made to retain? We then follow up, using services like LinkedIn to see where they ended up. How well are they doing there? It is often surprising what information women are willing to tell us in confidence once they have left an organization and how different it can be from their formal exit interviews. The employee satisfaction app Glassdoor's recommendations and complaint postings can help, too. It's critical that this information is analyzed by gender to discern which areas are specifically concerning for women.

What are the employees who leave telling you about your organization? Do different groups leave more often? Why? Is your organization listening to the feedback? And what are the risks?

| TURNOVER RISK | OPPORTUNITY RISK |

The Reframe?

Assumption	Reframe
I don't know why women leave. They just make another choice, or they leave because of family.	We can seek to discover the real reasons why people leave and make changes to keep them.

Performance evaluations have a range of potential bias land mines that need to be carefully negotiated.

Chen successfully launched her division's new product line and was looking forward to her performance review, despite some of the disappointments she'd felt in her first year at the organization. Joe had told her that when he launched a slightly smaller product line a year ago, he got a $25,000 bonus. But when Chen met with her boss, and even though she had completed all of her key performance indicators, she was given only a small bonus. Chen questioned it and was told that her product line was not as complex as Joe's. The bonus, he said, was for truly exceptional work. Joe was also perplexed with this feedback; he said what Chen did was actually far more challenging than what he had done, and he couldn't imagine why she wouldn't have received the same bonus. Chen felt very

167

discouraged that the company didn't seem to recognize what she felt was a very big investment of her discretionary energy and time and that they overvalued the admittedly subordinate work of her male colleague.

Performance metrics should be widely agreed upon, published, and made part of the standard on-boarding and training program for the company. And they shouldn't change midstream. Further, each manager should be held accountable for their level of knowledge of the metrics and ability to correctly evaluate employee experiences accordingly. Bringing leaders together to review all their subordinates at the same time, compare metrics, and share feedback would also be helpful to level-set, provided the politics of groupthink are recognized and mitigated.

We also recommend hiring a consultant, if possible, to oversee the review process at each level, to provide a nonpartisan mediation of the process and to highlight whenever an intangible or potentially biased comment is included in the process. This neutral mediator can also add consistency to the process as they move from team to team. It's almost impossible for people within organizations to not be swayed by closeness to the process. If you want to start to build an actual meritocracy, you must standardize the metrics and the evaluation criteria, as well as remove some of the subjectivity from the process

In another incident, Joe confessed to Chen that he was not looking forward to meeting with one of his direct reports. He had to deliver some negative feedback and was worried about how the associate was going to take it. The last time he corrected something she did, she responded quite emotionally. But Joe had put it off for almost a month, and the situation hadn't resolved itself on its own.

We've talked about how some women are culturally conditioned for perfectionism. Anything shy of 100 percent can be perceived as failure. Think about that. Failure. As an ally, you can help uncover the unconscious bias they have about themselves and reframe the flawed assumptions about perfectionism—that they are a work in progress while on this team—so they can shift the constructive feedback experience from a conversation about final judgment to one of critical career support. Reframing the response both for yourself and the person being evaluated can help. Instead of tiptoeing around and closing down when tears flow, think of this as part of the developmental process. By crying or becoming defiant, a woman has shown she hasn't yet developed the assumption/reframe skill. If she had hidden her response, nobody would know the perfectionism problem was brewing until some-where else down the line, perhaps when she burns out and leaves without warning. This way managers get an opportunity to work on it sooner.

A good tool for removing unconscious bias from the performance evaluation process is 360-degree performance feedback.* This is where a large sampling of people from all around the employee—peers, subordinates, and colleagues, in addition to managers—get to weigh in on how they think the employee is doing. It allows others to highlight their personal interactions with the employee and give managers information they otherwise wouldn't know. Done well, it should surface trends, both positive and negative. It also might highlight whether or not other employees have bias-awareness issues.

It is important to conduct a 360 without influence. Calling people on the phone, for example, allows the interviewer to sway the direction of the conversation. Bringing a group together to discuss a candidate introduces the "focus group problem" of louder voices influencing or dismissing valid input. There also can be negative consequences for participants, since it can be hard to disguise identities, so participants may temper feedback and squash valuable truths. The critical skill for the manager is to recognize when these problems have occurred, or whether bias has slipped in, and to measure feedback accordingly. Unfortunately, we've seen too often where 360 feedback is cherry-picked to justify an existing narrative about the employee, rather than looked at fully in order to uncover valuable new insights.

Sometimes we find that managers evaluate team members against the job description or a standard list of criteria. They do this, ostensibly, to be as unbiased as possible when evaluating employees. But research has found that this process is unfairly skewed against women, who are judged more harshly for missing attributes or falling short of perfection, whereas men are allowed to be a work in progress. Comparing individual evaluations with each other rather than a standard counter-intuitively reduces bias because the comparison enables evaluators to see how the current group compares as a whole and reduces unconscious biases against women's ability to be promoted.[217]

Evaluating people is a skill. Sometimes it is assumed that managers innately know how to do it, or have received sufficient experience during their own rise in the organization to become proficient. Research shows this is not true: a significant number of senior leaders have been shown as uncomfortable communicating with employees and providing employee feedback.[218] Yet it is one of the most important aspects of their job.

Managers who understand gender bias are better equipped to recognize the difference between confident self-promotion and actual performance.

---

* A 360-degree feedback process is designed to provide feedback from a myriad of perspectives. Traditionally, 360-degree feedback is collated from a manager, peers, and reportees. It's been expanded to include customers (internal and external) and even families (in a coaching situation).

They are aware of word choices in performance evaluations and know how to neutralize unconscious bias. Measuring these capabilities and creating systems to reduce the bias makes a huge difference.

Lastly, annual reviews or formal evaluation conversations should be consistent with hundreds of mini-feedback conversations that occur throughout day-to-day operations. Often these conversations haven't happened at all or have not included an HR professional to ensure consistency. Managers need this skill, so performance management and evaluation should be part of how an organization evaluates its leaders. As with the bias-awareness skill, leaders who are not good at evaluating others should not be promoted, because of their influence on a company's culture. Training should be focused on how to review people and share hard feedback so group leaders can improve this skill as part of their own personal development.

How is performance measured and rewarded in your organization? What does the data tell you? Are performance scores distributed equally in the organization? Tracking performance ratings by gender and ethnicity as well as other areas that could suffer from bias, such as personality type (overvaluing extroverts versus introverts), is an important tool to uncover problems and point the organization to areas that need improvement.

The risks of poor performance evaluation?

| LEGAL RISK | | TURNOVER RISK |

The Reframe?

Assumption	Reframe
We already evaluate performance based on objective criteria. It's a meritocracy.	I am biased. We are all biased. We can change the process and decision-making approach to bring in more objectivity.

Promotion and pipeline development are also key processes that are important to track and measure.

One of Chen's mentees from a different department, Amy, was up for a promotion to manager. Chen felt Amy was ready and had met all of the requirements for the role. But at a highly visible presentation,

Amy's performance was mediocre. Chen knew Amy was capable of more and suspected she suffered from nerves because of the proximity of the promotional review date and the highly visible nature of the presentation. So when Amy's boss announced Amy's promotion to supervisor instead of manager, citing a lack of "gravitas," even Chen couldn't find a concrete way to argue. Ironically, it felt like Amy would have got the promotion if she had been out sick the day of the presentation or given it at a later date.

We recommend challenging everyone's cultural assumptions about risk and perfectionism. Women are more likely to be penalized for a mistake as if it confirms that they were ill-suited from the start. This is part of the reinforcing-stereotypes problem we talked about earlier. Instead, you can provide positive coaching: catching an employee doing things right and encouraging her to learn from anything that went wrong. (Frankly, this works for everyone—not only women. It's good management.) Creating a positive learning environment or lab will give women a place where they are allowed to be a work in progress and let others know that they are too.

And of course, instead of allowing women to sit back in meetings or even sit away from the table[219] you can proactively engage their opinions and act upon what is heard. Be careful not to misinterpret this hesitancy to engage as an indicator that she isn't ambitious. Remember the perfection tendency and encourage her. Sometimes the opposite happens. Women are often labeled negative when they ask for a promotion. African American women are often counseled to dim "their light."[220] The reframe works the same here: challenge your assumptions about what women should do, and listen to any ask based on its own merits.

But this is just one aspect. McKinsey says that if we change promotion and hiring, much of the differential in numbers will disappear.[221] So we measure the effectiveness of the promotions and pipeline development process by tracking a sample of men and women through the process, measuring their length of time spent at each step, types of assignments and experience gained, and level of responsibility imparted at each step. We commonly find that women's career progression takes longer, even after adjustment for maternity leave or part-time stints. It is especially slow in companies without a well-managed talent management process, transparent promotional criteria, and formal mentoring/sponsorship programs. We recommend that organizations do their own career time-tracking by demographic, review promotion notes from the process for areas of potential bias, and audit their pipeline development decision-making systems. Often the results are quite telling in their inexplicable differences by gender.

If a single department seems to promote fewer women than others, take a closer look for potential problems. Learn from those departments that are already effective. Also conduct a postmortem for each promotion cycle and document the decision process for future review so you can highlight patterns and opportunities to improve the process. We also recommend that those responsible for promoting people be fully trained in unconscious bias and rewarded when they work to mitigate its effects.

Have you seen the numbers? Does your organization promote men and women at the same rate? Or do you notice women falling behind? Is the disparity dismissed as a motherhood issue, even for women who are not mothers? What parts of the promotion process might contain bias in your organization?

The risk?

| TURNOVER RISK | STAGNATION RISK |

The Reframe?

Assumption	Reframe
Women aren't asking for more money or promotions; they lack ambition. Or the opposite: She's a bit aggressive, don't you think?	Women may have different ways of showing they are ready for promotion. I can make promotional requirements clear and standardized so asking is not part of the process.

The final category in the process section is mentoring, which as we explained earlier, impacts career progression, whether it is formal in the organization or informal.

A rumor developed at Chen and Joe's company that in order to be promoted, you needed to be Joe's friend. That's because the majority of employees promoted in the last few promotion cycles were men who socialized or worked on projects with him. Joe was proud of having invested so much time in these guys and that it paid off for them. But he was also a bit reluctant about doing the same for women, because he feared they might take it the wrong way. Plus, few women wanted to hang out at sporting events after work, so he couldn't see where he could find additional time in his schedule to spend with them.

If men feel uncomfortable mentoring women, this needs to be identified so that they can be coached and their fears mitigated. Given the predominance of men in senior leadership, more cross-gender mentoring is essential. Some men feel a little uncomfortable mentoring young women. This needs to be addressed! There is no reason for a truly authentic mentoring relationship to be uncomfortable. In fact, discomfort signals that the men lack the skills to manage a professional male/female relationship. Either the pair needs to be reassigned or the mentor needs additional training. We recommend that companies encourage more men to mentor women and women to mentor men to work toward removing the gender bias.

Mentoring relationships can be made more overt by explaining the process and noting that it can feel awkward but that it's essential for career growth. By helping male mentors develop an ally mentality (see Chapter 7), women will feel more supported and feel like these relationships are an essential part of the culture. One way to practice is to form a mixed group of men and women as a brainstorm team to develop what this could look like for the company.

We measure the effectiveness of an organization's mentorship both formally and informally. We can map who employees are meeting with on a regular basis. We can also document the impact of mentors on sponsorship decisions. Senior leaders can be evaluated on their specific mentoring efforts and the level of diversity of their mentees, not to mention the speed of their mentees' career trajectories. We also incorporate questions around career growth opportunities and mentoring systems in our surveys to gauge how effective the process is to various demographic groups. The process can also highlight when people feel uncomfortable with the mentoring approach.

It's important to recognize that because women don't always see networking and mentorship as legitimate work, they may be more likely to participate in a formal structure at first, especially if given management's blessing (or if the program is made mandatory). To avert this, you can expose young women to formal programs early in their career and give them specific training on how to effectively utilize mentoring and networking opportunities.

Women also need to buy into the value and importance of informal networking and mentorship. Highlighting more instances of where time invested in the process is helpful; even showcasing particular informal mentoring relationships on a regularly basis reinforces its value. You could include this as part of the evaluation process—how much time a candidate has spent connecting with others to share and grow their value. Role modeling effective mentoring relationships by talking about them, incorporating them into training, and evaluating effectiveness as part of the review process also can make the value more visible.

Since women don't get much experience or cultural support for self-promotion, they need safe spaces for this to happen. We have heard senior leaders complain that female mentees have squandered their time together or haven't asked for the right things, and use that as a reason to discontinue mentorship support, rather than seeing it as an opportunity to train. These skills should not be seen as natural or innate, particularly when they are less culturally acceptable for women.

Does your organization have a formal mentoring program? Do you participate? Is it gender-neutral? Does mentoring result in development, sponsorship, and promotion?

The risk?

STAGNATION RISK

The Reframe?

Assumption	Reframe
People should have to find their own mentors based on their work product. It will happen naturally.	There is bias in the mentor and sponsor systems. Being more conscious and inclusive about how we do sponsorship and mentorship means we can help more people.

SUPPORTING ENVIRONMENT

The third and final section of our gender scorecard is the creation of a supporting environment and includes the categories of role modeling, culture, work-life synergy, and external impact. Do members of out-groups feel welcome and psychologically safe at work? Can they envision career progression? Do people like them succeed? What vibe does the workplace give? Does the work here integrate with their life?

And how does the broader world—customers, suppliers, the community—feel about the company?

Let's start with role modeling. Chen's senior-team colleagues were all married men with children and stay-at-home wives. So when her teammates needed help at home, such as holiday shopping, party planning, or weekly meal-preparation, they had it. In fact, many of them had no home responsibilities, or even personal hobbies, so they were able to spend an almost unlimited amount of time at the office.

Chen overheard some young women in her company complain that they didn't want to get promoted to management because of the long hours, which they felt they couldn't accommodate and still have a life outside of work. They were seeing only one type of leadership model and had assumed that was the only way to be successful. They were knocking themselves out to perform their career like the men, but their home life was closer in form to that of the men's wives.

If leaders truly want diversity—the kind of diversity of thought and group impact that makes a difference—it needs to be authentically modeled from the top.

The only way to address the role-modeling problem is to put women, people from other underrepresented groups, and people with different career paths and lifestyles on the senior team. Period. We often get pushback on this point. Many companies seek us out to get help because shareholders, clients, and employees are pressuring them to become more diverse. And while they agree with the concept in principle, they usually want us to help everywhere in the organization except the top. After all, making a change at the top affects them the most. One prospective client we met wondered how they could possibly achieve gender equity at the top of the organization by saying, "We're all guys, and we're not going anywhere." This fixed-pie thinking assumes there is only one way to lead an organization. (Incidentally, their next senior-team hire was also a man!)

You need to rethink your organizational structure and expand the senior team so it is more diverse. We know of another organization, taxed with lowering headcount to save money, that intentionally promoted a significantly more diverse group of up-and-comers from the ranks of the organization to their senior leadership team rather than hiring expensive outsiders. Broadening their team in this way brought in new, previously untapped perspectives and opportunities.

Organizations with role models who ascended to top positions differently tend to have more women pursuing positions. For example, allowing a male leader to take a sabbatical to help manage his child's recent ADHD diagnosis can illustrate a new model of career parenting. Or positively showcasing a leader who works a four day/ten hour schedule. Or showcasing when a senior male leader takes paternity leave. Or giving a female leader dedicated time to devote to training and development or philanthropy. Having alternative and female role models is extremely important to fuel and support so-called ambition: it's not that women aren't ambitious, it's that if they don't like the limiting lifestyle they see exhibited by the leaders, so they opt for a different choice. (By the way, younger generations of men concur.)

Role modeling also affects the bottom of the organization. In many companies, support staff is primarily made up of women. When men take a support-staff position, the title often gets upgraded. When only women do the undervalued work at the bottom of the organization, the stereotype that lower-level tasks are women's work is reinforced.

How diverse are the senior leaders in your organization? Do their backgrounds diverge or are they all from the same mold? We measure this kind of background diversity in our work by looking closely at employees' resumes, measuring how many different schools, background experiences, industries, and home lifestyles are represented. In one of our

WHY IS ROLE MODELING SO IMPORTANT?

Role modeling is powerful because it gives people something to emulate. Especially when individuals are paving a new pathway to senior leadership, they are unsure of how to go about it because they are not like the person at the top. Yet it is possible to address this uncertainty by showcasing alternative career-path trajectories. It can be helpful to publish intimate senior leader profiles, for example, including lifestyle components, particularly where the leaders followed an unusual career path or have unusual background experience. Offering more information about people can dispel myths and give younger employees more opportunities to connect with a particular background experience or elements of a person's life they may not have known about. For example, a white senior man who describes a time when he struggled to get promoted because he had a baby at home might help a younger woman believe that her own struggle is not unique, not gender-specific, and is possible to overcome. It also signals to men that their career paths do not have to follow a single trajectory.

clients, for example, we found a department where every male leader had a wife who was a teacher. We note interesting dynamics like this and how that might impact role modeling from that team. To counter homogeneity, we recommend organizations make an active goal to ensure the next hire or promotion to that group has a different background experience. It is also important to publicize and reward leaders who successfully facilitate greater background diversity on their teams, because this reflects their own ability to role model as well.

The risk?

TURNOVER RISK	PRODUCTIVITY RISK

The Reframe?

Assumption	Reframe
We have clear and effective role models for effective leadership at our firm.	Role modeling multiple paths to leadership will improve our leadership pool.

Culture is the oil that enables all this to work.

Chen noticed something interesting about the social culture at her company. All the women, who happened to be in lower-level positions, ate lunch together every day in the cafeteria and went out together after work. The men, who mainly held senior positions, generally went out for lunch together and then stayed late to work, often shooting a couple of rounds of pool and drinking beers in the company foyer late at night. Though Chen joined the men on a couple of occasions, Chen really wished she could spend less time at lunch and socializing after work so she could get work done and go home. The women sometimes invited her to eat with them, but she recognized that she made them feel awkward and intimidated when she joined them. It felt as if there were no place for a senior-level woman in the social fabric of the company.

Culture is typically defined as the characteristics—both overt and hidden—that indicate the behaviors and attitudes deemed acceptable in an organization.[222] As we described earlier, identifying biased cultural practices and then overtly working to change them can signal to those outside the current power structure that they are acceptable employees and can bring their full selves to work. We can measure this through anecdotal stories, survey data, complaints, and individual attitudes.

One visible way to improve culture is to hold company social events that appeal to a wide audience and build inclusiveness. Gender-neutral events such as going to an escape room, working at a food bank, or going to a paint bar, rather than golf outings and professional sporting events, can include more women. Nonphysical events can include people of all ages and abilities. Ensuring there are plenty of nondrinking events can help include people who don't drink. Make sure that senior leaders attend social events with their subordinates to role model, provide support, and build connections; their presence will signal to others how much they are valued. And make sure that women aren't the only ones organizing these events. Rotate so everyone shares responsibilities.

Employee resource or affinity groups are often used to foster a safe learning space for groups to discuss difficult issues related to race and gender. While we acknowledge that these groups play a role in reinforcing group identity and negative priming, they can bring together people who are otherwise feeling isolated and discouraged. They provide an opportunity to facilitate important connections and discussions in a safe environment. We recommend including all women (including administrative staff) in affinity groups as well, not only high achievers. Men should be included and encouraged to participate, but reminded to not dominate. If possible, these groups should be professionally facilitated so they do not descend into a session that perpetuates bias. They should be planned according to best practices.[223]

Look at all the subtle ways culture is reinforced, such as the stories told and the language used. Are women called girls? Are the stories all about heroism and sacrifice to the company? Is competition worshipped? These are subtle signals of culture that tell women they do not belong. Changing these can be done a myriad of ways. Professors Robin Ely and Debra Meyerson studied an offshore drilling company, a stereotypically masculine environment, where bravado and risk-taking was compromising safety and costing the company a lot of money. As a result, it changed from a competitive, last-man-standing culture to one of questioning, support, and safety first—and saved money.[224]

Be honest with yourself as you assess your organizational culture. Is this a good old boys club? How can you tell? One way is to look around— is everyone the same? Do they all hang out together in and out of work? Are social events more like frat parties? And if so, how did you get here? In a good old boys club, leadership rewards and promotes leaders who are just like themselves. So the cycle never breaks. Changing the behavior of more traditionally minded managers can be challenging, because that's the way they've always done things. Yet it is clearly very critical. So add "managing a diverse team" to your managers' review process. If they don't have this experience and skill, then they don't get promoted.

The risk?

TURNOVER RISK

The Reframe?

Assumption	Reframe
We have a unified culture here. Everyone just needs to fit in.	Opening the culture to allow influence by diverse participants can make the company more robust and inclusive.

While the need for work-life balance has been primarily driven by women and addressed as an accommodation for motherhood, in reality, organizations that don't address work-life balance will continue to repel diversity—and younger generations.

Chen worked hard to win over the company president and prove she was the best choice for her job, particularly through the launch of her division's newest product line. Similar to other leaders, Chen stayed late most nights and was in the office early every morning. She gave up her morning workout and grabbed food from the vending machine. It wasn't particularly healthy, but she felt this pace was relatively temporary. She was mystified, then, when her boss told HR to deduct a half day of personal time when she attended a supplier meeting one afternoon near her home and chose to work from there for the rest of the day rather than battling traffic to return to the office. When confronted, her boss stated that they don't allow working from home. So Chen was forced to return to the office after all meetings, costing the company mileage and lost productivity. One afternoon a few weeks later, Chen sought her boss's input on a client matter and was told he was downstairs working out. He returned an hour later but the client had already gone home for the day. Chen was frustrated that the company seemed to value any time spent at (or near) the office more than actual work.

PRODUCTIVITY RISK

Chen was also asked to travel on many occasions. Most of the time, she agreed with the need and was happy to rearrange her personal life to make these trips. But occasionally, the trips seemed unnecessary. She once overheard one of her male colleagues talking about how he liked to travel, and because he really didn't like spending time at home, he proactively looked for travel opportunities. Chen also found that trips were often purposely scheduled to minimize days out of the office, at the expense of personal time, holidays, and weekends. She also noticed that when people at the company traveled, they were expected to entertain well into the evening in bars or sports events. She was even chastised for not using enough of her travel or entertainment budget.

LEGAL RISK	PRODUCTIVITY RISK

Joe was asked to travel extensively for work. It was repeatedly hinted that this was essential for his career. But his second child had just been born, and he really wanted to be there for his growing family. He felt he had no choice and traveled whenever asked. It really started to weigh him down, and he hated leaving every other week to hit the road. He also somewhat resented that some of his female colleagues didn't seem to be asked as often.

TURNOVER RISK	STAGNATION RISK

The risk categories attached to the stories above summarize the risks of misunderstanding the importance of work-life synergy: productivity, stagnation, turnover—even legal problems. Flexibility for work-life purposes is only one step on the continuum of how work is changing to meet the needs of both businesses and employees. Flexibility as a strategic approach encourages people to think more holistically about when and where the best place is to get their work done. Additionally, it separates flexibility from being a benefit for mothers to a benefit for everyone.[225] It is important to encourage all workers to integrate work and life more fully, since employees who integrate perform better.[226] Further, offering employees the ability to control how and where they work increases engagement and work satisfaction.[227] Such a strategy also enables organizations to increase retention and productivity and differentiate themselves from competition for talent.

An organization that has traditionally worked a formal hours-focused structure and not encouraged flexibility may need training on how to balance home and work responsibilities more equitably as well as eliminating penalties for using flexibility options. It could also implement more creative and gender-neutral work-life benefits, such as parenting leave, meal delivery, house cleaning, car services for kids, homework club, on-site yoga/meditation, and more.

When one of Chen's direct reports, Petra, got back from maternity leave, Chen's colleagues became hyper-focused on how much time Petra was or wasn't spending at the office. They counseled Chen to make sure Petra wasn't taking too much time off for doctor's appointments or leaving early to pick up kids. In fact, they suggested that Chen should ask Petra to cut back her hours, so she would be able to spend more time with her family. They also decided not to pay Petra's bonus for the quarter where her maternity leave fell, even though she achieved her goals by working extra hours before and after her time out. Another of Chen's direct reports, Todd, also recently had a baby but he garnered no such attention. In fact, it was suggested that maybe Todd should be given some special assignments now that he was a father so he could position himself to be promoted.

LEGAL RISK   TURNOVER RISK

Maternity biases encourage women to step back from career when they become mothers. Organizations reinforce this bias when they offer maternity leave instead of parenting leave, or when they support new mothers in flawed ways such as helping them step back, go part-time, or stop traveling for business. It is important that companies move beyond simply accommodating maternity to supporting all employees with developing the skills to manage the early days of parenting while remaining employed.

We recommend challenging women's own cultural assumptions about maternity. Instead of feeding the traditional narrative, as many managers do when they say things like, "Don't decide now if you are coming back; you may feel differently about your career after having a child," managers should encourage mothers to consider their careers more positively. They could say instead, "Your kids are young for such a short time in the long scheme of your career; we are confident we can figure out how to navigate this temporary pressure and that you will emerge with even better leadership skills." This sentiment sends an entirely different message: one of support. We recommend providing training and support for new mothers (and fathers) to help them navigate this time while preserving their career trajectories.

And offer flexibility to men as well! So many men we've spoken to have wanted flexibility when their kids were little and have been refused. Years later, they regret how much they missed. Supporting fathers with equal attention sends the message that flexibility is for everyone and men don't need to have a stay-at-home spouse in order to get promoted.

Helping managers understand that parenting and other outside interests enrich the lives of employees in a positive way and make them better employees can help mitigate the short-term concerns about employee productivity. Actively encouraging workers at all levels to take leave, and even offering sabbatical programs, is something forward-thinking organizations do. Sabbatical is a great term as it is gender-neutral and open for any reason, rather than prescribing that maternity or any other reason is more valid for someone taking time off. Really advanced organizations have even removed recording time off at all—their focus is on getting the job done and as long as employees are getting results, they don't care how it happens.

How effective is your organization at promoting work-life synergy? Who uses paid leave, part-time work, and flexible-work options? Are people over-rewarded for never taking time off for their level of apparent commitment to the organization? If only women use these programs, is that a signal that the organization is still in accommodation mode? Examine women's career trajectories and note any penalties for using maternity leave or flexibility. Compare men's use of flexibility and what happens when they do. When you look at role modeling, what do you learn about the expected lifestyle of the organization's leadership?

The risks? You've read them.

| LEGAL RISK | TURNOVER RISK | PRODUCTIVITY RISK |

The Reframe?

Assumption	Reframe
We accommodate people's lives, but work is most important and those who work hardest and longest reap the rewards. That's the way it is.	Everyone considers work and life differently. And everyone has a life. We can focus on results, not how people integrate their work and life. Flexibility is a strategy, not a benefit.

The last of our gender scorecard categories is external impact. Companies who haven't completed the inclusion process often miss one of the most important areas of benefit: customers.

One of Chen and Joe's company's largest suppliers invited the senior team to a customer appreciation event at its headquarters in Maine. They greeted the group with a complimentary swag bag of gifts including personalized jackets and gloves, meant to help out with comfort during the scheduled factory tour. Unfortunately for Chen, everything was size men's large. Attendees' spouses were also invited on the trip and treated to a spa day while the executives were in meetings. Both Chen and her husband felt excluded from the experience.

Why would a supplier make assumptions? Imagine how Chen will react when that supplier wants a renewed contract. She might reasonably ask to open up the bidding process.

We evaluate how an organization's brand shows up in the marketplace, and we audit customer feedback for telltale signs of bias. In addition to an organization's internal tracking data, we use online reviews, consumer complaint agencies, media instances, and other external sources to unearth potential problems. We noticed, for example, that one company used "booth babes" to advertise products at industry trade shows, despite the fact the vast majority of participants were female. The company clearly seemed out of touch, yet to their all-male team, this external manifestation of their brand seemed completely normal.

We also evaluate how much diversity exists among an organization's key partners, such as suppliers.

Because bias can be exacerbated from company to company, and because visible scandals can be so damaging, eliminating it from the supply chain should also be a goal. Coca-Cola, Walmart, and others have invested in women across their supply chains.[228] And when Amazon learned that its AI-based resume-selection software perpetuated bias from its program inputs, the project was scrapped before it was used internally or made available as a product. But these types of problems can sometimes be less obvious. Buying ergonomic office chairs designed primarily for men, to the detriment of female employees' health, or using an overseas manu-facturer that publicly violates women's human rights are smaller, more hidden decisions that can also have a negative impact on the organization and women in general.

The long-term effects of excluding women from positive marketing experiences for the business can actually help the competition. Think about how many coworking spaces are specifically targeted at women business owners. Or how well Saturn's car brand did with women when they opened retail stores in malls and eliminated negotiation from the selling process.[229] In conversations with senior leaders, we have heard many comments like this: "We won the business because we had women on our team. Our client told us that our competitors all looked alike."

What does your sales team look like? How do your external events appear? Who might you be leaving out? Who could you include in the sales process to see the opportunities to adapt to a broader customer base?

The risks?

| TURNOVER RISK | STAGNATION RISK | PRODUCTIVITY RISK |

The Reframe?

Assumption	Reframe
We sell to everyone. That includes women.	Female customers often have unique needs. We can address those needs better if we understood women better. We may identify new markets that serve everyone better as a result.

UNDERSTANDING THE NARRATIVE

An organization's narrative is the cumulative story that people tell about the company. When assessing organizations, we interview a wide range of people at all levels and actively solicit and listen to gossip. We unearth drama. In gossip and drama, we hear what people are really thinking, particularly when trends recur across the organization. We hear about cliques and how people feel about the company's leadership. We hear about how work really gets done. And we hear about what narratives people accept about the company from leadership and what gets discarded.

We also ask in our surveys if people feel respected by their organization. We note the disconnects between women and men or certain groups, which can highlight different perspectives. We also ask key clients, vendors, and other stakeholders for input. Oftentimes management is blind to the company narrative and finds information extremely illuminating. If you suspect your leadership team is out of step with its narrative and not listening to company gossip, we recommend bringing in an outside consultant to elicit feedback objectively.

The three sections and twelve categories of our evaluation and scorecard process can be overwhelming, but if you spend time with it, put it into the context of the unconscious bias definitions we presented and our taxonomy of leadership capabilities, they form an excellent tool for giving your organization objective insight into hidden biases, process problems, cultural flaws, and missteps that hinder or exclude women. We've outlined the risks so you can quantify them.

The scorecard can reveal situations and moments of discovery that, once highlighted, can seem obvious and potentially embarrassing. It is important that company leaders look at the process as a positive self-awareness opportunity, and think of it in terms of the potential return on investment they can earn as they can mitigate risk. Notice that this process is not dissimilar to most other operational consulting processes. We take apart the entire pipeline, at every level for every department, to unearth the problems and inefficiencies and document the potential gains the organization can make by fixing them.

As you review your own organization, you will likely find areas where your company will get an A. There will also be problem areas that you can target for improvement. (If there aren't, ask yourself if you're being fully honest.) Our recommendation would be to track progress using the tool set we give you in this book, and assess again annually to remind yourself how far the organization has come and to ensure it continues to move forward.

Lastly, think about our scorecard as gap analysis, not an audit. Humility, in this case, is good for the organization. It is okay to have problems; it is not okay not to know where they are or what to do about them. Let's face it—if there were no problems, there would be equity at all levels. The risk for leaders isn't that identifying the bias problems will increase liability, it's that pretending there isn't bias—when everyone can count—will leave the organization exposed to all the risks we have outlined in this chapter.

CONCLUSION

WELL, WE'VE COME A LONG WAY from the two Terrys' stories at the beginning of this book. We hope we've helped you understand the nature of the challenges that all women face in the workplace and how a vision of true gender equity can be achieved by understanding the barriers, reframing false assumptions, and using an evaluative set of tools to examine your organization. The challenge, as we have noted, is both individual and organizational, but those are inevitably bound together and require a consistent and integrated set of solutions.

We've helped you envision a team or organization with gender equity and greater diversity. We've also shown you how gender roles are all made up, based on bias, and built on flawed assumptions. You've seen the different ways and places where bias shows up. Women have bias about themselves and others. Men have self-limiting biases too. Leaders can't help but have bias. And organizations are full of biased processes and barriers that keep women from gaining power and influence.

We have given you some powerful tools as well. When you learn to recognize flawed assumptions and unconscious bias, you can reframe to open up countless new possibilities. You get to rewrite the rules for yourself. We hope you can help others to see this too. We have taught you how to have positive, even-keeled conversations using Direct Speak. And we outlined how men can be powerful allies for women at work.

We have also showed how leaders or potential leaders can effect organizational change and get the buy-in the company needs from others. We shared our taxonomy of leadership competencies to reshape how you think about and measure diversity skills. With this new definition of effective leadership, you can identify those who need training in order to become twenty-first-century leaders.

Finally, we have provided you with a tool set that will enable you to look inside your organization, discover barriers to diversity, strip them away, and sustain a long-term gender equity strategy with the help of comprehensive measurement.

Now that you've seen what you've seen, you can't unsee it. The emperor has no clothes. But seeing clearly opens the path to action: rewriting the rules and helping others do the same. Once people see biases and flawed assumptions, it's hard to keep operating in the same old way. They can chose to walk around and pretend the problem's not there, but deep down they know. In our work, we have often had people initially reject our work who come back in time and describe its powerful impact on their lives. Because you can't un-ring the bell.

Building Blocks of Change

We wrote this book with the idea that change is possible with a new mindset. It's about looking at the challenge of inclusion with a different lens and an updated skill set. We aren't talking about throwing everything out, but reframing and changing behaviors and processes to reflect the reframe. And since now you know these biases are all made up anyway, there is so much more power inherent in changing.

It's actually not that hard; it's more about being conscious. One of the best parts of being conscious—as we've highlighted—is that it's so freeing. The limits are removed.

Getting there requires a combination of internal and external approaches. As the diagram above illustrates, there are pieces that everyone needs to work on about themselves and pieces we need to work on together to adapt and fix the organization. We are all in this together. We encourage you to think about what you have learned in these pages and how you can help achieve this new vision.

Here are some summary guidelines:

FIXING OURSELVES

- **Observe.** Observing your own actions and the impact of your words and behaviors is crucial. Remember, this is not about tiptoeing around, being politically correct, or feeling shame. It is about privately reflecting on the impact of words and actions and understanding that being more thoughtful can help everyone. People are allowed to make mistakes and notice after the fact. Everyone is allowed to learn and be a work in progress.

- **Identify and reframe underlying assumptions.** Naming the assumptions that underlie behaviors starts the process. What assumptions can be identified? Did you change your assumptions in the course of this book? Why or why not?

- **Be a bias-buster.** When you notice bias at work or at home, and when you are comfortable, help combat bias by speaking up and changing behavior. If it was your mistake, own it and apologize. Others can learn from your example. If it was someone else, ask how you can help them recognize bias and move beyond it. We shared examples of ways to reframe and bust bias. Start with just a few and see what happens.

FIXING THE TEAM

- **Ask why.** Be curious about why a process is done in a particular way. Or why a woman on your team says no to a promotion. Explore and find the underlying assumption. Discover the underlying reasons why the bias is there.

- **Help stop the worthiness competition and instead create a safe space.** Competition can be a good thing, but turning it away from the work into a context about who's better can be very damaging. Instead, help create the psychological safety that will make your team shine and leverage inclusion.

- **Speak up and out.** Change the way your team operates. Implement the changes we've highlighted here in your team and make it a role model for others. For example, change the way your team decisions are made, ensure that everyone on your team has a voice, and discuss how the whole team can shift their behavior to remove bias.

- **Build synthesis.** Truly leverage your diverse team. Synthesize talent, ideas, and technology to not only bring diverse people to the table, but integrate thoughts and functions that take the business to an altogether more impactful place.

FIXING THE ORGANIZATION

- **Notice biased processes.** If a team has few women, figure out what barriers exist. How has the system blocked participation? What can you do about it?

- **Always observe.** If women are not in the room, ask why not. When a commercial for your product gets made or a sales team makes a pitch, seek out diverse voices and faces to represent your brand. Don't let decisions get made by an insular, homogeneous group. Keep up to date on demographics in the ever-changing marketplace to ensure your organization stays in front. Measure progress across all the operational changes.

- **Approach all this as a business problem like any other.** You already know how to make changes for business problems. Use the same skill set, apply the specifics we've outlined, and make it strategically important. Then you can be on your way!

When NASA started the space program in the 1950s and 60s, it sought one type of man: a fighter pilot who could physically withstand g-force. Fast forward to today's astronauts who are preparing to go to Mars. The criteria are totally different. Now it's about mental strength and diversity of background.[230] NASA needs people who can handle a multitude of situations—most of which they can't even anticipate. And in some cases, people who are physically smaller can move around better in small quarters. (Let that sink in for a second. How could that shift the power dynamic if we continue to let homogeneity prevail or use gender as a litmus test for capability? Would all astronauts be women? Let's hope not!) Diversity provides resilience, creativity, and the ability to innovate for better solutions.

NASA's new mindset means envisioning an organization where you no longer notice that there are superficial differences between people but focus instead on creating cognitive diversity. Individuals and the organization can then move beyond an unconscious recognition of difference to a reframed vision of inclusion.[231] For NASA, it's about leveraging the nongovernment sector and involving diverse people from diverse career specialties. It's also about increasing collaboration with a broad group of stakeholders.[232] What could this mean for your organization?

The world is moving in this direction. While we think it is too slow, change is inevitable. Everyone is on this journey. It's just a matter of when you join. You can get on board today and be part of the change, helping to shape and define it. Or you can wait and implement what others have done after the fact. If you are still around. There isn't really a choice of whether; there's only the choice about when you personally choose to move forward.

There actually is one other choice. People can choose to resist this change. But in addition to harming their own career trajectory, they will pose significant harm to others in all the ways we've identified that old norms block creativity, energy, and dreams. That choice is an option. It damages others, but it is available.

We think this second option is only a short-term choice. The world is moving beyond ideas of either/or. The world we see is one where people get the chance to fully use their talents and potential and add value. In our work with hundreds of organizations, people consistently tell us that this is what they want.

This book has been about how to remove barriers that block progress for women and how achievable it really is. It has been about the skills leaders need and how to measure them. And it has been about changing the system. Now that you have these tools, won't you join us in spreading this message? Are you willing to enlist others to join the battle as well? Can you use your own power to help create gender equity in your organization?

We hope you are with us. Thank you for reading.

POSTSCRIPT

THE NEXT SMART STEP HAS SOUGHT TO HELP you see how the underlying assumptions we've used to structure our careers, lives, and organizations around are just that: assumptions. They are all made up. It's up to you to decide if they are true—for you—or flawed and need to be changed. One fundamental assumption that seemed pervasive before (and a key reason women have been held back[233]) is that work is something you do primarily in-person, at a workplace, during set business hours, with life revolving around those established prerequisites. School, shopping, exercise, free time, and health all must be slotted in accordingly. If you wanted to work, you had to adhere; to be successful, you needed to be "all-in."

The COVID-19 pandemic disrupted this workcentric assumption fundamentally. It helped us see all the impacts of that assumption, such as how critical our health and well-being really are. We lost friends, coworkers, parents, grandparents, scientists, and leaders—people who still had contributions to make. Our priorities shifted, and taking care of ourselves and family suddenly mattered most. "How is your health? Is your family doing OK?" These questions became the opening virtual handshake for every meeting. The prior invisibility of the tasks required to take care of life were suddenly and often inconveniently illuminated. The fullness of life stared us in the face. Kids, school, laundry, dinner, the messy house, and buying toilet paper all became visible in a way that's rarely been the case. As did, "Whose job is it?" Suddenly, Dad had to balance a kid on his knee during a meeting and shush Fido at the same time. We had to go out of our way to connect with friends, because we couldn't just bump into each other anymore. The pandemic showed us that life is *really* at the center. Now we can see that being "all-in" and "work-first" was simply an assumption—people across the globe figured out how to work and manage life simultaneously overnight.

During the pandemic, many leaders were more patient with people who had to deal with their kids or their parents or themselves. Some organizations were more relaxed about sick leave. Others adapted to automating functions and moving operations online. Many leaders shifted their focus away from *how* to get work done and instead prioritized *getting outcomes*. Many realized that they can actually trust people to work independently.

We hope that the crisis also provided you with an opportunity to see that the people function of an organization—whether its human resources, learning and development, diversity and inclusion, or just plain leadership—needs to shift from being thought of as a nice-to-have cost-center to an invaluable resource for keeping the wheels on the bus for your organization. After all, overnight initiatives like teleworking and flexible work schedules have become strategically necessary—not a "benefit"—as has the ability to scale your workforce up and down while redefining roles central to your organization's survival. How important is employee engagement now? How about leveraging inclusion to innovate in ways never previously imagined? We are guessing more critical than ever. There is no playbook for this unprecedented period, so we need new ideas now.

This crisis also helped us realize the true benefit of diversity in our workplace. Diversity of thought, experience, and ideas is how we collectively build resilience. Biodiversity builds resilience in nature.[234] When we think about biodiversity, we think about the homeostasis of a forest.[235] Diverse species are interconnected. Everything works together to help everything else. When we think about diverse teams, we think about possibilities for experimentation and piloting, testing and discovering. We think about new ideas and making sure we leverage the great ideas that those outside the mainstream have.[236] For example, think about the international collaboration that enabled the understanding of the human genome and working of the international space station.[237] Diversity is the enabler of change. How, for example, can a homogeneous senior executive team respond effectively if everyone thinks similarly? Where do the creative ideas come from? There's less resilience. It can make the organization weak and vulnerable to attack, unable to creatively solve major challenges like the pandemic.

Did you notice who struggled most during the pandemic? People who expected things would go back to normal in a few days...which became weeks and months before it was clear that this was the "new normal." People who wanted to keep doing business as usual, but business was anything but. Some of those people fought against allowing others to work from home unmonitored. Many engaged in "headcount reduction" instead of re-engineering and redeploying their talent. They cut training and development and maybe even diversity and inclusion initiatives. Many wallowed or hid behind outdated sick-time laws when considering what to do about employees who fell ill, or had to tend to family members. Some stuck to rigid work schedules despite having workers who suddenly had massive childcare or eldercare barriers. And they employed technological solutions that couldn't be accessed by workers without strong internet connections. How many smart, innovative people were excluded in this context?

Others who struggled were those who succumbed badly to the stress of the situation. Many were rendered less productive because they lacked the skills to deal with rapid change. They resisted bringing work (or Zoom cameras) into their homes. Maybe they were laid off or furloughed so they sat out the changing workplace and never learned to work remotely. Or their leaders lacked the skills to lead inclusive change, so they floundered directionless. Was your organization prepared and supportive? Or did leaders think of inclusive leadership skills as "nice to haves" rather than critical executive competencies?

Some of the people who flourished during this time found themselves on the inside circle of their organization's transformation. One leader we spoke to transformed the traditional leadership hierarchy in her organization into cross-functional pods to allow for more agile decision-making during the crisis. Another took apart their organization's customer-facing processes and found opportunities to permanently automate some face-to-face transactions. Others used the "COVID-19 pauses" as opportunities for long-overdue facility upgrades and to conduct training certifications and long-term planning that had been deprioritized. Many individuals found they ate better, got more exercise, spent more time with family, and prioritized wellness in ways they hadn't felt they had space for previously. Most described improved productivity from shortened commutes and fewer interruptions. Many have decided to retain these changes in their post-COVID-19 lives. Most recognized they wanted to live a fuller life.

This event gave us an opportunity to rethink. In change management theory, disequilibrium can be intentionally introduced in an organization to shake it up, to instigate a change of process. Well, the pandemic certainly gave us disequilibrium. Now we have the *opportunity* to create a new normal. If you miss this opportunity, you will have to figure out how to compete against those who took on the challenge and *reframed*.

Now's the time to create a new normal that's inclusive of everyone, and to reframe work as an important part of a whole life. It's not too late for anyone to embrace inclusive leadership skills and the *reframe* process so they can pivot to the new world of work. If you haven't yet, you can still catch up. The opportunity to completely redefine work and life in a post-COVID-19 world looms large. The only certainty is that resisting the change and doubling down on the old ways will leave the resisters in the dust.

ACKNOWLEDGMENTS

It is with deep gratitude that we publicly thank the many people who helped us make this book a reality, from the moment we asked ourselves, "Are we really going to write another book?" through the iterations that took many months.

To our clients and colleagues who are kindred spirits in our efforts to make the workplace better and more inclusive, we thank you for your willingness to try new things. Thank you, Karen Lynskey: your relentless passion for creating the learning organization inspired new training techniques for integrated leadership development. Laura Gregoriadis and the team at CREW Boston: thank you for making your women leaders the best they can possibly be. Thanks to Rachel Cooke at Brandon Hall for partnering with us in important research. Heide Abelli at Skillsoft: keep building innovative learning approaches and solutions. Nancy Carlson: thank you for outcome-driven diversity initiatives. We are grateful for Pamela Popp and Peter Clune, who believe inclusion is a top business priority and are walking the talk. Stacey Gordon and Farzana Nayani: thank you for being our allies and thinking partners as you also do this great work.

We thank Celina Guererro, who helped us shape and tell our story to organizations ready for change, and Camilla Heinzmann, who shared her vast training and facilitation experience to help us develop a world-class team. To Susanna Katsman, Ank Stuyfzand, Ashana Crichton, Roshan Shah, Daffany Chan, Julia Robillard, Keely Denenberg, Suzanne Wilkins, and Heatherjean MacNeil: our gratitude for your ongoing energy, flexibility, and brainpower that run so deep. We could not have written a book "in our spare time" without you running the ship for us.

We thank Kevin Stevens for reaching out and challenging us to write a book he would be proud to publish. And for believing so thoroughly in the importance of this work and how men can help. Your patience with us and diligence to push us—even when the virus pandemic disrupted the process—was invaluable.

From Jodi: I thank Kelly for being an incredible thinking partner. The discussions and debates we have make our ideas deeper, more nuanced, and more useful to others. My business partnership with Kelly is a real joy in my life and I thank her for that. Our incredible business partnership has meant the world to me.

I thank my three "boys": Mike, Sam, and Eric, who have listened to my soliloquies for decades and yet continue to challenge my thinking and support me as I share my thinking with the world.

From Kelly: I thank Jodi for being the instigator of all things dangerous. You continually throw grenades over the wall to see what will happen and then indulge my need to follow every angle—chase down every detail— until the idea is either fully fleshed out or beaten to death before your next inspiration arrives. Keep instigating brilliance and I will keep wrestling it!

I also thank my husband, Martin, who continues to practice inclusive leadership and live the principles I preach while modeling them for our three children: Patrick, Fiona, and Deirdre.

APPENDICES

APPENDIX A
Initiative Mind Mapping

Here is a mind-map tool to guide your visioning exercise and help you think about what your organization could look like with gender equity and/or diversity at all levels. Take a moment to answer some of these questions and jot down thoughts. Where else does this thinking lead? Can you think of other areas that will have to change?

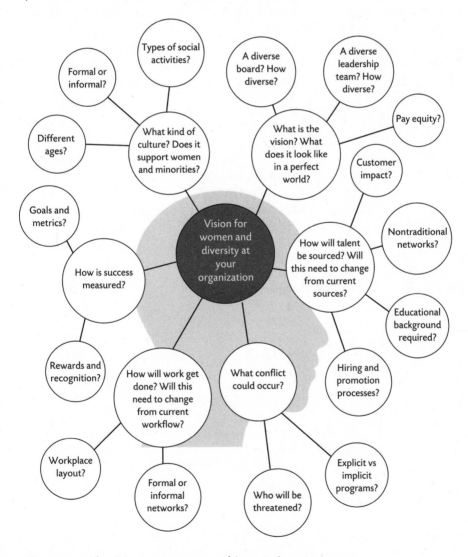

For more tools, visit orangegroveconsulting.com/nextsmartstep.

APPENDIX B
How Our Understanding of Gender Biology Has Changed Over Time*

Supposed Biological Limitation	Historical Context	Present-day Reality
Women shouldn't be trusted with the vote because they are too sentimental, impressionable, and rely too much on intuition.	Countries where women can vote: **1893** New Zealand **1902** Australia **1906** Finland **1913** Norway **1915** Denmark **1917** Canada **1918** Austria, Germany, Poland, Russia **1919** Netherlands **1920** United States **1921** Sweden **1928** Britain, Ireland **1930** South Africa **1931** Spain **1934** Turkey **1944** France **1945** Italy **1947** Argentina, Japan, Mexico, Pakistan **1949** China **1950** India **1954** Colombia **1957** Malaysia, Zimbabwe **1962** Algeria **1963** Iran, Morocco **1964** Libya **1967** Ecuador **1971** Switzerland **1972** Bangladesh **1974** Jordan **1976** Portugal	Countries where women can vote: **1989** Namibia **1990** Western Samoa **1993** Kazakhstan, Moldova **2005** Kuwait **2006** United Arab Emirates **2011** Saudi Arabia Countries where women still cannot vote: Vatican City

---

* See page 241 for citation information.

Supposed Biological Limitation	Historical Context	Present-Day Reality
Women shouldn't run marathons because "their uterus might fall out, their legs would get big, and maybe they would grow hair on their chests."[1]	**1967** Women weren't allowed to run in a marathon. Officials try to tackle the first woman to run the Boston Marathon.[2]	**2019** 38.2% of marathon runners are women.[3] To date there has been no recorded instance of a lost uterus during a marathon.
Women shouldn't be in the military because "the standards of physical fitness have been set to suit men, and women attempting to reach them will overstretch themselves."[4]	**1917** Women are only allowed to join the military as nurses.[5] **1976** The first women are admitted to service academies.[6]	**2018** Women make up 16 percent of the US Army.[7]
Women shouldn't be able to own property or have a bank account because "married women lack independent souls."[8]	**1800s** US legislators debated whether women should own property separate from their husbands and decided against it.[9]	**1848** The Married Woman's Property Act was passed in New York, allowing married women to act as if single with respect to property.[10] **1974** The Equal Opportunity Act was passed, allowing women to apply for credit without a man to cosign.[11]
Women are less "technical" than men.[12]	**Mid 1950s** As many as half of computing jobs were held by women.[13] **1991** 36 percent of computing jobs were held by women.[14]	**2017** Only 25 percent of computing jobs were held by women.[15]

APPENDIX C
A History of Women's Rights*

August 26, 1920
The 19th Amendment is ratified; women have the right to vote.

1932
Hattie Wyatt Caraway becomes the first woman elected to the Senate for a full term.[1]

1947
Women are excluded from serving on juries in 16 states.[2]

1963
Katharine Graham becomes the first female CEO of a Fortune 500 company (the *Washington Post*).[3]

1964
The Civil Rights Act passes, outlawing discrimination based on race or sex.

1968
Shirley Chisholm becomes the first African American woman in Congress and the first woman to seek the presidency.

1972
Title IX legislation passes, opening up the doorway for equal opportunities in education for women.

1974
Legislation passes that prohibits discrimination in credit based on gender and race.

1978
Discrimination against pregnant women is banned for the first time.

1981
Sandra Day O'Connor becomes the first female Supreme Court justice.

1988
Ronald Reagan signs H.R. 5050 into law, superseding state laws that female entrepreneurs no longer need a man to cosign a business loan.[4]

---

* See page 242 for citation information.

1993
Senators Barbara Mikulski, Nancy Kassebaum, and Carol Moseley Braun wear "pants on the Senate floor, breaking an unofficial rule that women must wear dresses or skirts."[5]

1994
Supreme Court bans states from excluding women in juries.[6]

2010
Women are now 47% of the workforce.[7]

2011
House of Representatives gets a female restroom on the House floor.[8]

2013
Women can now serve in military combat.[9]

2017
"Congress has a record number of women, with 104 female House members and 21 female Senators, including the chamber's first Latina, Nevada senator Catherine Cortez Masto."[10]

2017
Women wear sleeveless tops to protest the House dress code barring it.[11]

2018
Under Armour bans expensing strip-club visits on corporate card.[12]

2019
Women are 22.5% of Fortune 500 boards. African American appointees to boards have doubled over the past decade. Hispanic appointees stayed stagnant at 4%. Asian American appointees have 8%.[13] Women are only 5% of CEOs in the S&P 500.[14]

APPENDIX D
Quantify Risks

Use this scorecard to evaluate your organization on each of the categories and quantify the risks. What does this tell you? Are there areas of immediate priority because they have a high potential return and are relatively easy to implement?

How would you evaluate your company or team?

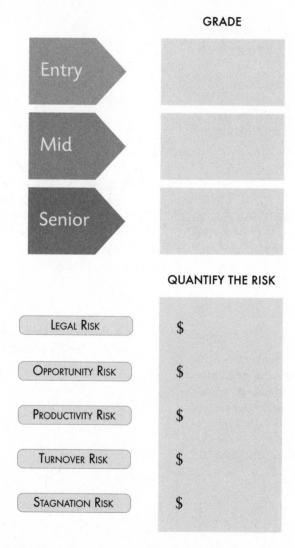

GRADE

Entry

Mid

Senior

QUANTIFY THE RISK

LEGAL RISK — $

OPPORTUNITY RISK — $

PRODUCTIVITY RISK — $

TURNOVER RISK — $

STAGNATION RISK — $

For more tools, visit orangegroveconsulting.com/nextsmartstep.

APPENDIX E
Mini Self-Assessment Tool

Please take a moment to answer, as truthfully as you can, the following true/false questions.

1. I think women and minority groups should be represented in companies in the same proportions as they are represented in the general population.

   TRUE | FALSE

2. I want to improve the amount of diversity on my team.

   TRUE | FALSE

3. In general, I feel people get hired and promoted based on merit.

   TRUE | FALSE

4. We should not focus on promoting diversity and inclusion because it will happen on its own.

   TRUE | FALSE

5. My team is comprised of 50 percent women and 30 percent minority group representation.

   TRUE | FALSE

6. Most members of my team have background experience and skills similar to mine.

   TRUE | FALSE

7. People in my LinkedIn network come from a broad variety of industries and background experiences and represent many different demographic groups including age, gender, and race.

   TRUE | FALSE

8. I treat everyone the same, regardless of differences.

   TRUE | FALSE

(continued)

Mini Self-Assessment Tool *(continued)*

9. My team actively takes a customized approach to different demographic group communities, such as offering custom products or service responses.

   TRUE | FALSE

10. It takes too much time to include everyone's perspective and doesn't necessarily give a better result.

    TRUE | FALSE

11. I am comfortable facilitating a boisterous team discussion about bias.

    TRUE | FALSE

12. I prefer for people to be professional and leave their personal lives at home.

    TRUE | FALSE

13. Sometimes my team gets better results going in a different direction than I would have done.

    TRUE | FALSE

14. Sometimes I find actively including women or different demographic groups negatively impacts performance.

    TRUE | FALSE

15. My team often debates the process of decision-making before we tackle the decision itself.

    TRUE | FALSE

16. I find that people who fit well into our culture also perform well.

    TRUE | FALSE

To score:

Question	TRUE	FALSE	LEVEL
1	1	0	D
2	1	0	D
3	0	1	D
4	0	1	D
5	1	0	I
6	0	1	I
7	1	0	I
8	0	1	I
9	1	0	E
10	0	1	E
11	1	0	E
12	0	1	E
13	1	0	S
14	0	1	S
15	1	0	S
16	0	1	S

	Diversity	Inclusion	Engagement	Synthesis	Total
Score					

Circle the level with your highest score. This is your focus taxonomy level. What will it take for you to move to the next level?

Overall Recommendation:

0-7 Keep reading! Hopefully our book can provide a new perspective for you.

8-13 You are on your way to developing crucial leadership skills. Keep going!

14-16 You have high potential for leading the workplace of the future!

For more tools, visit orangegroveconsulting.com/nextsmartstep.

APPENDIX F
Diversity Capability Rubric

Below is an organizational framework and rubric to help you categorize the leadership capabilities and visualize different levels of performance for each. How does this apply to you? To the leaders who work for you?

		BELOW EXPECTATIONS
Diversity Level	**Diverse Inspiration:** Inspire others to take action – Understands why this matters to this person, what need is not being met. – Genuineness; real concern for people. Intellectual curiosity.	Doesn't see value in diversity, thinks this is a low priority. Ignores or maligns women and/or minorities. Ignorance about the problem. Blind to their privilege. Can't discern between being "politically correct" and small acts of disrespect.
Inclusion Level	**Diversity Intelligence:** Includes: – Bias Awareness – Gender Intelligence – Cultural Intelligence – Intersectionality – Willingness to take steps to remove bias	Hires and promotes only white men or people with non-diverse backgrounds/ same context. Has a homogeneous team. Has token representation of women and minorities. Doesn't believe in bias despite evidence.
Engagement Level	**Engaged Direction:** Set vision, direction, and a compelling course of action – Believes in the cause – Calculates expected diversity gains into projections	Ignores dissonant voices on the team. Pays lip service to listening but doesn't change or include new perspectives. Says people have to behave "normally." Fights against changing norms. Determines value of contribution based on delivery being "normal" (e.g., extrovert v. introvert, accent, dress style, hair, etc.).
	Empowering Influence: Persuade and influence in all directions – Ability to have or facilitate difficult conversations between diverse individuals – Ability to manage conflict between diverse groups – Ability to influence and persuade others to be more inclusive/tell a compelling diversity story – Credibility of influencer audience	Unable to transcend group politics or persuade others on non-popular decisions or issues.

Meets Expectations	Exceeds Expectations
Brings attention to issue of diversity and asks organization to focus on it. Displays genuine interest in learning more. May still operate with homogeneous workgroups.	Demonstrates commitment to the cause with highly visible stake-in-the-ground move such as hiring 50% women on the team. Consciously disbands the homogeneous work-groups.
Hires and promotes a wide variety of different backgrounds and perspectives to the team. Comfortable with different cultures/genders. May still have homogeneous "power cliques."	Has a sustained history of hiring and promoting people from diverse backgrounds. Views including difference as integral to the team. Consciously disbands the homogeneous "power cliques."
Facilitates new ways of engaging and considering different perspectives in team. Includes different perspectives in team direction. Envisions what diversity can/will add to team in future. Recognizes bias in others and how this may be impacting team (e.g., man commenting on a woman's looks and she shuts down; mansplaining).	Anticipates and plans for different future as team diversity evolves. Discussion facilitation at expert level. Ability to discern substance from style in contributions. Acts on bias in others (e.g., allyship behaviors, sponsorship, standing up).
Able to influence others to do the right thing for all group members.	Has a history of managing many conflict situations to exceptional outcomes.

(continued)

Diversity Capability Rubric (continued)

Engagement Level	**Building Talent with Voice:** Develop people for competitive advantage – Can tell the difference between poor performance and diverse/different performance – Has the ability to recognize real performance	Has a homogeneous team. Has subpar women and minorities on team to look good but not getting performance gains. Cannot discern performance.
Synthesis Level	**Agile Execution:** Get teams to achieve results – Fosters an inclusive culture; creates psychological safety – Adaptability: Uses testing and experimentation, and willing to change while we learn; being a work in progress; accepting feedback to further learning – Intellectual courage – Endurance; perseverance. Willingness to persist even after mistakes or pushback – Open mindset; open to feedback	Fails to create a safe environment for all team members (low team member trust). Culture contains bullying, self-censorship, and exclusion.
	Collaboration: Collaborate with others – Integrates diverse perspectives to approach problems creatively. – Perspective Taking: The ability to hold multiple viewpoints at the same time	Unable to integrate diverse perspectives or collaborate with anyone different than themselves. Unable or unwilling to acknowledge different perspectives and truths.
	Competitive Edge: Know their markets and innovate to stay ahead – Committed to developing the skills to lead diverse teams. – Committed to creating a diverse and inclusive team – Considers customer diversity and is committed to developing an innovative approach to diverse customer sets	Excludes groups from customer offerings and ignores rising trends.
	Inclusive Business Judgment: Make business decisions that drive positive bottom-line performance – Sees value and has quantified potential return on investment in improving skills for leading diverse teams (reduced turnover, team productivity, innovation, etc.)	Decision-making contains bias and self-interest/self-preservation. Focuses only on certain stakeholders.

Meets Expectations	Exceeds Expectations
Manages a diverse and high-performing team. Can exercise effective performance discernment.	Has a history of developing diverse and high-performing individuals who have gone on to do great things for the organization and on other teams.
Fosters a safe and supportive team culture for all members. Is willing to learn and adapt to evolving minority group dynamics. Holds group to high performance standards.	Creates an organization-wide performance culture supportive to all employees. The way business is done fundamentally changes.
Integrates diverse perspectives but one or two perspectives still dominate. Ideas often stay within a particular group and are not shared.	Integrates diverse perspectives to create new ideas and more robust decisions. Mainstreams the variety of ideas. Spreads ideas so that everyone gets better (e.g., multiple factories, sharing best practice and continuing to improve).
Able to integrate diverse customer market knowledge into innovative product and service offerings.	Has a demonstrated history of building industry-leading, innovative products and services offers that include all groups.
Decision-making is based on objective standards and includes diverse perspectives. Able to weigh multiple stakeholders' interests.	Has a history of decisions that have driven positive performance and included diverse interests. Able to leverage multiple stakeholders' interests, even if competing.

APPENDIX G
Women's Bad Habits, Rules, Assumptions, and Possible Reframes

Bad Habits	→	Rules
Acquiescing and doing it alone Working harder, not smarter Self-sacrificing	→	Do it all.
Avoiding risk and over-compensating Catastrophizing Creating a diversion Seeking external validation	→	Look good.
Lowering career and reward expectations Avoiding asking for challenges or what we need	→	Be nice.

Assumptions	→	Reframes

Women are primarily responsible for home and family; career is secondary.

Our commitment to something is measured by how much time we devote to it.

Anything I do for myself is selfish.

→

We are all responsible for home and family and earning a living.

I work smarter to fulfill my purpose.

My needs are equal.

We need to be perfect in behavior and appearance at all times.

We are never "good enough."

→

Doing my best and "good enough" are perfectly acceptable.

I am a good person and I am a work in progress.

We are not entitled to time, money, and power-based rewards.

If we follow the rules, we will be taken care of.

→

I am paid what the work is worth.

I take responsibility for myself and ask for what I need.

APPENDIX H

Men's Bad Habits, Rules, Assumptions, and Possible Reframes

Bad Habits	→	Rules
Working all the time; letting wife run family responsibilities Putting self second; assuming women, not men, need work-life balance Taking credit and displaying false confidence Self-promoting and working late	→	Earn it all.
Competing, not collaborating; interrupting Hiding true self at work Overreacting with anger and showing no empathy Protecting women; failing to provide feedback Mansplaining and patronizing	→	Look strong.
Sabotaging women, overtly or benignly; setting women up for failure Reinforcing stereotypes and excluding Talking negatively about women and second-guessing women's work Hitting on women at work; objectifying women	→	Be the Man.

Assumptions	→	Reframes

Assumptions	Reframes
Men are the providers. Men are primarily responsible for earning a living; home life is secondary. Look successful and important.	We are all responsible for home and family and earning a living. Be authentic.
Demonstrate strength. Protect those who are weaker, i.e., women and children.	Vulnerability is acceptable. Challenge others to grow and learn.
Women are a threat. Women are less competent. I am worthy and important when I get sexual attention.	Together we can do more. Competence is independent of gender; I can discern the difference. I am worthy and important just as I am.

APPENDIX I

Overcoming Bias in the Recruitment Process

1. **Identifying Need**—Sometimes people have a particular gender in mind when they envision a role or types of roles offered. They look to hire another "accounting girl" or "technical guy." Sometimes, people assume that to fill a role with intensive hours or travel, that only young men will be interested. Similarly, if the role involves caregiving, they tend to assume women will fit the bill. These stereotypes run deep and are completely unconscious. But if a particular gender is in mind as early as when the need is identified, it becomes easy for bias to slip in all along the recruiting chain, from how the job description is written to the criteria for determining the final candidate, and hard to create a neutral and inclusive recruiting platform. For example, when hiring an administrative position, the hiring committee needs to stop saying "she." We work with companies to assess new-hire needs by work function, job characteristics, and skill requirements.

2. **Posting the Job**—How a job is posted, where it is advertised, and what words are used to describe the role can also signal the unconsciously desired gender of candidates. Even the faces that appear on recruiting posters and who sits at the recruiting table can be leading. Aggressive words like dominate, competitive environment, and ninja can turn off female candidates as these words are deemed by experts as masculine. Words like team, collaborative environment, and supportive are considered more feminine.[239233] We recommend eliminating adjectives about personality from job descriptions and instead sticking to the skills required for the job.

   This is further complicated by who applies. A research study done by Hewlett-Packard tells us that women will apply only for roles where they have 100 percent of the job characteristics whereas men will apply when they only have 60 percent.[240] So a laundry list of skills, more than any single candidate can possibly have, will reduce the number of women who apply. In her book *What Works: Gender Equality by Design*, Iris Bohnet suggests limiting the number of qualifications needed to just those absolutely required for the job.

We recommend posting jobs where women and minorities can find them. That could include recruiting from colleges that graduate a more diverse student body, not simply the colleges existing employees attended. Organizations can hire specialists to train about how to hire underrepresented people, such as Rework Work,[241] and build relationships with matching firms that identify underrepresented candidates with required skill sets such as ReacHire.[242] Companies can also employ recruiting companies that go further than simply looking at like firms but know how to tap more unorthodox candidate pools. Some organizations require their recruiting firms to return lists that have at least 30 percent women with representation from other underrepresented groups as well.

A word of caution about recruiters: One of the problems with recruiting comes from using recruiters. Recruiters can be helpful because they often have a vast network of candidates who work in the same job at other companies in the same industry. The problem is that this can narrow the candidate pool. And if those companies did not recruit diversely, then the effect is compounded and self-reinforcing. Remember our simulation story from Chapter 4 with the devastating impact of a 1 percent bias? The bias gets exacerbated when companies allow other companies' biases into their organization. We suggest reminding recruiters about the organization's diversity goals and requiring a diverse slate of candidates. Further, we recommend making recruiters work harder to find candidates from other jobs in other industries who have transferable skills and could potentially bring a fresh perspective to the company and industry.

We've already talked about how using recruiters can compound bias and limit candidate pools. Often companies look to their own employee relationships and networks to find candidates as well. But the thing about our personal networks is that they don't tend to be very diverse. People initially gravitate towards meeting people who look like they do and are more likely to continue the relationship if they act similarly, like the same things, do similar work, and generally agree. So teams and companies become uniform. Often networks contain the same connections as those of other network members, meaning the network doesn't have a lot of breadth.[243] So if you hope to add a new, diverse dimension to your organization, and if the organization is not terribly diverse, then you are not likely to find that diversity from your employees' networks.

3. **Reviewing & Selecting Candidate Resumes**—Research has consistently identified that resume review and selection is inherently biased.[244] Gender and race can be guessed by names, clubs and affiliations, schools, the font used, and even home addresses. Then there is the "he reminds me of me" factor—who is doing the resume review can skew whose resumes move on. Age bias also can play a role when a resume has too many dates or it's been a long time since the candidate's graduation from college. Since pre-identifying gender, age, and race unconsciously influences decision-making, we recommend removing all potentially gender, age, or race-identifying information from resumes before review. This includes the name of the candidate's college. That may seem controversial, but consider again what we shared about there being a disproportionate number of senior leaders who are tall, named John, and come from one of only a few schools.[245] School pedigree is given disproportionate weighting in most situations and is a strong signal of racial and even socioeconomic background.[246] For most jobs out there, it is the degree that matters, not the school. So take out the school—assuming the candidate has the educational qualifications, you don't need it.

> One way to ensure that a diverse candidate is hired is to ensure a diverse resume set is forwarded. Again, this is not about setting a quota for each underrepresented group, but rather to ensure that the candidate resumes that move to the interview stage present a broad range of backgrounds, experiences, and cultural contexts. The percentage of resumes reviewed should reflect the national or local candidate market (e.g. the percentage of women and engineers of color) overall. When there is only one female or candidate of color in the pool, the status-quo bias effect suggests that person has zero probability of being selected.[247] Look at that again: *zero* chance. Mirroring the percentages nationally helps to offset this effect. Many organizations that have implemented mirrored target candidate pools have found a significant increase in the number women and people of color hired.

4. **Interviewing**—Warning! Interviewing is a significant danger area for the introduction of bias. First, our brains love to jump to instant conclusions about people based on millions of nonverbal cues from dress, cleanliness, handshake strength, posture and body position, and facial expressions. If someone reminds us of someone we know, we form an opinion based on that other person. All of this can happen even before someone speaks.

Second, there is no real way to disguise gender, age, or race in an interview. So our unconscious biases build. A well-known experiment was conducted with auditions for an orchestra, which demonstrated that when interviewers knew the gender of the player, men were selected more often, but when they auditioned behind a screen with a carpet to disguise shoe sounds, the proportion of women selected grew measurably.[248]

Since instant decision-making without objective reflection, coupled with a lack of structure, can introduce significant bias into the process and can result in a less-objective decision-making process, we recommend slowing down the interview process to ensure that interviewers don't jump to conclusions while collecting data.[249] Structure matters significantly—in study after study, unstructured interviews yielded poor results.

Hiring managers need to reflect on their pre-agreed, specific, measurable criteria, stick to asking objective questions and grade candidates accordingly. It is important to approach the process as a scientist, using impartial inquiry to unearth as much information as the candidate is willing to share. One problem arises when a candidate shares too little information because that allows interviewers to fill in blanks with assumptions. Getting candidates to do the talking (instead of the interviewer) and ensuring everyone shares equally can be a critical interview skill.

Using multiple interviewers doesn't guarantee elimination of bias, but it does help, particularly if each interviewer is prepared to evaluate candidates from a slightly different perspective. This means preparing as a team before interviews to ensure each interviewer elicits different background stories and experiences from the candidate so they can compare and paint a more nuanced candidate picture. Interview candidates individually so candidates are put at ease and to ensure that comparison of the interview results is not skewed by groupthink.[250] Videotaping interviews can also help to observe where bias might take place.

Interviewing is a key element for determining who are the right people to hire. Training for those doing interviewing so they are evaluated on the efficacy of their interview skills makes this a clear skill not an ad hoc task.

5. **Candidate Selection / Decision-Making**—Some common problems we have seen include situations where standard hiring criteria is set before the job gets posted, but then when it comes time to make the decisions, these criteria are ignored or weighted lower than candidate-specific characteristics or factors.

For example, a male candidate has less experience than a female one, but the male candidate played football for Notre Dame, as did the interviewer, and they have a lot in common. So the fact that the man is a good guy and more familiar culturally to the interviewer outweighs the female candidate's experience. Words like fit and social skills are nebulous, subjective categories that often allow lots of bias without providing good information relevant to decision-making. There are also biases about what leadership should look like that creep into candidate selection at the decision-making stage. We have heard statements like, "They'd rather have a mediocre balding man who looks like their vision of a leader than a giggly but highly qualified, high-performing woman."

BIBLIOGRAPHY

Abbate, Janet. *Recoding Gender: Women's Changing Participation in Computing.* Cambridge, MA: MIT Press, 2012.

Abouzahr, Katie, Matt Krentz, Claire Tracey, and Miki Tsusaka. "Dispelling the Myths of the Gender 'Ambition Gap.'" Boston Consulting Group, April 5, 2017.

"America's Women and the Wage Gap." National Partnership for Women and Families, September 2019.

Aronson, Joshua, Michael J. Lustina, Catherine Good, Kelli Keough, Claude M. Steele, and Joseph Brown. "When White Men Can't Do Math: Necessary and Sufficient Factors in Stereotype Threat." *Journal of Experimental Social Psychology* 35, no. 1 (1999): 29–46.

Babcock, Linda, and Sara Laschever. *Ask for It: How Women Can Use the Power of Negotiation to Get What They Really Want.* New York: Bantam, February 2008.

Babcock, Linda, and Sara Laschever. *Women Don't Ask: The High Cost of Avoiding Negotiation—and Positive Strategies for Change.* New York: Bantam, February 2007.

Banyard, Victoria, Elizabethe G. Plante, and Mary M. Moynihan. "Bystander Education: Bringing a Broader Community Perspective to Sexual Violence Prevention." *Journal of Community Psychology* 32, no. 1 (January 2004): 61-79.

Barsh, Joanna, and Lareina Yee. "Unlocking the Full Potential of Women at Work." McKinsey & Company, 2012.

Bauer, Gerrit. "Gender Roles, Comparative Advantages and the Life Course: The Division of Domestic Labor in Same-Sex and Different-Sex Couples." *European Journal of Population* 32, no. 1 (2016): 99-128.

Bear, Julia, and Peter Glick. "Gendered Rewards: Breadwinner Versus Caregiver Status Affects Workplace Rewards for Men and Women." *Academy of Management Proceedings* 2016, no. 1 (2016).

Beard, Alison. "Why Are We Still Promoting Incompetent Men?" *Harvard Business Review,* March 12, 2019.

Behson, Scott. "Why Two-Income Families Are Happier Than Single Earner Households." *Good Men Project,* February 25, 2013.

Berdahl, Jennifer L., Marianne Cooper, Peter Glick, Robert W. Livingston, and Joan C. Williams. "Work as A Masculinity Contest." *Journal of Social Issues* 74, no. 3 (2018): 442-448.

Berdahl, Jennifer L., Peter Glick, and Marianne Cooper. "How Masculinity Contests Undermine Organizations, and What to Do About It." *Harvard Business Review,* November 2, 2018.

"Beyond Wages: Effects of the Latina Wage Gap." National Partnership for Women and Families, November 2018.

"Black Women and the Wage Gap." National Partnership for Women and Families, April 2019.

Bohnet, Iris. *What Works: Gender Equality by Design.* Cambridge, MA: The Belknap Press of Harvard University Press, 2016.

Bohnet, Iris. "How to Take Bias Out of Interviews." *Harvard Business Review,* April 18, 2016.

Bosson, Jennifer K., Amber B. Johnson, Kate Niederhoffer, and William B. Swann Jr. "Interpersonal Chemistry Through Negativity: Bonding by Sharing Negative Attitudes about Others." *Personal Relationships* 13, no. 2 (May 9, 2006): 135-150.

Bourke, Juliet, and Ardie van Berkel. "Diversity and Inclusion: The Reality Gap." Deloitte Insights, February 28, 2017.

Braunstein, Elissa. "The Feminist Political Economy of the Rent-Seeking Society: An Investigation of Gender Inequality and Economic Growth." *Journal of Economic Issues* 42, no. 4 (December 2008): 959-979.

Bridges, William. *Managing Transitions: Making the Most of Change.* Boston: Da Capo Press, September 22, 2009.

Brown, Brené. *I Thought It Was Just Me (But It Isn't): Making the Journey From "What Will People Think?" to "I Am Enough."* New York: Avery, February 2007.

Castilla, Emilio J. "Gender, Race, and Meritocracy in Organizational Careers." *American Journal of Sociology* 113, no. 6 (2008): 1479–1526.

Cecci-Dimeglio, Paola. "How Gender Bias Corrupts Performance Reviews, and What to Do About It." *Harvard Business Review,* April 12, 2017.

Centola, Damon, Joshua Becker, Devon Brackbill, and Andrea Baronchelli. "Experimental Evidence for Tipping Points in Social Convention." *Science* 360, no. 6393. (June 8, 2018): 1116-1119.

Cha, Youngjoo. "Reinforcing Separate Spheres: The Effect of Spousal Overwork on Men's and Women's Employment in Dual-Earner Households." *American Sociological Review* 75, no. 2 (April 1, 2010): 307.

Cheeks, Maura. "How Black Women Describe Navigating Race and Gender in the Workplace." *Harvard Business Review,* March 26, 2018.

Clifton, Jim. "The World's Broken Workplace." Gallup, June 13, 2017.

Cohen, Philip N., and Matt L. Huffman. "Working for the Woman?: Female Managers and the Gender Wage Gap." *American Sociological Review* 72, no. 5 (2007): 681-704.

Contu, Diane. "Why Teams Don't Work." *Harvard Business Review,* May 2009.

Delizonna, Laura. "High-Performing Teams Need Psychological Safety. Here's How to Create It." *Harvard Business Review,* August 24, 2017.

DeGroot, Jessica, and Jodi Detjen. "Transformative Flex." Third Path, Philadelphia, 2018.

Detjen, Jodi Ecker, Michelle A. Waters, and Kelly Watson. *The Orange Line: A Woman's Guide to Integrating Career, Family, and Life.* Newton, MA: JMK Publishing, May 2013.

Dobbin, Frank, and Alexandra Kalev. "Why Diversity Programs Fail." *Harvard Business Review* 94, July-August 2016.

Duffin, Erin. "Bachelor's Degrees Earned in the United States by Gender 1950-2029." Statista, May 20, 2019.

Duguid, Michelle. "Female Tokens in High-Prestige Work Groups: Catalysts or Inhibitors of Group Diversification?" *Organizational Behavior and Human Decision Processes* 116, no. 1 (2011): 104-115.

Dweck, Carol S. *Mindset: The New Psychology of Success.* New York: Ballantine Books, December 26, 2007.

Dyble, Mark, Gul Deniz Salali, Nikhil Chaudhary, Abigail E. Page, Daniel Smith, J. Thompson, Lucio Vinicius, Ruth Mace, and Andrea Bamberg Migliano. "Sex Equality Can Explain the Unique Social Structure of Hunter-Gatherer Bands." *Science* 348, no. 6236 (2015): 796–98.

Edmondson, Amy. "Psychological Safety and Learning Behavior in Work Teams." *Administrative Science Quarterly* 44, no. 2 (1999): 350-383.

Edmonson, Amy. *The Fearless Organization: Creating Psychological Safety in the Workplace for Learning, Innovation and Growth.* Hoboken, NJ: Wiley, 2018.

Eliot, Lise. *Pink Brain, Blue Brain: How Small Differences Grow into Troublesome Gaps–and What We Can Do about It.* Boston: Mariner Books, 2010.

Ellingrud, Kweilin, Mekala Krishnan, and Anu Madgavkar. "Miles to Go: Stepping Up Progress Toward Gender Equality." McKinsey & Company, September 2016.

Ely, Robin J., and Debra E. Meyerson. "An Organizational Approach to Undoing Gender: The Unlikely Case of Offshore Oil Platforms." *Research in Organizational Behavior* 30 (October 2010): 3–34.

England, Kim, and Kate Boyer. "Women's Work: The Feminization and Shifting Meanings of Clerical Work." *Journal of Social History* 43, no. 2 (2009): 307–340.

England, Paula, Paul Allison, and Yuxiao Wu. "Does Bad Pay Cause Occupations to Feminize, Does Feminization Reduce Pay, and How Can We Tell with Longitudinal Data?" *Social Science Research* 36, no. 3 (2007): 1237-1256.

Evans, Claire L. *Broad Band: The Untold Story of the Women Who Made the Internet.* New York: Portfolio, 2018.

Eveleth, Rose. "Computer Programming Used to be Women's Work: Computer Programmers are Expected to be Male and Antisocial—a Self-fulfilling Prophesy that Forgets the Women that the Entire Field was Built Upon." *Smithsonian Magazine,* October 7, 2013.

Francis, David R. "Employers' Replies to Racial Names." National Bureau of Economic Research, September 2003.

Frankel, Lois P. *Nice Girls Still Don't Get the Corner Office: Unconscious Mistakes Women Make That Sabotage Their Careers.* New York: Business Plus, 2014.

Gaucher, Danielle, Justin Friesen, and Aaron C. Kay. "Evidence That Gendered Wording in Job Advertisements Exists and Sustains Gender Inequality." *Journal of Personality & Social Psychology* 101, no. 1 (July 2011): 109–128.

Giles, Sunny. "The Most Important Leadership Competencies, According to Leaders Around the World." *Harvard Business Review,* March 15, 2016.

Glauber, Rebecca. "Trends in the Motherhood Wage Penalty and Fatherhood Wage Premium for Low, Middle, and High Earners." *Demography* 55, no. 5 (October 2018): 1663–1680.

Goldin, Claudia, and Cecilia Rouse. "Orchestrating Impartiality: The Impact of 'Blind' Auditions on Female Musicians." *American Economic Review* 90, no. 4 (September 2000): 715-741.

Groot, Gertjan de, and Marlou Schrover. "Between Men and Machines: Women Workers in New Industries, 1870–1940." *Social History* 20, no. 3 (1995).

Grote, Dick. "Let's Abolish Self-Appraisal." *Harvard Business Review*, July 11, 2011.

"Global Generations: A Global Study on Work-Life Challenges Across Generations." Ernst & Young, 2015.

Harrington, Brad, Jennifer Sabatini Fraone, and Jegoo Lee. "The New Dad: The Career-Caregiving Conflict." Boston College Center for Work & Family, 2017.

Heinemann, Sue. *Timelines of American Women's History.* New York: Penguin, 1996.

Hewlett, Sylvia Ann, Laura Sherbin, Fabiola Dieudonné, Christina Fargnoli, and Catherine Fredman. "Athena Factor 2.0: Accelerating Female Talent in Science, Engineering & Technology." Center for Talent Innovation, 2014.

"Highlights of Women's Earnings in 2017." U.S. Bureau of Labor Statistics, August 2018.

Honeyman, Katrina, and Jordan Goodman. "Women's Work, Gender Conflict, and Labour Markets in Europe, 1500-1900." *Economic History Review* 44, no. 4 (1991): 608-628.

Houghton, Luke, and David Tuffley. "Towards a Methodology of Wicked Problem Exploration through Concept Shifting and Tension Point Analysis: Concept Shifting and Tension Point Analysis." *Behavioral Science* 32, no. 3 (October 2013): 294.

Hunt, Vivian, Dennis Layton, and Sara Prince. "Why Diversity Matters." McKinsey & Company, January 1, 2015.

Huselid, Mark, Brian Becker, and Richard Beatty. *The Workforce Scorecard: Managing Human Capital to Execute Strategy.* Brighton, MA: Harvard Business Review Press, 2005.

Ibarra, Herminia, and Jennifer Petriglieri. "Impossible Selves: Image Strategies and Identity Threat in Professional Women's Career Transitions." INSEAD Working Paper, March 4, 2016.

Ibarra, Herminia, and Mark Hunter. "How Leaders Create and Use Networks." *Harvard Business Review* 85, no. 1 (January 2007): 40–47.

Johnson, W. Brad, and David Smith. *Athena Rising: How and Why Men Should Mentor Women.* Brookline, MA: Bibliomotion, 2016.

Johnson, W. Brad, and David Smith. "How Men Can Become Better Allies to Women." *Harvard Business Review*, October 12, 2018.

Johnson, Stefanie K., Ksenia Keplinger, Jessica F. Kirk, and Liza Barnes. "Has Sexual Harassment at Work Decreased Since #MeToo?" *Harvard Business Review*, July 18, 2019.

Johnson, Stefanie K., David R. Hekman, and Elsa T. Chan. "If There's Only One Woman in Your Candidate Pool, There's Statistically No Chance She'll Be Hired." *Harvard Business Review*, April 26 2016.

Joshi, Aparna, and Andrew P. Knight. "Who Defers to Whom and Why? Dual Pathways Linking Demographic Differences and Dyadic Deference to Team Effectiveness." *Academy of Management Journal* 58, no. 1 (April 28, 2014).

Kahneman, Daniel. *Thinking, Fast and Slow.* New York: Farrar, Straus and Giroux, 2011.

Kay, Katty, and Claire Shipman. *The Confidence Code: The Science and Art of Self-Assurance What Women Should Know.* New York: Harper Business, April 2014.

Kegan, Robert, and Lisa Laskow Lahey. *Immunity to Change: How to Overcome It and Unlock the Potential in Yourself and Your Organization.* Brighton, MA: Harvard Business Review Press, 2009.

Knight, Rebecca. "7 Practical Ways to Reduce Bias in Your Hiring Process." *Harvard Business Review,* June 12, 2017.

Krivkovich, Alexis. "Women in the Workplace 2018: Progress on Gender Diversity at Work Has Stalled. To Achieve Equality Companies Must Turn Good Intentions into Concrete Action." McKinsey & Company, October 2018.

Kumra, Savita, and Susan Vinnicombe. "Impressing for Success: A Gendered Analysis of a Key Social Capital Accumulation Strategy." *Gender, Work & Organization* 17, no. 5 (September 2010): 521–546.

Lent, Richard M. *Leading Great Meetings: How to Structure Yours for Success.* Stow, MA: Meeting for Results, 2015.

Levanon, Asaf, Paula England, and Paul Allison. "Occupational Feminization and Pay: Assessing Causal Dynamics Using 1950-2000 U.S. Census Data." *Social Forces* 88, no. 2 (December 1, 2009): 865–91.

Levant, Ronald F., and Katherine Richmond. "A Review of Research on Masculinity Ideologies Using the Male Role Norms Inventory." *Journal of Men's Studies* 15, no. 2 (July 31, 2016): 130–146.

Livermore, David. *Leading with Cultural Intelligence: The Real Secret to Success.* New York: AMACOM, 2015.

Martell, Richard F., David M. Lane, and Cynthia Emrich. "Male-Female Differences: A Computer Solution." *American Psychologist* 51, no. 2 (February 1996): 157-158.

Morwick, Jason M., Emily A. Klein, Robyn Bews, and Tim Lorman. *Workshift: Future-Proof Your Organization for the 21st Century.* New York: Palgrave Macmillan, 2013.

Moss-Racusin, Corinne A., John F. Dovidio, Victoria L. Brescoll, Mark J. Graham, and Jo Handelsman. "Science Faculty's Subtle Gender Biases Favor Male Students." *Proceedings of the National Academy of Sciences of the United States of America* 109, no. 41 (October 9, 2012): 16474-16479.

Murrell, Audrey J., and Stacy Blake-Beard. *Mentoring Diverse Leaders: Creating Change for People, Processes, and Paradigms.* London: Taylor and Francis, 2017.

Nickerson, Jordan. "Market Forces and CEO Pay: Shocks to CEO Demand Induced by IPO Waves." *Review of Financial Studies* 30, no. 7 (2017): 2272–2312.

Noonan, David. "The 25% Revolution—How Big Does A Minority Have to be to Reshape Society?" *Scientific American,* June 8, 2018.

Oliver, Tom H., Matthew S. Heard, et al. "Biodiversity and Resilience of Ecosystem Functions." *Trends in Ecology & Evolution* 30, no. 11 (November 2015): 673-684.

Padavic, Irene, Robin J. Ely, and Erin M. Reid. "Explaining the Persistence of Gender Inequality: The Work–family Narrative as a Social Defense against the 24/7 Work Culture." *Administrative Science Quarterly* 65, no. 1 (February 14, 2019): 61-111.

Paustian-Underdahl, Samantha C., Lisa Slattery Walker, and David J. Woehr. "Gender and Perceptions of Leadership Effectiveness: A Meta-Analysis of Contextual Moderators." *Journal of Applied Psychology* 99, no. 6 (November 2014): 1129–1145.

Phillips, Katherine W. "The Biases That Punish Racially Diverse Teams." *Harvard Business Review*, February 22, 2016.

Pink, Daniel H. *Drive: The Surprising Truth About What Motivates Us*. New York: Riverhead Books, 2009.

Rabinowitz, Noah, et. al. *Leadership Capability Modeling: Introducing the Next-Generation Competency Model*. Atlanta: Deloitte Development LLC, 2018.

Reid, Erin. "Whether a Husband Identifies as a Breadwinner Depends on Whether He Respects His Wife's Career—Not on How Much She Earns." *Harvard Business Review*, August 15, 2018.

Robbins, Mike. *Be Yourself, Everyone Else is Already Taken*. San Francisco: Jossey-Bass, 2009.

Robbins, Mike. *Bring Your Whole Self to Work: How Vulnerability Unlocks Creativity, Connection, and Performance*. Carlsbad, CA: Hay House, 2018.

Sandberg, Sheryl. *Lean In: Women, Work, and the Will to Lead*. New York: Alfred A. Knopf, 2013.

Schein, Edgar H. *The Corporate Culture Survival Guide*. San Francisco: Wiley, 2009.

Schwarz, Roger. "Getting Teams with Different Subcultures to Collaborate." *Harvard Business Review*, July 22, 2016.

Scully, Maureen, and Mary Rowe. "Bystander Training within Organizations." *Journal of the International Ombudsman Association* 2, no. 1 (2009): 1-9.

Seeberger, Colin. "Nearly Two-Thirds of Mothers Continue to be Family Breadwinners, Black Mothers Are Far More Likely to be Breadwinners." Center for American Progress, May 10, 2019.

Shih, Margaret, Todd L. Pittinsky, and Nalini Ambady. "Stereotype Susceptibility: Identity Salience and Shifts in Quantitative Performance." *Psychological Science* 10, no. 1 (January 1999): 80–83.

Siebert, Scott E., Maria L. Kraimer, and Robert C. Liden. "A Social Capital Theory of Career Success." *Academy of Management Journal* 44, no. 2 (April 2001): 219–237.

Smith, David G., Judith E. Rosenstein, and Margaret C. Nikolov. "The Different Words We Use to Describe Male and Female Leaders." *Harvard Business Review*, May 25, 2018.

Sneader, Kevin, and Lareina Yee. "One Is the Loneliest Number: Put an End to Costly Workplace Isolation Experienced by Many Women by Clustering Them on Teams and Improving the Promotion Process." McKinsey & Company, January 2019.

Snow, Shane. *Dream Teams: Working Together Without Falling Apart*. New York: Portfolio Books, 2018.

Solomon, Lou. "Two-Thirds of Managers Are Uncomfortable Communicating With Employees." *Harvard Business Review*, March 2016: 2–5.

Steele, Claude. *Whistling Vivaldi: How Stereotypes Affect Us and What We Can Do*. New York: W.W. Norton, 2011.

Steinberg, Mia, and Amanda B. Diekman. "The Double-Edged Sword of Stereotypes of Men." In *APA Handbook of Men and Masculinities*, edited by Amanda B. Diekman, 433-56. Washington, DC: American Psychological Association, 2016.

Taillie, Lindsey Smith. "Who's Cooking? Trends in US Home Food Preparation by Gender, Education, and Race/Ethnicity from 2003 to 2016." *Nutrition Journal* 17, no. 41 (April 2018).

"The State of Women in Technology Leadership." Brandon Hall Group and Blue Circle Leadership, 2018.

Thomas, David A., and Robin J. Ely. "Making Differences Matter: A New Paradigm for Managing Diversity." *Harvard Business Review*, September-October 1996.

Thomas, Rachel, Marianne Cooper, Ellen Konar, Ali Bohrer, Ava Mohsenin, Lareina Yee, Alexis Krivkovich, Irina Starikova, Jess Huang, and Delia Zanoschi. "Women in the Workplace." McKinsey & Company, October 2019.

Thompson, Whitney. "Mister Secretary: The Gendered History of Clerical Work." *Odyssey*, February 9, 2017.

Torres, Nicole. "It's Better to Avoid a Toxic Employee Than Hire a Superstar." *Harvard Business Review*, December 2015.

"Understanding Implicit Bias." Ohio State University Kirwan Institute for the Study of Race and Ethnicity, 2015.

Waikar, Sachin. "A Tilted Playing Field: New Research Finds Bias in Elite Professional Services Hiring." Kellogg Insight, May 1, 2015.

Wang, Lucy Lu, Gabriel Stanovsky, Luca Weihs, and Oren Etzioni. "Gender Trends in Computer Science Authorship." Cornell University, June 19, 2019.

Warner, Judith, Nora Ellmann, and Diana Boesch. "The Women's Leadership Gap." Center for American Progress, November 20, 2018.

Williams, Joan, and Rachel Dempsey. *What Works for Women at Work: Four Patterns Working Women Need to Know.* New York: NYU Press, 2014.

Wittenberg-Cox, Avivah. "Rethinking What Masculinity Means at the Office." *Harvard Business Review*, June 2016.

Woetzel, Jonathan, Anu Madgavkar, Kweilin Ellingrud, Eric Labaye, Sandrine Devillard, Eric Kutcher, James Manyika, Richard Dobbs, and Mekala Krishnan. "How Advancing Women's Equality Can Add $12 Trillion to Global Growth." McKinsey & Company, September 2015.

"Women in Leadership Study." Brandon Hall Group, 2016.

"Women in the Labor Force: A Databook (2011 Edition)." U.S. Bureau of Labor Statistics Report 1034, December 15, 2011.

"Women in the Workforce—United States: Quick Take." Catalyst, June 5, 2019.

Yavorsky, Jill E., Lisa A. Keister, Yue Qian, and Michael Nau. "Women in the One Percent: Gender Dynamics in Top Income Positions." *American Sociological Review* 84, no. 1 (February 1, 2019): 54-81.

Zeneger, Jack, and Joseph Folkman. "Research: Women Score Higher Than Men in Most Leadership Skills." *Harvard Business Review*, June 25, 2019.

ENDNOTES

1. Throughout this book, we have used a variety of case studies, names, and examples from our workshops and research. All names have been changed to protect people's identity and maintain confidentiality.
2. Catalyst, *Quick Take: Women in the Workforce—United States* (June 5, 2019).
3. Liz Long, "Why Products Designed by Women Are the Next Big Thing," *Forbes* (December 22, 2017).
4. Katherine Shaver, "Female Dummy Makes Her Mark on Male-Dominated Crash Tests," *Washington Post* (March 25, 2012).
5. Leslie Young, "Drugs Aren't Tested on Women Like They Are on Men, and It Could Have Deadly Consequences," Global News (November 2, 2016).
6. Maria Miller, "The Workplace Was Designed by Men, for Men—We Need to Modernize," *Guardian* (November 19, 2013).
7. Adela Talbot, "Study: Women's Impact on Economy Undervalued," *Phys.org* (June 22, 2018).
8. Fatima Najiy, "Women's Impact on the Economy, By the Numbers," *ThinkProgress* (March 8, 2012).
9. Rachel Thomas et al., *Women in the Workplace* (Palo Alto, CA: McKinsey & Company, 2019).
10. For information about Boston University's education program, see https://www.bu.edu/academics/hub/; for Suffolk University, see https://www.suffolk.edu/academics/academic-catalogs/undergraduate-course-catalog/management#Management-Major-Requirements.
11. Juliet Bourke et. al., "Diversity and Inclusion: The Reality Gap," *Deloitte Insights* (February 28, 2017).
12. Vivian Hunt, Dennis Layton, and Sara Prince, "Why Diversity Matters," McKinsey & Company (January 2015).
13. Justin Wolfers, "Fewer Women Run Big Companies Than Men Named John," *New York Times* (March 2, 2015).
14. Joe Pinsker, "The Financial Perks of Being Tall," *Atlantic* (May 18, 2015).
15. Jack Zenger and Joseph Folkman, "Research: Women Score Higher Than Men in Most Leadership Skills," *Harvard Business Review* (June 25, 2019).
16. "Women's History Month: March 2017," United States Census Bureau (March 17, 2017).
17. Randy Olson, "Percentage of Bachelor's Degrees Conferred to Women, By Major (1970-2012)," *Randal S. Olson* (June 14, 2014).
18. Ilana Kowarski, "U.S. News Data: A Portrait of the Typical MBA Student," *U.S. News* (March 14, 2017). The school where Jodi teaches has 50 percent women in

their MBA program.

19. Alan Jope, "Gender Equality is 170 Years Away. We Cannot Wait That Long," *World Economic Forum* (January 19, 2017).

20. Catalyst, *Quick Take: Women in the Workforce—United States* (June 5, 2019).

21. "How Did Tech Become So Male-Dominated?," *Atlantic*, March 14, 2017, video, 4:12, https://www.youtube.com/watch?v=OZ7zX6LalLI&feature=youtu.be.

22. Heather Murphy, "Picture a Leader. Is She a Woman?," *New York Times* (March 16, 2018).

23. Mark Dyble et. al., "Sex Equality Can Explain the Unique Social Structure of Hunter-Gatherer Bands," *Science* 348 (May 15, 2015): 796-798.

24. Suzanne McGee and Heidi Moore, "Women's Rights and Their Money: A Timeline from Cleopatra to Lilly Ledbetter," *Guardian* (August 11, 2014).

25. Katrina Honeyman and Jordan Goodman, "Women's Work, Gender Conflict, and Labour Markets in Europe 1500-1900," *Economic History Review* 44, no. 4 (November 1991): 608-628.

26. Honeyman and Goodman, "Women's Work, Gender Conflict, and Labour Markets in Europe 1500-1900," 609.

27. Lise Eliot, *Pink Brain, Blue Brain: How Small Differences Grow into Troublesome Gaps—And What We Can Do About It* (Boston: Mariner Books, 2010).

28. Tia Ghose, "Google Manifesto: Does Biology Explain Gender Disparities in Tech?," *LiveScience* (August 9, 2017).

29. Claire Cain Miller, "As Women Take Over a Male-Dominated Field, the Pay Drops," *New York Times* (March 20, 2016).

30. Katie Burns and Malinda Larkin, "Why Do Female Veterinarians Earn Less Than Male Veterinarians?," *American Veterinary Medical Association* (March 20, 2013).

31. Asaf Levanon, Paula England, and Paul Allison, "Occupational Feminization and Pay: Assessing Causal Dynamics Using 1950-2000 U.S. Census Data," *Social Forces* 88, no. 2 (December 2009): 865–891.

32. Gertjan De Groot and Marlou Schrover, "Between Men and Machines: Women Workers in New Industries, 1870-1940," *Social History* 20, no. 3 (1995): 284.

33. Rachel Payne, "Positive Opportunities for Women's Empowerment and Recognition" (lecture, Loyola Marymount University, Playa Vista, CA, November 15, 2018).

34. Janet Abbate, *Recoding Gender: Women's Changing Participation in Computing* (Cambridge, MA: MIT Press, 2012), 1.

35. "Global Generations: A Global Study on Work-Life Challenges Across Generations," Ernst & Young (2015).

36. "Understanding Implicit Bias," Ohio State University (2015).

37. Claire Cain Miller, "How Elementary School Teachers' Bias Can Discourage Girls From Math and Science," *New York Times* (February 6, 2015); Joan C. Williams, Marina Multhaup, and Rachel Korn, "The Problem with 'Asians Are Good at Science': Stereotypes of 'Worker Bees' and 'Dragon Ladies' are Holding Asian Americans Back in STEM Careers," *Atlantic* (January 31, 2018); "Teacher Racial Bias Matters More for Students of Color," *NYU Steinhardt News* (May 18, 2017); Joshua Aronson et. al., "When White Men Can't Do Math: Necessary and Sufficient Factors in Stereotype Threat," *Journal of Experimental Social Psychology* 35, no. 1 (January 1999): 29-46.

38. Renee Davidson, "Why We Need to Stop Equating Leadership with Masculinity," *AAUW* (March 18, 2016).

39. Kieran Snyder, "The Abrasiveness Trap: High-Achieving Men and Women are

Described Differently in Reviews," *Fortune* (August 26, 2014).

40. Adam Bornstein and Jordan Bornstein, "22 Qualities That Make a Great Leader," *Entrepreneur* (August 21, 2019).

41. Sunnie Giles, "The Most Important Leadership Competencies, According to Leaders Around the World," *Harvard Business Review* (March 15, 2016).

42. Daniel Kahneman, *Thinking, Fast and Slow* (New York: Farrar, Straus and Giroux, 2011).

43. Rebecca Knight, "7 Practical Ways to Reduce Bias in Your Hiring Process," *Harvard Business Review* (June 12, 2017).

44. "Women in the Workplace," McKinsey & Company (September 2015).

45. Lucy Lu Wang et. al., "Gender Trends in Computer Science Authorship," Cornell University (June 19, 2019).

46. Erin Duffin, "Bachelor's Degrees Earned in the United States by Gender 1950-2029," *Statista* (May 20, 2019).

47. Judith Warner, Nora Ellman, and Diana Boesch, "The Women's Leadership Gap," *Center for American Progress* (November 20, 2018).

48. Nicole Torres, "It's Better to Avoid a Toxic Employee Than Hire a Superstar," *Harvard Business Review* (December 2015), 2–4.

49. Damon Centola et. al., "Experimental Evidence for Tipping Points in Social Convention," *Science* 360, no. 6393 (June 8, 2018): 1116-1119.

50. Iris Bohnet, *What Works: Gender Equality by Design* (Cambridge: Belknap, 2016).

51. Bohnet, *What Works*.

52. Howard Ross, "'Everyday Bias: Identifying and Navigating Unconscious Judgments' | Talks at Google," Authors at Google, October 6, 2014, video, 58:43, November 16, 2014, https://www.youtube.com/watch?v=v01SxXui9XQ.

53. "Stereotype Threat: A Conversation with Claude Steele," interview by Not In Our School, July 18, 2013, video, 8:18, https://www.youtube.com/watch?v=failylROnrY.

54. Joan Williams and Rachel Dempsey, *What Works for Women at Work: Four Patterns Working Women Need to Know* (New York: NYU Press, 2014).

55. Bohnet, *What Works*, 24.

56. Bohnet, *What Works*, 24.

57. Paola Cecchi-Dimeglio, "How Gender Bias Corrupts Performance Reviews, and What to Do About It," *Harvard Business Review* (April 12, 2017).

58. Daniel A. Gross, "How Elite US Schools Give Preference to Wealthy and White 'Legacy' Applicants," *Guardian* (January 23, 2019).

59. Claude Steele, *Whistling Vivaldi: How Stereotypes Affect Us and What We Can Do* (New York: W. W. Norton, 2010).

60. Steele, *Whistling Vivaldi*.

61. "Company News: Mattel Says It Erred; Teen Talk Barbie Turns Silent on Math," *New York Times* (October 21, 1992).

62. Margaret Shih et. al., "Stereotype Susceptibility: Identity Salience and Shifts in Quantitative Performance," *Psychological Science* 10, no. 1 (January 1999).

63. Steele, *Whistling Vivaldi*.

64. Jordan Nickerson, "Market Forces and CEO Pay: Shocks to CEO Demand Induced by IPO Waves," *Review of Financial Studies* 30, no. 7 (July 2017): 2272–2312.

65. Marianne Cooper, "The False Promise of Meritocracy: Managers Who Believe Themselves to be Fair and Objective Judges of Ability Often Overlook Women and Minorities Who Are Deserving of Job Offers and Pay Increases," *Atlantic* (December 1, 2015).

66. Emilio J. Castilla, "Gender, Race, and Meritocracy in Organizational Careers,"

American Journal of Sociology 113, no. 6 (May 2008): 1479–1526.

67. Jodi Ecker Detjen, Michelle A. Waters, and Kelly Watson, *The Orange Line: A Woman's Guide to Integrating Career, Family, and Life* (Newton, MA: JMK Publishing, May 2013).

68. Lindsey Smith Taillie, "Who's Cooking? Trends in US Home Food Preparation by Gender, Education, and Race/Ethnicity from 2003 to 2016," *Nutrition Journal* 17, no. 41 (April 2018).

69. Taillie, "Who's Cooking?"

70. Lindsay Colameo, "New Study Says Confident Women Spend Less Time Getting Ready," *Glamour* (January 28, 2016).

71. Katty Kay and Claire Shipman, *The Confidence Code: The Science and Art of Self-Assurance—What Women Should Know* (New York: Harper Business, April 2014).

72. Lois P. Frankel, *Nice Girls Don't Get the Corner Office: Unconscious Mistakes Women Make That Sabotage Their Careers* (New York: Business Plus, 2004).

73. Detjen, Waters, and Watson, *The Orange Line.*

74. Laura Stampler, "Microsoft's CEO Tells Women it's Bad Karma to Ask for a Raise," *Time* (October 9, 2014).

75. Linda Babcock and Sara Laschever, *Women Don't Ask: The High Cost of Avoiding Negotiation—and Positive Strategies for Change* (New York: Bantam, February, 2007).

76. "America's Women and the Wage Gap," *National Partnership for Women and Families* (September 2019).

77. "Beyond Wages: Effects of the Latina Wage Gap," *National Partnership for Women and Families* (November 2018).

78. "Black Women and the Wage Gap," *National Partnership for Women and Families* (April 2019).

79. Linda Babcock and Sara Laschever, *Ask for It: How Women Can Use the Power of Negotiation to Get What They Really Want* (New York: Bantam, February 2008).

80. Kenneth R. Harney, "Single Women Account for More Real Estate Purchases than Single Men," *Washington Post* (May 9, 2018).

81. Colin Seeberger, "Nearly Two-Thirds of Mothers Continue to be Family Breadwinners, Black Mothers Are Far More Likely to be Breadwinners," Center for American Progress (May 10, 2019).

82. Youngjoo Cha, "Reinforcing Separate Spheres: The Effect of Spousal Overwork on Men's and Women's Employment in Dual-Earner Households," *American Sociological Review* 75, no. 2: 307.

83. Rebecca Glauber, "Trends in the Motherhood Wage Penalty and Fatherhood Wage Premium for Low, Middle, and High Earners," *Demography* 55, no. 5 (Oct. 2018): 1663–1680.

84. "Balancing Work and Family Life," in *Modern Parenthood*. Pew Research Center (March 2013), https://www.pewsocialtrends.org/2013/03/14/chapter-2-balancing-work-and-family-life/.

85. Ronald F. Levant and Katherine Richmond, "A Review of Research on Masculinity Ideologies Using the Male Role Norms Inventory," *Journal of Men's Studies* 15, no.2 (July 31, 2016): 130–146.

86. Stephanie Coontz, "Do Millennial Men Want Stay-at-Home Wives?," *New York Times* (March 31, 2017).

87. David A. Thomas and Robin J. Ely, "Making Differences Matter: A New Paradigm for Managing Diversity," *Harvard Business Review* (September-October 1996).

88. Brad Harrington, Jennifer Sabatini Fraone, and Jegoo Lee, "The New Dad: The

Career-Caregiving Conflict," Boston College Center for Work & Family (2017).

89. See, for example, the Gillette commercial "We Believe: The Best Men Can Be" (https://www.youtube.com/watch?v=koPmuEyP3a0), the Pixar short video "Purl" (https://www.youtube.com/watch?v=B6uuIHpFkuo), or The Representation Project's "The Mask You Live In" (http://therepresentationproject.org/film/the-mask-you-live-in-film/).

90. Mia Steinberg and Amanda B. Diekman. "The Double-Edged Sword of Stereotypes of Men," *APA Handbook of Men and Masculinities,* American Psychological Association (2016): 433–456.

91. In 2015, Michael Kimmel, a leading scholar on masculinity and the director of the Center for the Study of Men and Masculinities, helped start the nation's first master's degree program in Masculinities Studies. The program, at Stony Brook University, explores what it means to be male in today's world.

92. We are not saying that women's leadership development programs are bad. We believe they are important for helping teach women how to reframe their own internalized biases that block their career potential. They would actually be helpful for men, too, but we haven't found (yet) that companies are willing to invest in them for their male employees.

93. Kweilin Ellingrud, Mekala Krishnan, and Anu Madgavkar, "Miles to Go: Stepping Up Progress Toward Gender Equality," McKinsey & Company (September 2016).

94. Richard F. Martell, David M. Lane, and Cynthia Emrich, "Male-Female Differences: A Computer Solution," *American Psychologist* 51, no. 2 (February 1996): 157-158.

95. Steve Calechman, "Old Managers, Old-School Expectations, and Why Men Don't Take Paternity Leave," *Fatherly* (June 17, 2018).

96. "Highlights of Women's Earnings in 2017," U.S. Bureau of Labor Statistics (August 2018).

97. *Black Women and the Wage Gap* (Washington, D.C.: National Partnership for Women and Families, April 2019).

98. This is increasingly illegal at the state level.

99. Julia Bear and Peter Glick, "Gendered Rewards: Breadwinner versus Caregiver Status Affects Workplace Rewards for Men and Women," *Academy of Management Proceedings* 2016, no. 1 (2016).

100. Bear and Glick, "Gendered Rewards."

101. Asaf Levanon, Paula England, and Paul Allison, "Occupational Feminization and Pay: Assessing Causal Dynamics using 1950–2000 US Census Data," *Social Forces* 88, no.2 (2009): 865-891.

102. Paula England, Paul Allison, and Yuxiao Wu, "Does Bad Pay Cause Occupations to Feminize, Does Feminization Reduce Pay, and How Can We Tell with Longitudinal Data?," *Social Science Research* 36, no.3 (2007): 1237-1256.

103. Dick Grote, "Let's Abolish Self-Appraisal," *Harvard Business Review* (July 11, 2011).

104. Samantha C. Paustian-Underdahl et al. "Gender and Perceptions of Leadership Effectiveness: A Meta-Analysis of Contextual Moderators," *Journal of Applied Psychology* 99, no. 6 (November 2014): 1129–1145.

105. Williams and Dempsey, "What Works for Women at Work."

106. Sara Randazzo, "Being a Law Firm Partner Was Once a Job for Life. That Culture Is All But Dead: At the Modern Law Firm, Not All Partners are Created Equal, and Data and Billings Rule," *Wall Street Journal* (August 9, 2019).

107. Paola Cecchi-Dimeglio, "How Gender Bias Corrupts Performance Reviews, and What to Do About It," *Harvard Business Review* (April 2017).

108. Frank Dobbin and Alexandra Kalev, "Why Diversity Programs Fail," *Harvard*

Business Review 94 (July- August 2016).

109. David G. Smith, Judith E. Rosenstein, and Margaret C. Nikolov, "The Different Words We Use to Describe Male and Female Leaders," *Harvard Business Review* (May 25, 2018).

110. Herminia Ibarra and Jennifer Petriglieri, *Impossible Selves: Image Strategies and Identity Threat in Professional Women's Career Transitions,* INSEAD Working Paper (March 4, 2016): 1.

111. Ibarra and Petriglieri, *Impossible Selves*, 7.

112. David Noonan, "The 25% Revolution—How Big Does A Minority Have to be to Reshape Society?," *Scientific American* (June 8, 2018).

113. Jennifer L. Berdahl et al., "Work as A Masculinity Contest," *Journal of Social Issues* 74, no. 3 (2018): 422-448.

114. Jennifer Booton, "Twitter Funds Frat Party for Employees, Highlighting Silicon Valley Bro Culture," *MarketWatch* (July 22, 2015).

115. Mike Issaac, "Inside Uber's Aggressive, Unrestrained Workplace Culture," *New York Times* (February 22, 2017).

116. Chris Gardner, "Rose McGowan Calls Out 'X-Men' Billboard That Shows Mystique Being Strangled," *Hollywood Reporter* (June 2, 2016).

117. Edward Baig and Jessica Guynn, "At CES, 'Booth Babes' are Less Obvious, But They're Not Gone," *USA Today* (January 12, 2018).

118. "The State of Women in Technology Leadership," Brandon Hall and Blue Circle Leadership, 2018.

119. Katie Abouzahr et. al., "Dispelling the Myths of the Gender 'Ambition Gap,'" Boston Consulting Group (April 5, 2017).

120. Alison Beard, "Why Are We Still Promoting Incompetent Men?," *Harvard Business Review* (March 12, 2019).

121. Joanna Barsh and Lareina Yee, "Unlocking the Full Potential of Women at Work," McKinsey & Company (2012).

122. Brené Brown, *I Thought It Was Just Me (But It Isn't): Making the Journey From "What Will People Think?" to "I Am Enough"* (New York: Avery, February 2007).

123. "Dove Real Beauty Sketches: You're More Beautiful Than You Think (3mins)," *Dove US*, April 14, 2013, video, 3:00, https://www.youtube.com/watch?v=XpaO-jMXyJGk.

124. See, for example, https://www.hopskipdrive.com/

125. Scott Behson, "Why Two-Income Families Are Happier Than Single Earner Households," *Good Men Project* (February 25, 2013).

126. Gerrit Bauer, "Gender roles, comparative advantages and the life course: the division of domestic labor in same-sex and different-sex couples," *European Journal of Population* 32, no. 1 (2016): 99-128.

127. Philip N. Cohen and Matt L. Huffman, "Working for the Woman?: Female Managers and the Gender Wage Gap," *American Sociological Review* 72, no. 5 (2007): 681-704.

128. Steele, *Whistling Vivaldi*.

129. Steele, *Whistling Vivaldi*, 110.

130. Steele, *Whistling Vivaldi*.

131. Steele, *Whistling Vivaldi*, 113.

132. Kevin Sneader and Lareina Yee, "One Is the Loneliest Number: Put an End to Costly Workplace Isolation Experienced by Many Women by Clustering Them on Teams

and Improving the Promotion Process," McKinsey & Company (January 2019).

133. Research finds that women's income goes down on average after divorce while men's income goes up. Stacy Rapacon, "Why Women Should Rethink Their Finances After Divorce," *U.S. News* (August 14, 2017).

134. Detjen, Waters, and Watson, *The Orange Line.*

135. Ross Brenneman, "Teacher Bias Devalues Math Skills of Girls and Students of Color, USC Research Finds," *USC News* (December 12, 2019).

136. Marianne Cooper, "Why Women (Sometimes) Don't Help Other Women: It's Not Because They're Inherently Harsher Leaders Than Men, But Because They Often Respond to Sexism by Trying to Distance Themselves from Other Women," *Atlantic* (June 23, 2016).

137. Olga Khazan, "Why Do Women Bully Each Other At Work?: Research Suggests that Conditions in the Workplace Might be to Blame," *Atlantic* (September 2017).

138. Michelle Duguid, "Female Tokens in High-Prestige Work Groups: Catalysts or Inhibitors of Group Diversification?," *Organizational Behavior and Human Decision Processes* 116, no. 1 (2011): 104-115.

139. Duguid, "Female Tokens in High-Prestige Work Groups."

140. Babcock and Laschever, *Women Don't Ask.*

141. We conducted a qualitative study interviewing 26 men in a one-hour, semi-structured interview over the phone about their career and life.

142. Erin Reid, "Whether a Husband Identifies as a Breadwinner Depends on Whether He Respects His Wife's Career—Not on How Much She Earns," *Harvard Business Review* (August 15, 2018).

143. We interviewed 118 college-educated business women for *The Orange Line* using a one-hour, semi-structured interview where we asked about their career and life.

144. Sue Shellenbarger, "A Strategy for Happy Dual-Career Couples," *Wall Street Journal* (February 21, 2017).

145. Information from the study referenced in 141.

146. Mike Robbins, *Be Yourself, Everyone Else is Already Taken,* (San Francisco: Jossey-Bass, 2009): 40.

147. Brown, *I Thought It Was Just Me (But It Isn't).*

148. Robbins, *Be Yourself, Everyone Else is Already Taken.*

149. Jim Clifton, "The World's Broken Workplace," Gallup (June 13, 2017).

150. Bonobos, "#EvolveTheDefinition," July 17, 2018, video, 1:30, www.youtube.com/watch?v=j6jz2Jma5-s

151. Jennifer L. Berdahl, Peter Glick, and Marianne Cooper, "How Masculinity Contests Undermine Organizations, and What to Do About It," *Harvard Business Review* (November 2, 2018).

152. Avivah Wittenberg-Cox, "Rethinking What Masculinity Means at the Office," *Harvard Business Review* (June 2016): 2–5.

153. Elissa Braunstein, "The Feminist Political Economy of the Rent-Seeking Society: An Investigation of Gender Inequality and Economic Growth," *Journal of Economic Issues* 42, no. 4 (December 2008): 959-979.

154. Jonathan Woetzel et. al., "How Advancing Women's Equality Can Add $12 Trillion to Global Growth: A McKinsey Global Institute Report Finds that $12 Trillion Could be Added to Global GDP by 2025 by Advancing Women's Equality. The Public, Private, and Social Sectors Will Need to Act to Close Gender Gaps in Work and Society," McKinsey & Company (September 2015).

155. Nicholas Kristof, "When Women Win, Men Win, Too," *New York Times* (July

30, 2016).

156. W. Brad Johnson and David Smith, *Athena Rising: How and Why Men Should Mentor Women* (Brookline, MA: Bibliomotion, 2016), 156.

157. Johnson and Smith, *Athena Rising*, 157.

158. See http://www.brandonhall.com/.

159. Jennifer K. Bosson et. al., "Interpersonal Chemistry Through Negativity: Bonding by Sharing Negative Attitudes about Others," *Personal Relationships* 13, no. 2 (May 9, 2006): 135-150.

160. Audrey J. Murrell and Stacy Blake-Beard, *Mentoring Diverse Leaders: Creating Change for People, Processes, and Paradigms* (London: Taylor and Francis, 2017), 189.

161. Murrell and Blake-Beard, *Mentoring Diverse Leaders*, 189.

162. Scott E. Seibert et al., "A Social Capital Theory of Career Success," *Academy of Management Journal* 44, no. 2 (April 2001): 219–237.

163. Seibert et al., "A Social Capital Theory of Career Success."

164. Savita Kumra and Susan Vinnicombe, "Impressing for Success: A Gendered Analysis of a Key Social Capital Accumulation Strategy," *Gender, Work & Organization* 17, no. 5 (September 2010): 521–546.

165. Stefanie K. Johnson et. al., "Has Sexual Harassment at Work Decreased Since #MeToo?," *Harvard Business Review* (July 18, 2019).

166. W. Brad Johnson and David G. Smith, "How Men Can Become Better Allies to Women," *Harvard Business Review* (October 12, 2018).

167. William Bridges, *Managing Transitions: Making the Most of Change* (Boston: Da Capo Press, September 22, 2009).

168. Carol S. Dweck, *Mindset: The New Psychology of Success* (New York: Ballantine Books, December 26, 2007).

169. Empathy mapping is a component of design thinking.

170. Amy Edmondson, "Psychological Safety and Learning Behavior in Work Teams," *Administrative Science Quarterly* 44, no. 2 (1999): 350-383.

171. Charles Duhigg, "What Google Learned From its Quest to Build the Perfect Team," *New York Times* (February 28, 2019).

172. Laura Delizonna, "High-Performing Teams Need Psychological Safety. Here's How to Create It," *Harvard Business Review* (August 24, 2017).

173. Edmondson, "Psychological Safety and Learning Behavior in Work Teams," 375.

174. Katherine W. Phillips, "The Biases That Punish Racially Diverse Teams," *Harvard Business Review* (February 22, 2016).

175. Roger Schwarz, "Getting Teams with Different Subcultures to Collaborate," *Harvard Business Review* (July 22, 2016).

176. Sheryl Sandberg and Rachel Thomas, "Sheryl Sandberg on How to Get to Gender Equality: The Facebook Chief Operating Officer and Founder of LeanIn.Org Says the First Step is Realizing How Far We Have to Go," *Wall Street Journal* (October 10, 2017).

177. Diane Contu, "Why Teams Don't Work," *Harvard Business Review* (May 2009).

178. Thomas and Ely, "Making Differences Matter."

179. Thomas and Ely, "Making Differences Matter."

180 Luke Houghton and David Tuffley, "Towards a Methodology of Wicked Problem Exploration through Concept Shifting and Tension Point Analysis: Concept Shifting and Tension Point Analysis," *Behavioral Science* 32, no. 3 (October 2013): 294.

181. Shane Snow, *Dream Teams: Working Together Without Falling Apart* (New York: Portfolio Books, 2018), 294.

182. David Livermore, *Leading with Cultural Intelligence: The Real Secret to Success* (New York: AMACOM, 2015), 38.

183. Noah Rabinowitz et al., *Leadership Capability Modeling: Introducing the Next-Generation Competency Model* (Atlanta, GA: Deloitte Development LLC, 2018).

184. Rabinowitz et al., *Leadership Capability Modeling.*

185. Thomas and Ely, "Making Differences Matter."

186. David Ng, "WarnerMedia Creates New Executive Position Focused on Diversity and Inclusion," *Los Angeles Times* (March 21, 2019).

187. Fred Chartrand, "Trudeau's 'Because it's 2015' Retort Draws International Attention," *Globe and Mail* (November 5, 2015).

188. Livermore, *Leading with Cultural Intelligence.*

189. Mark Huselid, Brian Becker, and Richard Beatty, *The Workforce Scorecard: Managing Human Capital to Execute Strategy* (Brighton, MA: Harvard Business Review Press, 2005).

190. Victoria Banyard, Elizabethe G. Plante, and Mary M. Moynihan, "Bystander Education: Bringing a Broader Community Perspective to Sexual Violence Prevention," *Journal of Community Psychology* 32, no. 1 (January 2004): 61-79.

191. Maureen Scully and Mary Rowe, "Bystander Training within Organizations," *Journal of the International Ombudsman Association* 2, no. 1 (2009): 1-9.

192. Thomas and Ely, "Making Differences Matter."

193. Susan Bruno, "Needed Now: Female Financial Planners," *AICPA* (May 17, 2018).

194. Anna Holland Smith, "Where Are All the Female Crash Test Dummies? (Or Why the Need for Diversity in STEM is a Matter of Life or Death)," *Medium* (May 4, 2018).

195. Rich Barlow, "Why Medical Research Often Ignores Women," *BU Today* (March 28, 2014).

196. Leah Crane, "NASA Cancels First All-Women Spacewalk Due to Spacesuit Sizing Issue," *New Scientist* (March 26, 2019).

197. Rebecca Greenfield, "Brainstorming Doesn't Work; Try This Technique Instead: Ever Been in a Meeting Where One Loudmouth's Mediocre Idea Dominates? Then You Know Brainstorming Needs an Overhaul," *Fast Company* (July 29, 2014).

198. For more information on in-group and out-group bias, see https://janeelliott.com/.

199. Beard, "Why Are We Still Promoting Incompetent Men?"

200. Mike Robbins, *Bring Your Whole Self to Work: How Vulnerability Unlocks Creativity, Connection, and Performance* (Carlsbad, CA: Hay House, 2018).

201. Amy C. Edmondson, *The Fearless Organization: Creating Psychological Safety in the Workplace for Learning, Innovation and Growth* (Hoboken, NJ: Wiley, 2018).

202. Sneader and Yee, "One Is the Loneliest Number."

203. Lorenzo Del Marmol, "How Does Agile Project Management Support Creative Projects?," *Agile Scrum* (October 27, 2019).

204. For an overview on design thinking, see Ideo's https://www.ideou.com/pages/design-thinking.

205. Richard M. Lent, *Leading Great Meetings: How to Structure Yours for Success* (Stow, MA: Meeting for Results, 2015).

206. Aparna Joshi and Andrew P. Knight, "Who Defers to Whom and Why? Dual Pathways Linking Demographic Differences and Dyadic Deference to Team Effectiveness," *Academy of Management Journal* 58, no. 1 (April 28, 2014).

207. Alex Woodie, "Do Amazon's Biased Algorithms Spell the End of AI in Hiring?," *Datanami* (October 16, 2018).

208. "Purl," a Pixar SparkShort, directed by Kristen Lester, produced by Gillian

Libbert-Duncan (Emeryville, CA: Disney Pixar, 2019), YouTube video, 8:43, https://www.youtube.com/watch?v=B6uuIHpFkuo.

209. Jack Altman, "How Much Does Employee Turnover Really Cost?," *Huffpost* (January 19, 2017).

210. Patrick Mitchell, *The 2017 Hiscox Guide to Employee Lawsuits* (New York: Hiscox, 2017).

211. "Equity Theory," *Wikipedia* (December 9, 2019).

212. Maria Puente, "Does Your Generation Determine How You Perceive Sexual Harassment?," *USA Today* (November 6, 2017).

213. See the Twitter account @manwhohasitall for lots of examples of these flips.

214. "Women in Leadership Study," Brandon Hall, 2016.

215. Rebecca Knight, "7 Practical Ways to Reduce Bias in Your Hiring Process," *Harvard Business Review* (June 2017): 2–7.

216. Sylvia Ann Hewlett et. al., "Athena Factor 2.0: Accelerating Female Talent in Science, Engineering & Technology," *Center for Talent Innovation* (2014).

217. Bohnet, *What Works.*

218. Lou Solomon, "Two-Thirds of Managers Are Uncomfortable Communicating with Employees," *Harvard Business Review* (March 2016): 2–5.

219. Sheryl Sandberg, *Lean In: Women, Work, and the Will to Lead* (New York: Alfred A. Knopf, 2013).

220. Maura Cheeks, "How Black Women Describe Navigating Race and Gender in the Workplace," *Harvard Business Review* (March 26, 2018).

221. Alexis Krivkovich, "Women in the Workplace 2018: Progress on Gender Diversity at Work Has Stalled. To Achieve Equality, Companies Must Turn Good Intentions into Concrete Action," McKinsey & Company (October 2018).

222. Edgar H. Schein, *The Corporate Culture Survival Guide* (San Francisco: Wiley, 2009).

223. Jonathan A. Segal, "Legal Trends: Affinity Group Danger Zones," *HR Magazine* (September 1, 2013).

224. Robin J. Ely and Debra E. Meyerson, "An Organizational Approach to Undoing Gender: The Unlikely Case of Offshore Oil Platforms," *Research in Organizational Behavior* 30 (October 2010): 3–34.

225. Jason Morwick et. al., *Workshift: Future-Proof Your Organization for the 21st Century* (New York: Palgrave Macmillan, 2013).

226. Jessica DeGroot and Jodi Detjen, "Transformative Flex," Third Path (Philadelphia, PA, 2018).

227. Daniel H. Pink, *Drive: The Surprising Truth About What Motivates Us* (New York: Riverhead Books, 2009).

228. Jennifer McKevitt, "Supply Chain Leaders Commit to Empower Women-Owned Suppliers," *Supply Chain Drive* (April 5, 2017).

229. "Saturn: A Wealth of Lessons from Failure," *Knowledge @ Wharton* (October 28, 2009).

230. *Beyond a Year In Space*, directed by Mark Mannucci, featuring Scott Kelly, aired November 15, 2017, on PBS, https://www.amazon.com/Beyond-Year-Space-Scott-Kelly/dp/B07HRKPHLT.

231. Adapted from Robert Kegan and Lisa Laskow Lahey, *Immunity to Change: How to Overcome It and Unlock the Potential in Yourself and Your Organization* (Brighton, MA: Harvard Business Review Press, 2009).

232. Alexandra Witze, "NASA Rethinks Approach to Mars Exploration," *Nature* (October 6, 2016).

233. Bohnet, *What Works.*

234. Irene Padavic, Robin J. Ely, & Erin M. Reid, "Explaining the Persistence of Gender Inequality: The Work–family Narrative as a Social Defense against the 24/7 Work Culture," *Administrative Science Quarterly* 65, no. 1 (February 14, 2019): 61-111.

235. Tom. H. Oliver, et al., "Biodiversity and resilience of ecosystem functions," *Trends in Ecology & Evolution* 30, no.11 (November 2015): 673-684.

236. "Functions of Ecosystem: Ecological Succession, Homeostasis," PMF IAS (April 22, 2019), https://www.pmfias.com/ecological-succession-primary-secondary-succession-homeostasis/.

237. Sidney Perkowitz, "If Only 19th-Century America had Listened to a Woman Scientist: Where might the US be if it heeded her discovery of global warming's source?," *Nautilus* (November 28, 2019).

238. Together Science Can, "10 Badass International Science Collaborations that will Blow Your Mind: How many scientists does it take to change the world?," *Buzzfeed* (October 17, 2017).

239. Danielle Gaucher et al. "Evidence That Gendered Wording in Job Advertisements Exists and Sustains Gender Inequality," *Journal of Personality & Social Psychology* 101, no. 1 (July 2011): 109–128.

240. Jack Zenger, "The Confidence Gap in Men and Women: Why It Matters and How to Overcome It," *Forbes* (April 8, 2018).

241. See, for example, http://reworkwork.com/.

242. See, for example, https://www.reachire.com/.

243. Herminia Ibarra and Mark Hunter, "How Leaders Create and Use Networks," *Harvard Business Review* 85, no. 1 (January 2007): 40–47.

244. David R. Francis, "Employers' Replies to Racial Names," National Bureau of Economic Research (September 2003); Corinne A. Moss-Racusin et al., "Science Faculty's Subtle Gender Biases Favor Male Students," *Proceedings of the National Academy of Sciences of the United States of America* 109, no. 41 (October 9, 2012): 16474-16479.

245. Claire Cain Miller, Kevin Quealy, and Margot Sanger-Katz, "The Top Jobs Where Women Are Outnumbered by Men Named John," *New York Times* (April 24, 2018).

246. Sachin Waikar, "A Tilted Playing Field: New Research Finds Bias in Elite Professional Services Hiring," *Kellogg Insight* (May 1, 2015).

247. Stefanie K. Johnson et al., "If There's Only One Woman in Your Candidate Pool, There's Statistically No Chance She'll Be Hired," *Harvard Business Review* (April 2016): 2–6.

248. Claudia Goldin and Cecilia Rouse, "Orchestrating Impartiality: The Impact of 'Blind' Auditions on Female Musicians," *American Economic Review* 90, no. 4 (September 2000): 715–741.

249. Iris Bohnet, "How to Take Bias Out of Interviews," *Harvard Business Review* (April 18, 2016).

250. Bohnet, *What Works.*

Graphic Notes

Women in the Workplace: Shifts in Attitude

1. "American Women in World War II," *History.com* (February 28, 2020), https://www.history.com/topics/world-war-ii/american-women-in-world-war-ii-1.
2. Jone Johnson Lewis, "Women and World War II: Women at Work," *ThoughtCo.* (March 5, 2019), https://www.thoughtco.com/world-war-ii-women-at-work-3530690.
3. Howard N. Fullerton, Jr., "Labor Force Participation: 75 Years of Change, 1950–98 and 1998–2025," Labor Force Participation (1999): 3-12. https://www.bls.gov/mlr/1999/12/art1full.pdf.
4. "Women of Working Age," U.S. Department of Labor Women's Bureau, https://www.dol.gov/agencies/wb/data/latest-annual-data/working-women#wwcivilian.
5. Jill E. Yavorsky et. al., "Women in the One Percent: Gender Dynamics in Top Income Positions," *American Sociological Review* 84, no. 1 (February 1, 2019): 54-81.

The Feminization of Jobs: Clerical Work

1. Asaf Levanon, Paula England, and Paul Allison, "Occupational Feminization and Pay: Assessing Causal Dynamics Using 1950-2000 U.S. Census Data," *Social Forces* 88, no. 2 (December 2009): 865–891.
2. Kim England and Kate Boyer, "Women's Work: The Feminization and Shifting Meanings of Clerical Work," *Journal of Social History* 43, no. 2 (2009): 307–340.
3. England and Boyer, "Women's Work."
4. Whitney Thompson, "Mister Secretary: The Gendered History of Clerical Work," *Odyssey* (February 9, 2017), https://www.theodysseyonline.com/mister-secretary-the-gendered-history-of-clerical-work.

The Masculinization of Jobs: Computer Programming

1. Janet Abbate, *Recoding Gender: Women's Changing Participation in Computing,* (Cambridge, MA: MIT Press, 2012).
2. Rose Eveleth, "Computer Programming Used to be Women's Work: Computer Programmers are Expected to be Male and Antisocial—a Self-fulfilling Prophesy that Forgets the Women that the Entire Field was Built Upon," *Smithsonian* (October 7, 2013), https://www.smithsonianmag.com/smart-news/computer-programming-used-to-be-womens-work-718061/.

3. Steve Henn, "When Women Stopped Coding," *NPR: Planet Money* (October 21, 2014): https://www.npr.org/sections/money/2014/10/21/357629765/when-women-stopped-coding. Author Jodi Detjen was one of those programmers.

4. Slye Joy Serrano, "Why Women Stopped Coding," *Sysgen* (May 5, 2017), http://www.sysgen.com.ph/articles/why-women-stopped-coding/27216

5. Henn, "When Women Stopped Coding."

6. Byron Spice, "Women are Almost Half of Carnegie Mellon's Incoming Computer Science Undergraduates: Achievement Caps Decades of Effort to Increase Gender Diversity," Carnegie Mellon University (September 11, 2016): https://www.csd.cs.cmu.edu/news/women-are-almost-half-carnegie-mellons-incoming-computer-science-undergraduates

7. June Lin, "How Carnegie Mellon Grew The Number Of Women In Computer Science Classes By 35% In 5 Years," *Business Insider* (October 13, 2013): https://static1.businessinsider.com/carnegie-mellon-women-computer-science-2013-10.

8. Alec D. Gallimore, "An Engineering School With Half of Its Leadership Female? How Did That Happen?," *Chronicle of Higher Education* (May 1, 2019), https://www.chronicle.com/article/An-Engineering-School-With/246214?cid=wcontentlist.

The Masculinization of Jobs: The Business of Birthing Babies

1. Adrian E. Feldhusen, "The History of Midwifery and Childbirth in America: A Time Line," *Midwifery Today* (2000), https://midwiferytoday.com/web-article/history-midwifery-childbirth-america-time-line/.

2. Feldhusen, "The History of Midwifery and Childbirth in America."

3. Feldhusen, "The History of Midwifery and Childbirth in America."

4. "CPMs Legal Status by State," *Big Push for Midwives*, https://www.pushformidwives.org/cpms_legal_status_by_state.

Appendix B

1. Kathrine Switzer, "Boston, 1967: When Marathons Were Just for Men," BBC News (April 16, 2012), https://www.bbc.com/news/magazine-17632029.

2. Katie Reilly, "She Was the First Woman to Run the Boston Marathon. 50 Years Later, She's Back," *Time* (May 2017): 241.

3. See https://marastats.com/marathon/.

4. "Women in Combat Pros and Cons," Sisters in Arms (2009), https://sistersinarms.ca/history/women-in-combat-pros-and-cons/

5. "American Women in World War I," *Wikipedia* (June 7, 2020).

6. "American Women in World War I," *Wikipedia*.

7. "Women in the Army: Female Fighters in the World's Seven Biggest Armies," *Army Technology* (November 30, 2018), https://www.army-technology.com/uncategorised/women-in-the-army/.

8. Sue Heinemann, *Timelines of American Women's History* (New York: Penguin, 1996).

9. Suzanne McGee and Heidi Moore, "Women's Rights and Their Money: A Timeline from Cleopatra to Lilly Ledbetter," *Guardian* (August 11, 2014).

10. McGee and Moore, "Women's Rights and Their Money."

11. McGee and Moore, "Women's Rights and Their Money."

12. Lena Kozar, "How Gender Stereotypes are Still Affecting Women in Tech," *WITI* (June 2017), https://witi.com/articles/1017/How-Gender-Stereotypes-are-Still-Affecting-Women-in-Tech/.

13. Claire L. Evans, *Broad Band: The Untold Story of the Women Who Made the Internet* (New York: Portfolio, 2018).

14. Sage Lazzaro, "12 Statistics About Women in Tech That Show How Big the Gender Gap Truly Is: Women Own Only 5 Percent of Startups," *Observer* (June 5, 2017), https://observer.com/2017/06/women-in-tech-statistics/

15. Lazzaro, "12 Statistics About Women in Tech That Show How Big the Gender Gap Truly Is."

Appendix C

1. "Caraway, Hattie Wyatt," *History, Art, & Archives: The United States House of Representatives*, https://history.house.gov/People/Listing/C/CARAWAY,-Hattie-Wyatt-%28C000138%29/#top

2. David G. Savage, "Supreme Court Bars Sex Bias in Jury Selection," *Los Angeles Times* (April 20, 1994).

3. "Katharine Graham," *Wikipedia* (May 31, 2020).

4. "H.R.5050 - Women's Business Ownership Act of 1988," Congress.Gov.

5. Juliet Linderman, "How Women in Congress Have Fought for Equal Treatment Within the Halls of Capitol Hill," *Christian Science Monitor* (November 3, 2017), https://www.csmonitor.com/USA/Politics/2017/1103/How-women-in-Congress-have-fought-for-equal-treatment-within-the-halls-of-Capitol-Hill.

6. Savage, "Supreme Court Bars Sex Bias in Jury Selection."

7. "Women in the Labor Force: A Databook (2011 Edition)," U.S. Bureau of Labor Statistics, report 1034 (December 15, 2011), https://www.bls.gov/cps/wlf-databook2011.htm.

8. Linderman, "How Women in Congress Have Fought for Equal Treatment Within the Halls of Capitol Hill."

9. Eric Bradner, "U.S. Military Opens Combat Positions to Women," *CNN Politics* (December 3, 2015).

10. Susan Milligan, "Stepping Through History: A Timeline of Women's Rights from 1769 to the 2017 Women's March on Washington," *U.S. News* (January 20, 2017), https://www.usnews.com/news/the-report/articles/2017-01-20/timeline-the-womens-rights-movement-in-the-us.

11. Linderman, "How Women in Congress Have Fought for Equal Treatment Within the Halls of Capitol Hill."

12. Nick Turner, Zoya Khan, and Eben Novy-Williams, "Under Armour Bans Strip-Club Expenses in #MeToo Reckoning," BNN Bloomberg (November 5, 2018), https://www.bnnbloomberg.ca/under-armour-bans-strip-club-expenses-in-metoo-reckoning-1.1163554.

13. "Board Monitor US 2019: What's Changed in 10 Years, What Hasn't, and What's Next," *Heidrick & Struggles* (May 28, 2019), https://heidrick.com/Knowledge-Center/Publication/Board_Monitor_US_2019?fr=mm&utm_source=Email&utm_medium=Email&utm_campaign=Board_Monitor_US_2019.

14. "List: Women & CEOs of the S&P 500," *Catalyst* (June 2, 2020), https://www.catalyst.org/research/women-ceos-of-the-sp-500/

INDEX

A

African Americans, 30, 48, 131, 139, 149, 171
aggression, 84, 107
Agile Project Management, 148
allyship, 91, 95, 104–5, 107, 109, 168, 187
allyship continuum, 105
Amazon, 150, 183
anger, 75, 77, 84, 119
assumptions. See also reframe, reframing
    cultural, 171, 181
    false, 44, 46, 52, 54–55, 59, 84, 105, 110, 129, 137, 156
    flawed, 43, 55, 59, 70, 72, 75, 77–81, 84–85, 94, 96, 107–9, 111, 166, 168, 187–88
    gender-limiting, 50
    hidden, 77, 85, 100
    limiting, 105
    negative, 86
    organizational, 59
    reframing, 76
    self-limiting, 100
    stereotypical, 67
attention, sexual, 54, 103, 217
attrition, generational, 15
authoritarian leadership approach, 8

B

bad habits, 42–43, 55–56, 76, 85, 96, 100, 149, 158–59
barriers, systemic, 34
bias
    cascading, 37
    confirmation, 35
    hidden, 160, 165, 184
    ignoring, 40, 59, 61
    implicit, 29, 36
    in-group/out-group, 144
    internal, 11, 84–85, 94, 96
    parental wall, 37
    prove-it-again, 36, 64
    sexist, 150
    tightrope, 36
    tug-of-war, 37
    unconscious, defined, 29
bias advantage, 58
bias awareness, 8, 40, 156, 160–61
bias invisibility, 40
bias problems, 62, 84, 185
bias training, 161, 163
Blake, Sarah, 5
Bohnet, Iris, 36
"brand name" schools, 37
Brandon Hall Group, 105
breadwinners, 37, 49, 58, 62
breastfeeding, 28
bro culture, 25, 70, 124

C

candidates, job
    diverse, 105, 136
    female, 32, 62, 93, 124, 138
    male, 91, 163
    selecting, 9, 37
Chamorro-Premuzic, Tomas, 144
change process, 82, 112, 117, 156
coach, executive, 154
Coca-Cola, 183
collaboration, 6, 51, 81, 136–37, 147–48
compensation, 60, 63, 82–84, 158, 160

competencies, 117, 130, 132, 138, 153
    diversity management, 114
    leadership, 132, 139
complaints, 131, 167, 177
conflict, woman-versus-woman, 37
Cornell University, 33
COVID-19 pandemic, 193, 195
cross-functional pods, 195

D

daycare, 14, 45, 80, 122
decision-making, 5, 7, 30, 34, 38–39,
    40–41, 59, 75, 78, 88, 142, 148,
    161, 163
Dempsey, Rachel, 36
developmental interventions, 23
development pipeline, 40, 61, 154
Direct Speak Model, 88, 91, 95, 146
diverse perspectives, 118, 133, 135,
    142, 150
diverse teams, 3, 8, 10, 121, 131,
    133–34, 141–42, 144–48, 153–54,
    189, 194
diversity, 3–4, 7–8, 16, 112–14,
    130–32, 135–39, 141–43, 149–53,
    187–88, 190, 194–95
    background, 69, 176–77
    capabilities, 152, 154
    customer, 150
    goals, 114
    hiring, 124
    initiatives, 14, 59, 113, 150
    of thought, 3, 117, 153, 175, 194
    performance, 152
diversity and inclusion competencies,
    135, 137
diversity and gender inclusion, 142
diversity intelligence and experience,
    136–37, 139, 142

E

Ely, Robin, 93, 178
emotions, 52, 64–65, 77–78, 84, 88, 90,
    95, 100, 119, 145–146
empathy map, 116
Engaging in Conversations worksheet, 119
Entrepreneur Magazine, 31
Equal Employment Opportunity
    (EEO), 138

F

facilitation, 119, 143, 148
fathers, 36, 148, 181
feedback, 10, 31, 41, 58, 64, 88–89,
    101, 124, 132, 147, 154, 166–70
    360-degree, 169
    developmental, 64, 101
    eliciting, 184
    negative, 47, 64, 168
feedback loop, 65
    post-implementation, 111
female customers, 143, 184
female engineers, 122
female leaders, 4, 64, 122, 176
female mentees, 103, 174
female role models, 176
femininity, 22–23, 36, 42–43, 47,
    50–52, 65, 92, 120
flirting, 54, 104
Frankel, Lois P., 47

G

gap analysis, 111, 122–24, 185
gatekeeping, 92, 94
gender assumptions, 57, 72, 108
    binary, 81
    cultural, 48
gender balance, 113, 138
gender barriers, 28, 106
gender bias, 105, 108, 138, 162, 169, 173
gender clustering, 160
gender conflict, 107
gender diversity, 16, 138, 153
gender equity, 2–7, 10, 13, 15–16, 32–33,
    56–57, 59–61, 71, 91, 112, 122–23,
    138, 142–43, 155–57, 185, 187
    building, 111, 129–30, 135
    improving, 138, 155
    leveraging, 138, 152
    sustaining, 152, 188
gender equity taxonomy, 135
gender landscape, 155–56
gender risk, 155–56
gender roles, 12–13, 187
    institutionalized, 21
gender rules, unspoken, 13, 55
gender scorecard, 5, 123, 163, 174, 182
generational conflict, 93
generations, 15, 22, 49, 50–51, 92–93

gossip, 77, 114, 154, 184
group norms, 68, 119, 143
groups, 4, 7–8, 16, 30, 36–38, 86,
    90–91, 93, 116, 118–21, 138, 145–49,
    153, 164–65, 169, 175, 177–78
    affinity, 59–60, 178
    dynamics, 68–69
    homogeneity, 78
    minority, 34, 145
    privileged, 86, 109
    underrepresented, 16, 37, 175,
        219–20
groupthink, 7, 37, 118, 121, 164, 168

H
harassment, sexual, 33–34, 54, 59, 162
harassment claims, 162
Harvard Business Review, 31
hiring process, 71, 164
hours, work, 41, 45, 62, 109, 175,
    179–181

I
impostor syndrome, 120
inclusion, 3–4, 8, 112–14, 130, 132, 134,
    135, 138–39, 141, 188–90, 194
inclusive workplaces, 5
incomes, 12, 49–50, 97
inspiration, diverse, 136–38
interviews, job, 71, 91, 138, 155, 164,
    169, 221–22

K
Kahneman, Daniel, 32, 34–35, 41
key performance indicators (KPIs), 63,
    118, 167
Kimmel, Michael, 52
Kristof, Nicholas,102

L
leaders
    diverse, 153
    effective, 101, 146–47
    group, 170
    individual, 157
    organizational, 39, 130
    potential, 129, 152, 187
    successful, 69, 77

leadership
    effective, 137, 177, 188
    inclusive, 130, 132, 134–35
    male, 68, 72
    organizational, 8, 42, 135, 152, 182
    senior, 31, 48, 69, 83, 93, 112,
        123, 155, 158, 161, 169,
        173–76, 178, 183, 220
leadership bias, 30–31
leadership capabilities, 135, 137,
    152–53, 184, 210
leadership competencies, 68, 130, 132,
    136, 187
leadership gap, 71–72, 130
leadership models, 139, 147, 152, 175
leadership pipeline, 40, 138, 163
leadership roles, 13, 37, 68, 153, 155
leadership skills, 5, 7, 31, 67, 134
    inclusive, 8, 132, 195–96
    twenty-first-century, 3, 42–43, 104
    women's, 53
leadership team, 52, 58, 67, 105,
    138, 184
    all-male, 105, 138
legal risk, 100, 156–57, 160, 162,
    170, 180–82

M
male leaders, 30, 52, 94, 117, 122, 139,
    141, 175–76
managing diversity, 8, 131, 134
masculinity, 22-23, 25, 30, 45, 51–52,
    54-55, 69–71, 99
maternity, 49, 59–60, 62–63, 66, 102,
    148, 159, 171, 180–82
McKinsey & Company, 33, 72, 171
mentoring, 53–4, 66, 91, 94, 100–1,
    103, 106–7, 130, 171, 172–74
    female, 90
meritocracy, 11–12, 33, 40, 61, 66, 87,
    104–5, 110–11, 131, 168
microaggressions, 39, 46, 53, 107
mothers, 13, 23, 28, 36–37, 41, 44–45,
    55, 65–66, 72, 94, 148, 172, 180–81
    new, 148, 181

N
Nadella, Satya, 48
networking, 66, 173

networks, 39, 90, 107
    social, 71, 90
    informal, 7

O

organizational assessment, 154
organizational assumptions, 59, 110
organizational barriers, 5, 61, 72
organizational bias, 5, 35, 57
organizational change, 4, 60, 125
organizational culture, 7, 56, 69, 119, 178
organizational processes, 59, 154
organizational structures, 7, 57, 153, 175
organizations
    diverse, 4, 16, 124
    inclusive, 152
out-groups, 30, 144, 174

P

parenting, 12, 60, 80–81, 180–81
partners, 49, 80–81, 96
peers, 11, 31, 51, 88, 90, 95, 148,
    155–56, 158–59, 169
    male, 61, 64, 83, 92, 94
perfectionism, 65, 81, 146, 168, 171
performance, 36, 38–39, 41–42, 47, 53,
    61, 63, 66–67, 85–86, 121, 144, 146,
    148, 153, 160, 169–70
performance evaluation, 68, 163, 167, 170
"pink-collar" jobs, 4-5, 52, 63, 90,
    156, 159
pipeline, 41, 111, 114, 138, 163, 185
pipeline development, 163, 170–71
Pixar, 151
politics, 37, 118, 168
power, 21, 47, 53, 59–60, 81–83,
    87–88, 90, 94, 98, 103–7, 109, 143,
    147, 187, 190–91
process
    biased, 130, 187, 190
    recruitment, 164
productivity risk, 156–57, 160, 177,
    179–80, 182, 184
promotion cycles, 84, 172
psychological safety, 118–20, 145,
    147, 189

Q

quotas, 33, 61, 115

R

race, 6, 11, 40, 155, 166, 178
recruitment, 39, 71, 93, 124, 163–64,
    218–19
reframe, reframing, 13, 16, 76–89,
    94–105, 108–111, 129-30, 132,
    156-85, 187-90, 196
retention, 163, 165, 167, 180
review process, 168, 174, 178
rights, human, 22, 131–32, 183
role models, 28, 59, 68–69, 93, 98,
    107, 117, 137, 141, 163, 174–78,
    182, 189
roles, 27, 30, 37, 41–42, 46, 63, 68–69,
    107, 111, 157
Ross, Howard, 35

S

salary, 11, 54, 58, 156, 158–160
scorecard, gender assessment, 154–55
self-promotion, 63–64, 174
selves, authentic, 98, 100, 103, 147, 155
Shellenbarger, Sue, 98
sponsorship, 66, 107, 171, 174
stakeholders, 114, 143, 147–49, 184, 190
stereotypes, 12, 22, 29–30, 35–39, 41,
    60, 67, 69, 82, 85–86, 90, 140
    negative, 35, 38–39, 85, 90,
        93, 107
stereotype threat, 35, 38–39, 85–86
support staff, 94, 176

T

taxonomy of leadership capabilities,
    135–36, 142, 146, 152, 184, 187
team leaders, 117, 134, 147
team members, 106, 133–34, 138, 143,
    145–46, 148, 152, 169
teams
    all-male, 10, 106, 183
    gender-balanced, 11, 148
    inclusive, 4, 130, 132, 139, 150
    psychologically safe, 119, 145
    senior, 68, 113, 122, 175, 182

turnover risk, 156–57, 160–62, 165, 167, 170, 172, 177, 179–82, 184
Twitter, 70

U
Uber, 33, 70
unconscious bias, 4–5, 29–30, 32, 35, 37–42, 50, 55–58, 70, 72, 78, 86, 107, 109–10, 119, 129–30, 161, 168–70, 172
underlying assumptions, 39, 55–56, 75–77, 79–80, 83, 91, 95, 110, 134, 189, 193
underrepresented groups, 16, 37, 175
upstanding, defined, 108

V
vulnerability, 98–100

W
Wall Street Journal, 98
Williams, Joan, 36
Walmart, 183
Wittenberg-Cox, Avivah, 100
women
    engineers, 15, 23, 86, 150
    grouping, 86, 147
    leaders, 36, 64, 69, 93–94, 103, 138, 152
    mentors, 66, 107
workers, part-time, 10
workforce, 3, 11, 14, 22, 114, 194
    diverse, 132, 135
work-life balance, 5, 12, 50, 98, 179
World War II, 19, 22–24

ABOUT THE AUTHORS

Kelly Watson and **Jodi Ecker Detjen** are accomplished organizational development consultants, educators, and managing partners of Orange Grove Consulting, a consultancy firm specializing in helping organizations improve gender equity and inclusivity through a set of consulting tools and training programs. They have designed top-tier women's leadership training for clients and consulted for a wide range of organizations.

Kelly and Jodi are also coauthors of the book *The Orange Line: A Woman's Guide to Integrating Career, Family, and Life,* in which they addressed the unconscious biases many women internalize at the peril of their own career development. Kelly is an adjunct professor at Loyola Marymount University in Los Angeles, and Jodi is a clinical professor of management and academic MBA program director at Boston's Suffolk University.

Kelly holds a BA in Political Science from the University of Western Ontario in London, Canada, and an MBA from Loyola Marymount University. She is currently pursuing a PhD in Business at the University of Denver. She is a Recreation & Parks Commissioner for the city of El Segundo, California, and helps women and girls reach their full potential through AYSO coaching, refereeing, and playing soccer.

Jodi earned her BSc in Management Science from Virginia Tech, her MA in International Development Policy from Duke University, and is currently pursuing her Doctorate in Business Administration at Temple University.